Financial Accounting
in an Economic Context

4th Edition

Jamie Pratt

Professor of Accounting

Indiana University, Bloomington

Prepared by

Donald R. Loster

University of California, Santa Barbara

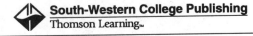

South-Western College Publishing
Thomson Learning™

Australia • Canada • Denmark • Japan • Mexico • New Zealand • Philippines
Puerto Rico • Singapore • South Africa • Spain • United Kingdom • United States

Instructor's Manual to *Financial Accounting in an Economic Context*, 4th edition, prepared by Donald R. Loster

Accounting Team Director: Richard Lindgren
Acquisitions Editor: Rochelle Kronzek
Senior Developmental Editor: Ken Martin
Marketing Manager: Dan Silverburg
Production Editor: Mark Sears
Production Services: Donna Helfst
Manufacturing Coordinator: Doug Wilke
Printer: Globus Printing, Inc.

Printed in the United States of America
1 2 3 4 5 02 01 00 99

For more information contact South-Western College Publishing, 5101 Madison Road, Cincinnati, Ohio, 45227 or find us on the Internet at http://www.swcollege.com

For permission to use material from this text or product, contact us by
• **telephone: 1-800-730-2214**
• **fax: 1-800-730-2215**
• **web: http://www.thomsonrights.com**

ISBN: 0-324-01525-9

This book is printed on acid-free paper.

CONTENTS

CHAPTER 1   Financial Accounting and Its Economic Context

SYNOPSIS

In this chapter, the author discusses the economics of financial accounting, which includes (1) the demand for financial information; (2) the environment of financial accounting; (3) the controls associated with the financial accounting process; and (4) generally accepted accounting principles. The author illustrates and discusses the roles that equity investors, debt investors, managers, and auditors have in the financial accounting process, providing a basis for the discussion of both a user orientation and economic consequence perspective.

The discussion of generally accepted accounting principles focuses on the evolution of GAAP and the political nature of standard setting in the United States. An international perspective of the general state of accounting practices and standards throughout the world is also considered.

The ethics vignette considers employee conduct contrary to a company's stated code of conduct.

The Internet research exercise considers examples of how some companies overstate profits through aggressive, yet not fraudulent, accounting methods.

The author compares and contrasts the four different types of accounting (i.e., financial, not-for-profit, managerial, and tax) along six dimensions in Appendix 1A.

The following key points are emphasized in Chapter 1:

1. The economic role of financial accounting statements and why managers must have both an economic consequence perspective and a user orientation.

2. The standard audit report, management letter, and footnotes to the financial statements.

3. The four financial statements and the kind of financial information each provides.

4. The two forms of investment—debt and equity—and how information on the financial statements relates to them.

5. Why ethics is important in the accounting process.

6. The Securities and Exchange Commission, the Financial Accounting Standards Board, and the development of generally accepted accounting principles.

7. The current status of international accounting practices and standards.

TEXT/LECTURE OUTLINE

Financial accounting and its economic context.

I.   The financial accounting process.

    A.   Overview of accounting.

        1.   Accounting is a <u>system</u> through which <u>managers</u> report <u>financial information</u> about an <u>economic entity</u> to a variety of <u>recipients</u> who use this information to make better <u>decisions</u>. These decisions affect the <u>economic wealth</u> of the reporting entity and its management.

        2.   Types of accounting.

            a)   Not-for-profit accounting.

                Not-for-profit accounting generates financial information for those entities that do not exist solely to generate profits.

            b)   Managerial accounting.

                Managerial accounting generates financial information useful to managers for making day-to-day operating decisions.

            c)   Tax accounting.

                Tax accounting generates financial information in compliance with the Internal Revenue Code.

            d)   Financial accounting.

                Financial accounting generates financial information for individuals external to a profit-seeking entity.

    B.   Components of the financial accounting process.

        1.   Providers of capital.

            a)   Equity investors.

                (1)   Equity investors purchase ownership shares (i.e., equity) in a company.

                (2)   Equity investors are most interested in acquiring information about a company's earning power.

            b)   Debt investors.

(1)   Debt investors loan capital to a company.

(2)   Debt investors are most interested in acquiring information about a company's solvency position.

2. Managers.

3. Contracts.

    a) Debt contracts.

    b) Compensation contracts.

4. Financial accounting statements.

5. Independent auditors.

6. Legal liability.

7. Ethics and professional reputation.

8. Generally accepted accounting principles (GAAP).

    a) Evolution of GAAP.

    b) Bodies responsible for establishing GAAP.

        (1)   Securities and Exchange Commission (SEC).

        (2)   Financial Accounting Standards Board (FASB).

    c) Standard setting is a political process.

II. International accounting practices and standards.

III. Ethics in the real world.

IV. Internet research exercise.

LECTURE TIPS

1. Students often expect accounting to be a boring "cookbook" course. Discussion of Chapter 1 can set the tone for the rest of the course through a relevant, interesting discussion of the economics of accounting and an early introduction of real world examples.

2. Although students usually understand the motives underlying the economic consequences arguments, they often do not apply these motives to accounting.

OUTSIDE ASSIGNMENT OPPORTUNITIES

Article search: current developments at NIKE

1. Search the financial press (*The Wall Street Journal, Barrons, Fortune, Forbes,* etc.) for an article reporting a current development that relates to NIKE. Consider the impact on NIKE's financial statements (presented in Appendix A), from both a user orientation and an economic consequence perspective and present your findings in writing and/or orally to the class.

Article search: current developments in accounting standards

2. Search the financial press (*The Wall Street Journal, Barrons, Fortune, Forbes,* etc.) for an article that reports a current development in accounting standards, for example, a new or proposed pronouncement by the FASB or IASC. Consider its impact from both a user orientation and an economic consequence perspective and present your findings in writing and/or orally to the class.

ANSWERS TO END-OF-CHAPTER QUESTIONS

1. a. A debt investment arises when an investor loans money to a company. In other words, a debt investor is a creditor of the company. Alternatively, an equity investment arises when an investor purchases an ownership interest in a company.

    Debt investments usually involve a formal contract that specifies the maturity date of the investment, required periodic interest payments, collateral for the loan (if any), and any other restrictions. Equity investments rarely include a formal contract; equity investors are not entitled to prespecified periodic payments. Instead, equity investors receive dividend payments at the discretion of the company's board of directors. In addition, if the company goes bankrupt, a debt investor can claim the collateral, while equity investors will only receive payment after the claims of the creditors have been satisfied.

    When taken together, the above items imply that equity investments entail greater risk than do debt investments. However, as compensation for bearing increased risk, equity investors have the potential to earn greater returns than do debt investors. The return on a debt investment is typically limited to the return specified in the debt contract. Alternatively, an equity investor, as the residual owner of the company, is entitled to all returns in excess of that paid to the debt investors. This means that an equity investor has unlimited earning potential.

    b. As owners of the company, equity investors share in the company's profits (or lack thereof). Consequently, if the company performs well over the long run, the equity investors should receive a larger return; if the company performs poorly over the long run, the equity investors should receive a lower return. Potential equity investors in IBM would be interested in financial information that would allow them to evaluate IBM's future earning power.

On the other hand, debt investors are more concerned with whether IBM will have sufficient cash to make principal and interest payments. This focus is more concerned with IBM's short-term cash availability. Consequently, potential debt investors in IBM would desire financial information that would allow them to evaluate IBM's solvency position.

2. a. Security analysts evaluate debt and equity investments for individuals, businesses, and other institutions. Therefore, they desire financial information that allows them to evaluate a company's earning power (for equity investments) and solvency position (for debt investments). Stockbrokers execute buy and sell orders for their customers and also dispense investment advice. Consequently, stockbrokers would desire the same financial information as security analysts but probably not to the same degree.

   b. Bank loan officers are current or potential creditors of a company. Because they are interested in whether the company will have sufficient cash to meet its interest and principal payments, loan officers desire financial information that allows them to evaluate a company's solvency position.

   c. Customers and suppliers are concerned with whether the company will continue to exist. If the company is not expected to continue in business, then customer warranties or other promises given by the company are essentially worthless; the debt to suppliers would also not be repaid. Consequently, customers and suppliers desire information that allows them to evaluate the company's continued existence and solvency.

   d. The rates that public utilities charge are usually based on the utility's asset base. Since a utility's asset base is a financial accounting number, public utilities are interested in reporting higher asset amounts in their financial statements.

   e. Labor unions negotiate with management for wage contracts and fringe benefits. If the financial statements indicate that the company is doing well, the union negotiators will use this information to demand higher wages and/or more benefits. Alternatively, if the financial statements indicate that the company is doing poorly, management will use this information to demand wage and/or benefit concessions from the union.

   f. Managers also use financial accounting information to make decisions. For example, managers often use financial accounting information to guide decisions concerning dividend payments, investments, and business operations.

3. Solvency refers to a company's ability to meet its debts as they become due. Because debt investors loan money to a company for a limited period of time, they are concerned with whether the company will have sufficient cash to make interest payments and to repay the principal. Alternatively, equity investors are the owners of the company and, hence, invest their money for a longer period of time. Therefore, the equity owners are more interested in the company's long-run performance, while debt investors are more interested in a company's solvency position.

   Debt investors would be interested in several types of financial information. First, they would desire information on how much cash and cash equivalents the company currently possesses. Second, they would desire information on the magnitude and timing of future debt payments. Third, they would desire information on the value of assets that could be sold to satisfy their (and other creditors') claims.

4. Net income is a measure of a company's performance based on net assets generated through operating activities. Net assets, however, are comprised of much more than just cash. To remain solvent, a company must have sufficient cash to both meet its debts as they come due and to continue operating. Thus, even though a company could be generating net assets through operating activities, if those net assets are in a form that cannot be used to make interest or principal payments, such as inventory, the company would not be solvent.

   If companies need cash, they essentially have four options: (1) borrow cash; (2) issue additional equity; (3) sell assets; or (4) generate cash through operations. However, a company cannot borrow, issue equity, or sell off assets forever. The company must eventually generate cash through operations or it will collapse. Therefore, net cash flows from operating activities would be a better measure of a company's solvency than net income. In addition, the value of the company's assets in relation to its debt would also provide important information about solvency.

5. The purpose of an audit is to assure the debt and equity owners that the financial statements have been prepared according to generally accepted accounting principles (GAAP) and are free from material misstatements. The audit opinion conveys these assurances to the debt and equity owners. By providing these assurances to the owners, managers can attract additional capital investments to the company.

   Companies whose securities are publicly traded are required by the Securities and Exchange Commission to have their financial statements audited by independent auditors. If a company's securities are not publicly traded, there is no requirement that the financial statements be prepared in accordance with GAAP. However, such nonpublic companies may have debt investors that require audited financial statements. In this case, though, the accounting principles used to prepare the financial statements can be negotiated between the creditor and the company; hence, the financial statements may not be required to be prepared in accordance with GAAP. If a company does not prepare its financial statements in accordance with GAAP, the auditor will give the company a qualified audit opinion.

6. An independent auditor is not biased towards the company's management. If auditors were not independent, the debt and equity owners would not place any reliance upon the auditors' assurances as to the fairness of the company's financial statements. This lack of reliance would, in turn, result in lower levels of capital being provided to companies.

   Management hires and pays an auditor to audit the company's financial statements. Since management pays the auditor, the auditor has incentives to bow to management's wishes. In the extreme, managers may threaten to shop for a new auditor that will be more compliant. These pressures to not be independent are offset, though, by (1) the auditor's legal liability to the debt and equity investors and (2) the auditor's professional reputation. If the auditor attests to the fairness of financial statements and those financial statements are later proved to be materially misstated, the auditor is liable for the losses incurred by investors. In addition, the auditor's reputation would be damaged, which may impair the auditor's ability to attract and retain clients.

7. The author strongly disagrees. Many of the amounts reported in the financial statements are based on estimates and assumptions. For example, the amounts reported for

inventory and the cost of the inventory sold are based on assumptions about how inventory costs flow through the company. Similarly, the amounts reported for plant and equipment and depreciation expense are based on estimates of how long the plant and equipment will last as well as how the company uses the plant and equipment over time. By definition, estimates and assumptions cannot be proven to be correct without the passage of time; auditors can only evaluate whether the estimates and assumptions are reasonable. Accordingly, it is incorrect to presume that an unqualified opinion means "totally accurate."

8. Ethics allow financial statement users to place greater trust in a company's financial statements than would otherwise be possible. Debt and equity owners will, therefore, require ethical companies to incur fewer costs in producing "reliable" financial statements than nonethical companies. But if management has incentives to maximize short-term profits, such as bonuses based on short-term profits, management may succumb to these incentives and abandon its ethical reporting practices.

9. Reported financial statement numbers have important economic consequences. The securities markets depend on reliable financial statement information to value a company's stock. Management may resort to earnings manipulation to try to favorably affect the stock price, but this is a double-edged sword. When manipulation is discovered, Wall Street loses faith in the company's numbers and punishes the stock price accordingly.

10. a. The investors may sue the management of Galaxy Enterprise and Mr. Howard for any losses incurred.

    b. In defending himself against the lawsuit, Mr. Howard would probably argue that the financial statements are the responsibility of Galaxy Enterprise and that he complied with the standard audit rules and procedures. Consequently, he exercised due care in the audit of Galaxy Enterprise and is, therefore, not liable for any losses.

    c. Mr. Howard should consider the expected costs and benefits of carrying liability insurance. If the expected benefits outweigh the expected costs, then he should carry liability insurance. If the expected benefits do not outweigh the expected costs, then Mr. Howard would not be expected to carry liability insurance. Since settlements against auditors are usually quite substantial, the expected benefits of liability insurance usually outweigh the expected costs of such insurance. Therefore, one would expect Mr. Howard to carry liability insurance.

11. Future projections allow debt and equity investors to better evaluate a company's solvency position and long-run earning power. Consequently, investors would prefer financial statements to contain future projections on the company. However, because investors realize that managers have incentives to bias such projections, investors would demand that an independent auditor audit future projections. The auditor is unable, though, to adequately verify the subjective projections. If these future projections are subsequently revealed to be materially misstated, the auditor may be legally liable to the investors for their losses. Consequently, the risk to the auditor of being sued is too great which, in turn, greatly increases the expected cost of the audit. Hence, auditors would be unwilling to attest to the fairness of future projections at a price that would be acceptable to managers.

12. Financial statement users desire information that is useful for making decisions—the information should be both reliable and relevant. In order to be reliable, the information needs to be objective and verifiable. However, obtaining completely objective and verifiable information may take so long that the information would no longer be relevant. That is, the information is not received when the financial statement users want to make a decision. Thus, there is a tradeoff between reliable information and timely (i.e., relevant) information. The solution to this tradeoff is to use objective and verifiable numbers where possible, and to use estimates and assumptions to generate other numbers in order to make the financial statements more timely. Thus, estimates and assumptions are necessary to provide financial statement users with timely information for decision-making purposes. In addition, estimates and assumptions allow managers to prepare financial statements that reflect the economic environment faced by the company.

13. Managers are parties to a multitude of explicit and implicit contracts in their role in the company. For example, many managers are paid incentive compensation equal to a certain percentage of net income. Also, companies and, hence, managers often enter into debt covenants with the company's creditors. Many of these contracts provide managers with incentives to manipulate the financial statements. If a manager can increase earnings, the manager can then increase his or her incentive compensation. Or if a manager can increase the company's working capital ratio, decrease the company's debt/equity ratio, or increase the company's net income, then the manager can decrease the probability of violating the company's debt covenants.

Generally accepted accounting principles provide some limits on a manager's ability to manipulate financial statements. The SEC requires publicly held companies to adhere to GAAP; consequently, a manager of a publicly held company must select accounting principles from within those principles acceptable under GAAP. However, managers have discretion in selecting from accounting policies and procedures acceptable under GAAP. Managers can make estimates and assumptions and select acceptable accounting principles that serve their interests. GAAP simply sets constraints on managers' ability to manipulate financial statements; it does not prevent the manipulation.

Since managers still possess some discretion in selecting accounting principles and in making estimates and assumptions, financial statement users must be wary. Financial statement users must consider management's incentives to bias the financial statements when relying on financial statement information for decision-making purposes.

14. a. Equity owners usually prefer more net income to less, holding everything else constant—higher net income usually reflects higher earning power, which, in turn, implies higher dividends or stock appreciation. By paying managers a bonus equal to a percentage of net income, the owners are trying to align the managers' goals with their own goals. The owners are trying to provide incentives for the managers to make decisions and take actions that are in the owners' best interests. In other words, the owners are trying to control the actions of the managers through a contract.

b. Financial statement users evaluate the investment potential of different companies. One factor that financial statement users examine is a company's earnings relative to other companies. Such an evaluation indicates whether the company has consistently outperformed similar companies and whether the company can be expected to have higher long-run earnings potential than its competitors.

c. The bank has dictated the company's accounting methods. The bank has also placed constraints on management's decisions and actions. The bank has limited management's ability to declare dividends, issue debt, dispose of assets, and so forth. By placing these constraints on the company, the bank has increased the probability that the company will not default on its interest and principal payments. Through the debt covenant, therefore, the bank is able to influence and partially control the managers' decisions and actions.

d. Increasing levels of debt make a company more risky, holding everything else constant. As a company increases its debt, it must generate more cash to meet the interest and principal payments as they come due. Financial statement users would want the change in debt levels disclosed in the financial statements in order to evaluate the increased riskiness of the company and to determine whether the company is using this additional debt to generate additional profits and cash.

e. A credit rating by an independent rating service provides potential investors and creditors with information about a company's riskiness. Credit ratings of various companies can be compared in order to determine the relative riskiness of individual companies.

15. Equity owners usually prefer more net income to less net income, holding everything else constant—higher net income usually reflects higher earning power, which, in turn, implies higher dividends or stock appreciation. Higher net income usually indicates that the company is doing well and will generate cash flows in the future. By paying managers a bonus equal to a certain percentage of net income, the owners are trying to align the managers' goals with their own goals. The owners are trying to provide incentives for the managers to make decisions and take actions that are in the owners' best interests.

Most people prefer receiving more money to less. Since Elmer Smith would receive a bonus equal to $1,000 under FIFO and only $700 under LIFO, we would expect Elmer to select FIFO to account for inventory. Elmer should also consider the effect of the accounting method choice on cash flows and other contracts. For example, if financial reporting net income equals taxable income, the selection of FIFO would cause the company to incur a higher tax liability. Therefore, Elmer should consider the relative costs and benefits of selecting FIFO or LIFO on cash flows and on all relevant contracts.

16. Creditors want to make sure that debtors will have sufficient cash available to make interest and principal payments as they come due. If a debtor borrows too much money from various sources, the probability that the debtor will be able to meet all the interest and principal payments to any one creditor decreases. One possible measure of whether a company has borrowed too much is its ratio of total liabilities to total assets. Consequently, a creditor may specify the maximum ratio that is acceptable. Similarly, a company could have insufficient cash available to meet the interest and principal payments if it has paid excessive dividends. By specifying the percentage of net income that may be paid out as dividends, a creditor also increases the probability that the company will have sufficient cash available.

Since FIFO results in higher total assets than LIFO, FIFO results in a lower total liability to total asset ratio. Consequently, selecting FIFO moves the company further away from the debt constraint and decreases the probability that the company will violate its debt covenant. Based upon this one contract, the managers of Acme Custom Design would be expected to select FIFO over LIFO to account for inventory.

17. a. Equity and debt investors are interested in evaluating a company's solvency position and long-run earning power. Consequently, they would prefer information about assets' current and future values because these values indicate the potential current and future cash flows associated with the assets. Because historical costs provide information on past values, they are not overly useful to equity and debt investors.

b. Although historical costs are not overly useful in assessing a company's solvency position and long-run earning power, they are objectively verifiable. These amounts are based on arm's-length transactions and are usually documented by contracts, invoices, and so forth. Since historical costs are objective, managers have little latitude in manipulating these amounts. Thus, owners have fewer concerns about managers biasing the financial statements and would be more willing to enter into contracts based upon historical cost amounts.

c. Auditors and managers also desire the use of historical cost numbers in financial statements. If financial statement users rely on the included information and it subsequently proves to be materially misstated, the financial statement users can sue the auditors and the managers for any losses incurred. Historical cost numbers, in most cases, are hard to prove false since they are based upon objective, verifiable transactions. Auditors and managers would object if nonhistorical cost numbers, such as fair market values, were used to prepare financial statements. Such valuation bases are usually quite subjective and are not verifiable. Consequently, auditors could not verify any of the numbers recorded by the managers. Since the auditor would be liable for any errors the managers made, the auditors might be unwilling to verify the financial statements and issue an audit opinion.

18. a. The only amount that is objective and that an auditor can verify, is the cost of the land, $10,000. The auditor cannot verify whether the land currently has a value of $25,000, $40,000, or some other amount. By requiring the $10,000 to be disclosed, the auditor decreases the probability of being sued for any losses incurred by the bank on a loan to Mary's company.

b. If the amount of the loan or the interest rate charged is based upon the company's reported assets, Mary would probably prefer that the land be reported at the highest reasonable amount, in this case, $40,000. Reporting the $40,000 would make the company appear to be a better risk, which, in turn, would allow Mary to obtain a larger loan or better terms on the loan.

c. The bank is interested in collecting all the interest and principal it is due over the life of the loan. Consequently, the bank is interested in the ability of the company to generate cash in the future through operations or in the value of assets that the company could sell to satisfy its debts. Thus, the bank would probably find the range of selling prices on similar pieces of land more useful than its historical cost.

19. The role of the board of directors is to represent the interests of equity investors. The board of directors sets company policy, declares dividends, and reviews performance

and compensation of senior management. If management is domineering and the board of directors is weak, the board may be unable to adequately evaluate or control management's actions. Consequently, management would essentially have free reign to do as it pleases. Auditors are concerned about management fraud since such fraud affects the financial statements to which the auditors are attesting. If auditors fail to detect fraudulent acts, the auditors may, in certain instances, be liable to the financial statement users for any losses they incur.

20. An audit committee is a sub-committee of a company's board of directors. The audit committee works with management to select an auditor, and it is the committee's responsibility to monitor the audit to ensure it is conducted in a thorough, objective, and independent manner. In order to monitor the audit and to allow the auditors to perform independently, the committee should not have a vested interest in the audit findings. Hence, the members of the audit committee should not be part of management.

21. The Securities and Exchange Commission (SEC) was established in 1934 in response to the Great Depression. The SEC is responsible for ensuring that financial statements provide uniform and credible information to financial statement users. This regulation of financial information is necessary to protect investors. That is, managers have incentives to bias the financial information they provide to current and potential investors in order to attract investment capital. For example, without certain generally accepted accounting principles managers would be free to select whatever accounting methods they desired. Such discretion would make it difficult to compare the financial statements of different companies. Further, the lack of reporting standards would make it virtually impossible for an auditor to verify a company's financial statements because the auditor would have no reporting standards upon which to base his/her opinion.

22. The Securities and Exchange Commission (SEC) is ultimately responsible for creating generally accepted accounting principles. The SEC, however, has largely passed this role to the accounting profession, and the Financial Accounting Standards Board (FASB) is currently responsible for creating financial accounting standards. The FASB is a private body consisting of seven full-time members and their support staff. The members of the FASB are required to sever all ties with former employers. Consequently, the members are somewhat independent from the people and organizations they govern. Further, the members of the FASB do not have to be CPAs from public accounting firms; the members come from private industry, academe, and public accounting firms.

Unlike the prior accounting standard-setting bodies—the Committee on Accounting Procedures and the Accounting Principles Board—the FASB has encouraged public input in the development of GAAP and has developed a conceptual framework to guide the establishment of GAAP. Although the FASB is a private group, it is a political body in that it has to confront and resolve the interests of different groups. The FASB has to consider the views of managers, auditors, industry associations, security analysts, other special interest groups, Congress, the SEC and other government agencies, investors, and creditors.

23. Economic consequences refer to the costs and benefits to equity investors, creditors, managers, auditors, and the general public associated with reported financial accounting

information. In short, economic consequences refer to the effect of reported financial accounting information on individuals' and companies' wealth.

a. Investors use reported financial information to help make valuation decisions about a company. Management has an incentive to use creative accounting to make the financial statements as attractive as possible in order to maximize those valuations. Some investors avoid those companies altogether, because they lack faith in the quality of information being provided. These same investors likely place a premium on companies that employ conservative accounting methods.

b. Creditors and credit rating agencies, such as Standard and Poors, consider trends in a company's reported profitability and cash flows in evaluating the company's ability to service its debt obligations or to incur new obligations. Negative trends result in higher cost of debt and more difficult access to new borrowing for the company, and a greater risk of loss and less willingness to lend by creditors.

c. Sales affect a company's level of reported profits and, in turn, its reported assets. By inflating sales, a company is distorting measures of its earning power and its solvency. Because earning power and solvency may affect the investment decisions of equity and debt investors, inflating sales could affect the wealth of equity and debt investors.

d. A new accounting proposal that either increases or decreases reported profits could likewise affect executives' bonuses if the bonuses are based on such profits. An accounting change would also be expected to affect stock prices if the change in profits were due to more than just a cosmetic accounting change. This would affect the wealth of equity investors to whom the executives are ultimately accountable; the executives' wealth would also be affected in relation to any equity interest they have in the companies that they manage.

e. By keeping debt off the balance sheet, companies make themselves appear to be less risky. By appearing to be less risky, companies are able to attract capital at more attractive terms (e.g., borrow at lower interest rates or issue debt or equity at higher prices). In addition, keeping debt off the balance sheet may enable companies to avoid violating debt covenants.

24. In order for financial statement users to believe and rely on an audit opinion, the auditor must conduct an unbiased audit; for auditors to conduct an unbiased audit, they must be independent of their clients. That is, the auditors must not have a vested interest in the outcome of the audit. The AICPA was concerned that allowing auditors to borrow from banks that their firms audit would, at a minimum, give the perception that the auditors were not independent.

25. Standard setting is a political process and those parties affected by proposed standards would be expected to participate. Economic consequences refer to the effects on the economic wealth of the reporting entity and its management from preparing, auditing, and disclosing financial accounting information. Therefore, if a proposed accounting standard has economic consequences for a particular entity, that entity would be expected to lobby to the FASB. This, in turn, may affect the FASB's decision.

Auditors would probably lobby to the FASB against the proposal to include earnings projections in the financial statements. Auditors are responsible for verifying the fairness of information contained in financial statements. Predicting future earnings is extremely subjective so it is not possible for the auditors (or even the managers) to verify such projections. If the financial statement users rely on such information and the information subsequently proves to be materially misstated, the financial statement users can sue the auditors for any losses incurred. Given the subjective nature of future earnings predictions, a probability exists that these projections will prove to be materially misstated. Therefore, the expected value to auditors of verifying such information is probably negative. Any groups involved in providing information to financial statement users would probably also lobby against this standard.

In lobbying the FASB, auditors would probably argue that while future earnings information is important to financial statement users, such predictions require many assumptions and estimates; consequently, such predictions would not be reliable. It would be better to simply provide objective financial data to the financial statement users and let the users determine their own prediction of future earnings. In this manner, each individual financial statement user can use the assumptions and estimates that he/she deems appropriate.

26. In order for financial statement users to feel secure in relying on a company's financial statements, the users want independent assurance that the information in the financial statements is materially correct. If the auditors providing the assurance are not independent, financial statement users will be unwilling to rely on the financial statements. There are concerns about public accounting firms providing management advisory services because such services may impair the accounting firm's independence. This concern arises for two primary reasons. First, public accounting firms may recommend and install accounting systems as part of their management advisory services—is the accounting firm then able to objectively verify the output of the accounting system it recommended? Second, management advisory services can be quite lucrative—are the accounting firms willing to jeopardize lucrative consulting fees by giving a company anything less than an unqualified opinion or by not bowing to management's wishes in how to report certain items in its financial statements?

27. The cost that a company must pay to attract investors is a function of the company's riskiness. Higher risk companies must pay more to attract investors than lower risk companies. If a company can make itself appear less risky, its cost of capital should decrease. Consequently, companies have incentives to manipulate the financial statements to make themselves appear less risky. An example would be to engage in off-balance-sheet financing as opposed to on-balance-sheet financing.

28. Accepted accounting practices vary across countries. That is, each country has its own set of generally accepted accounting principles. These varying principles reflect the different economic systems, cultures, environments, and heritages of the countries. Because accounting principles vary across countries, it can be quite difficult, if not impossible, to compare the performance levels of companies based in different countries. In short, each country has its own rules on how to measure performance. Without a detailed understanding of each country's rules, it is difficult to make comparisons across countries.

29. Generally accepted accounting principles (GAAP) are a collection of recommended financial accounting reporting standards. GAAP is not a set of laws—companies are not required by law to follow GAAP. Further, GAAP allows managers some discretion in selecting accounting methods. In many cases, GAAP provides several approaches to account for an economic event—managers are free to select from any of these accepted approaches.

The Financial Accounting Standards Board (FASB) currently sets GAAP. Ideally, the FASB would be insulated from pressures so that it could select those accounting methods and procedures that provide the most useful information to financial statement users. However, the FASB is often subject to intense political pressure from managers, trade associations, auditors, and so forth, who attempt to influence the FASB's decisions by lobbying either directly to the FASB or indirectly through the Securities and Exchange Commission (SEC) or Congress.

Companies that do not adhere to GAAP will receive a qualified opinion from their auditors. Depending upon the reasons for the deviation from GAAP, such companies could face some problems with the SEC—companies whose securities are publicly traded are required by the SEC to follow GAAP. However, the SEC does not oversee companies whose securities are not publicly traded. The only exception for nonpublicly traded companies is if a company is required to follow GAAP due to a debt agreement.

30. The International Accounting Standards Committee is the body that is primarily responsible for setting international accounting standards. Its progress in harmonizing accounting standards has been slowed due primarily to environmental and cultural differences across countries.

31. a. NIKE, a manufacturing company, has a major market position in athletic footwear and sports apparel.

b. The accounting firm of PricewaterhouseCoopers LLP audited NIKE's financial statements. The audit report states (1) which financial statements of NIKE are covered by the audit; (2) the audit firm's opinion that the financial statements of NIKE present fairly, in all material respects, financial condition, results of operations, and cash flows in accordance with generally accepted accounting principles; (3) that the financial statements are the responsibility of the management of NIKE; (4) that the audit firm's responsibility is to express an opinion on the financial statements based on its audit; (5) that the audit was conducted in accordance with generally accepted auditing standards; and (6) that the financial statements contain estimates which were evaluated in the audit.

c. According to its consolidated statements of income, NIKE reported 1998 net income of $399,600,000, compared to $795,800,000 for 1997 and $553,200,000 for 1996.

d. According to its consolidated balance sheets, NIKE's total liabilities as of year-end 1998 and year-end 1997 as a percent to total assets were as follows:

Current liabilities	$1,703,300,000	$1,866,900,000
Long-term debt	329,400,000	296,000,000
Deferred taxes and other liabilities	52,300,000	42,100,000
Total liabilities	$2,085,000,000	$2,205,000,000
Total assets	$5,397,400,000	$5,361,200,000
%	38.6%	41.1%

e. According to its consolidated statements of cash flows, NIKE generated $517,500,000, $323,100,000, and $339,700,000 in cash flows from operating activities in 1998, 1997, and 1996, respectively.

f. NIKE's 1998 net income was down considerably from 1997. Although sales were up in 1998, costs and expenses had risen even more, including a restructuring charge in 1998. Financial position at year-end 1998 was little changed over 1997. NIKE had significant working capital and a strong equity position as of the end of both years.

g. NIKE's board of directors consists of the following:

William J. Bowerman, Deputy Chairman of the Board of Directors
Thomas E. Clarke, President and COO of NIKE
Jill K. Conway, Visiting Scholar, MIT
Ralph D. DeNunzio, President, Harbor Point Associates, Inc.
Richard K. Donahue, Vice Chairman of the Board
Delbert J. Hayes
Douglas G. Houser, Assistant Secretary, NIKE; Partner, Bullivant Houser Bailey, Attorneys
John E. Jaqua, Secretary, NIKE; Partner, Jaqua & Wheatley, P.C., Attorneys
Philip H. Knight, Chairman of the Board and CEO of NIKE
Kenichi Ohmae, Former Chairman of the Board, McKinsey & Company
Charles W. Robinson, President, Robinson & Associates
A. Michael Spence, Dean, Graduate School of Business, Stanford University
John R. Thompson, Jr., Head Basketball Coach, Georgetown University

NIKE's advisory council consists of the following:

Michael Jordan, President, The Michael Jordan Foundation
Gareth C.C. Chang, Senior Vice President—Marketing, GM Hughes Electronics; President and CEO, Hughes International
Elizabeth G. Dolan, Dolan St. Clair, Inc.

32. E. W. Hauser and Associates' net income is based on generally accepted accounting principles while its taxable income is based on the Internal Revenue Code. These two sources of accounting procedures require or permit different accounting methods and procedures. For example, GAAP offers greater latitude in depreciating fixed assets than the IRS allows. Further, the IRS does not allow certain expenses to be deducted until the company incurs a cash outflow, while GAAP requires expenses to be deducted when incurred (e.g., warranty costs). Since the two types of accounting are based on different methods and procedures, the measures of a company's performance (such as net income) calculated under each type of accounting will usually be different.

33. Accounting is a <u>system</u> through which <u>managers</u> report <u>financial information</u> about an <u>economic entity</u> to a variety of <u>recipients</u> who use this information to make better <u>decisions</u>. These decisions affect the economic wealth of the reporting entity and its management. The differences between managerial and financial accounting are associated with the underlined items. Each of these items is discussed below.

System—accountants follow certain rules and procedures in preparing financial information. Managerial and financial accounting are both systems in that each follows certain rules and procedures to convert measurable economic events into financial reports. Financial accounting follows generally accepted accounting principles; managerial accounting follows the company's own information system.

Managers—management is responsible for creating the financial reports and the information contained within. The managers responsible for generating financial information under financial accounting are in the finance or accounting departments. Alternatively, the managers responsible for generating financial information under managerial accounting are in the company's internal accounting department.

Financial information—the type of information the accounting system provides. Financial accounting provides the financial information contained in annual financial reports (such as financial statements, footnotes, and supplementary schedules) and in filings made with the SEC; managerial accounting provides financial information contained in internal financial reports (such as manager reports, product costs, and performance evaluations).

Economic entity—the organization about which the accounting information reports. Managerial accounting is used by almost every entity while financial accounting reports on only profit-seeking entities.

Recipients—the type of people who will use the accounting information. People external to the entity are the primary users of the accounting information provided by financial accounting. Alternatively, people internal to the entity (i.e., managers) are the primary users of the accounting information provided by managerial accounting.

Decisions—the ultimate use of any information is for decision-making purposes. With financial accounting, the information is used to make investment decisions, negotiating decisions, dividend decisions, and so forth. With managerial accounting, the information is used to make operating decisions.

CHAPTER 2   The Financial Statements

SYNOPSIS

The author opens the chapter with an analogy of a business as a fruit tree. The author then presents overviews that include the various components of each financial statement: the classified balance sheet, the income statement, the statement of retained earnings, and the statement of cash flows.

An international perspective is presented on how financial statements differ in other countries. This discussion includes a specific comparison using a Japanese company.

The ethics vignette considers whether corporations are acting ethically when they publish annual reports that are factually correct, but presented so as to camouflage bad news with glitzy and slanted material.

The Internet research exercise considers the financial results and corporate strategy of an international company, Air France.

The following key points are emphasized in Chapter 2:

1. The three basic activities of a business and how they are reflected in the financial statements.

2. The balance sheet, income statement, statement of retained earnings, and statement of cash flows and how these financial statements are used.

TEXT/LECTURE OUTLINE

The financial statements.

   I.   How businesses are conducted.

        A.   Fruit tree analogy.

        B.   Three activities of a business.

             1.   Financing activities.

                  a)   Those activities involving the collection of capital through debt or equity issuances and any associated payments.

                  b)   Financing activities are analogous to the roots of a fruit tree.

2. Investing activities.

    a) Those activities involving the acquisition and the sale of producing assets (i.e., the assets used to produce and support the goods and services provided).

    b) Investing activities are analogous to the trunk and branches of a fruit tree.

3. Operating activities.

    a) Those activities involving the sale of goods and services.

    b) Operating activities are analogous to the fruit produced by a fruit tree.

II. The four fundamental financial statements.

A. Classified balance sheet.

1. The classified balance sheet is a statement of the company's financial position as of a point in time. The balance sheet is a statement of the fundamental accounting equation.

2. In a classified balance sheet, assets and liabilities are grouped into sub-classifications; in an unclassified balance sheet, assets and liabilities are not grouped into sub-classifications, they are simply listed.

3. Assets and liabilities are listed on the balance sheet in order of liquidity.

4. Asset groupings.

    a) Current assets.

        (1) Current assets are assets that are expected to be realized or converted into cash in the near future, usually within one year.

        (2) Current assets typically include cash, short-term investments, accounts receivable, inventory, and prepaid expenses.

    b) Long-term investments.

    c) Property, plant, and equipment.

    d) Intangible assets.

5. Liability groupings.

       a) Current liabilities.

          (1) Current liabilities are liabilities that are expected to be settled through the use of current assets.

          (2) Current liabilities typically include accounts payable, miscellaneous other payables (such as wages payable, interest payable, and so forth), and current maturities of long-term debts.

       b) Long-term liabilities.

   6. Stockholders' equity groupings.

       a) Contributed capital.

       b) Retained earnings (i.e., earned capital).

       c) Effect of organizational form (i.e., corporate versus partnership) on the equity section.

B. Income statement.

   1. The income statement explains the change in the company's net assets (i.e., total assets less total liabilities) during the accounting period due to operating activities.

   2. The change in net assets from operating activities is called net income (or loss) and is computed as revenues less expenses.

       a) Revenues are defined as inflows of assets or outflows of liabilities over a period of time due to a company's operating activities.

       b) Expenses are defined as outflows of assets or inflows of liabilities over a period of time due to a company's operating activities.

   3. Since revenues and expenses are defined by the changes in assets and liabilities, every transaction affecting the income statement also affects at least one asset or liability account on the balance sheet.

C. Statement of retained earnings.

   1. The statement of retained earnings explains the change in the retained earnings balance during the accounting period.

   2. The change in the retained earnings balance is due to the company's net income or loss and distributions to the company's owners (i.e., dividends).

D. Statement of cash flows.

1. The statement of cash flows explains (i.e., summarizes) the change in the cash balance during the accounting period.

    a) Cash flows from operating activities.

    b) Cash flows from investing activities.

    c) Cash flows from financing activities.

III. Relationships among the financial statements.

IV. International perspective.

V. Ethics in the real world.

VI. Internet research exercise.

LECTURE TIPS

1. The fruit tree analogy is an excellent and understandable way to introduce students to the concepts of operating, investing, and financing activities.

2. Students should be encouraged to read the text carefully so as to thoroughly understand what each account measures. A useful in-class drill requires students to explain what the amount reported on the balance sheet for a particular account represents.

3. Many introductory students have difficulty differentiating between cash collections and revenue and between cash disbursements and expenses. It is critical that these differentiations are made when discussing the income statement versus the operating activities section of the statement of cash flows.

4. It is critical to students' understanding of accounting and how to use financial statement information that they grasp how the four financial statements relate. However, most students often view each financial statement as independent and do not appreciate how the statements relate. Therefore, explain and demonstrate how the financial statements are linked together and complement one another.

5. When first discussing how to use the information in the financial statements, provide a general overview of how a potential investor would ascertain the company's solvency (i.e., compare its assets to its obligations) and earning power. Then provide a more detailed discussion by using a classified balance sheet (i.e., using current assets versus current liabilities), the income statement, the statement of cash flows, and ratio analysis.

OUTSIDE ASSIGNMENT OPPORTUNITIES

Study of annual reports: evaluation of profitability and solvency using financial statements and other information.

1. Obtain a recent annual report for a publicly held company. Read the financial statements and notes and evaluate profitability and solvency using concepts developed in the chapter. Read the letter to stockholders and other information in the annual report and compare with the results of your analysis; especially note instances where the letter to shareholders or the other information reads more favorably than indicated in the financial statements. Report your findings in writing and/or in a brief presentation to the class.

Comparative study of annual reports: a foreign company compared to a U.S. company.

2. Obtain a recent annual report for a publicly held foreign company. Compare the form, content, and terminology used in its financial statements to that of a U. S. public company, preferably one in the same industry. Report your findings in writing and/or in a brief presentation to the class.

ANSWERS TO END-OF-CHAPTER QUESTIONS

1. The roots of a tree are a system for collecting water and nutrients for the tree. Without the roots, a tree would die. The trunk and branches are necessary for a fruit tree to bear fruit. Finally, the fruit can be consumed or sold or bartered for other items (such as cash, fertilizer, and so forth). These other items can then be used to strengthen the trunk and branches or to strengthen the root system.

    A fruit tree is like a business in that investors are necessary for a company to exist. Thus, debt and equity investors are analogous to a tree's root system. In order for a company to be productive, it needs assets that the company can use to produce goods and services. Thus, a company's productive assets are analogous to the trunk and branches of a fruit tree. Companies can sell their goods and services for cash, and the cash can be used to acquire more productive assets, returned to debt investors (in the form of interest and principal payments), or consumed by equity investors (in the form of dividends). Thus, a company's goods and services are analogous to the fruit produced by a fruit tree.

2. Operating activities are associated with the sale of goods and services. These activities are reflected in the income statement, which measures the revenues and expenses involved in selling goods and services. The statement of retained earnings measures the extent to which the business reinvests its net earnings and pays dividends. Cash inflows and outflows from operating activities are shown in the statement of cash flows.

    Investing activities are associated with the acquisition and sale of producing assets. These activities are reflected in the balance sheet, which lists assets (goods and producing assets) as of a point in time. Cash inflows and outflows from investing activities are shown in the statement of cash flows.

Financing activities are associated with the collection of capital through equity or debt issuances and any associated payments, excluding interest, to debt and equity investors. These activities are reflected in the balance sheet, which lists financing sources (debt, equity, and reinvestments from net earnings) as of a point in time. Cash inflows and outflows from financing activities are shown in the statement of cash flows.

3. Since the balance sheet is associated with a specific date, it provides information on the company's financial position as of that specific date. Alternatively, the income statement, the statement of retained earnings, and the statement of cash flows are associated with a period of time. Thus, these three statements provide information on the inflows and outflows associated with transactions during that period of time.

4. Assets represent items and rights that a company has acquired through objectively measurable transactions which can be used to generate future economic benefits. Assets are listed on the balance sheet in order of liquidity. The most liquid assets are listed first, followed by the second-most liquid, and so forth. Presenting assets in this manner provides information to financial statement users about which assets are most readily available to satisfy the company's obligations. Assets are usually grouped into several categories. These categories are current assets; long-term investments; property, plant, and equipment; and intangible assets. Examples of current assets include cash, marketable securities, accounts receivables, inventory, and prepaid expenses.

5. If a company incurred debt to finance the investment, the amount payable would appear in the liability section of the balance sheet, and related maturities, interest rates, and covenant restrictions would be disclosed. Also, reported net income would be less because of interest expense on the debt.

Equity financing would appear in the stockholders' equity section of the balance sheet. The economic cost of equity is not reflected in the financial statements, and net income would not be affected.

6. Assets are acquired through borrowings, owner contributions, and operations. These three sources comprise the right-hand side of the balance sheet (i.e., right-hand side of the accounting equation). The claims on the assets acquired through borrowings are called liabilities. The claims on the assets acquired through owner contributions (part of stockholders' equity) are called contributed capital. The assets acquired through operations (also part of stockholders' equity) are called earned capital, which is captured in retained earnings. The balance in retained earnings represents the company's cumulative earnings not yet promised to stockholders in the form of dividends.

7. Revenues represent the inflow of assets or the outflow of liabilities over a specified period of time due to the company's operating activities. Expenses represent the inflow of liabilities or outflow of assets associated with generating revenues. Revenues increase stockholders' equity through retained earnings. Consequently, revenues affect the balance sheet in two ways: first, by affecting assets and/or liabilities and, second, by affecting retained earnings. Expenses decrease stockholders' equity through retained

earnings. Consequently, expenses affect the balance sheet in two ways: first, by affecting assets and/or liabilities and, second, by affecting retained earnings. Note that the recognition of revenues and expenses do not have to coincide with the collection of cash or the disbursement of cash, respectively.

A "core" revenue is revenue generated from core business activities as opposed to "one-shot" transactions. Similar to a "core" revenue, a "core" expense is an expense relating to core business activities as opposed to a "one-shot" transaction. Users are interested in "core" revenues and expenses because, presumably, they are expected to recur and are therefore useful in predicting future revenues and expenses.

8. Revenues and expenses are associated with inflows and outflows of assets or liabilities. To maintain the equality of the accounting equation (i.e., Assets = Liabilities + Stockholders' Equity), these inflows and outflows are offset by changes in the retained earnings account. So, although revenues and expenses are reported on the income statement, they are also reported as part of retained earnings to maintain the equality of the accounting equation. In short, revenue and expense accounts are actually temporary, sub-accounts of retained earnings. The balance in retained earnings signals users as to what extent the company has been profitable in the past and has chosen to reinvest those profits.

9. Short-term investments represent an equity investment by a company in another company. On the other hand, capital stock represents ownership rights given out by a company. If IBM purchases common stock directly from Xerox, IBM would report short-term investments while Xerox would report contributed capital.

10. A company should recognize revenue when the company becomes entitled, through operating activities, to collect cash from another entity. The actual cash collection could (1) take place at the same time (which would increase cash when the revenue is recognized); (2) take place at a later date (which would give rise to an account receivable when the revenue is recognized); or (3) take place at an earlier date (which would result in a decrease in deferred revenue when the revenue is recognized). Thus, the asset accounts that are related to Sales are Cash (for cash sales) and Accounts Receivable (for credit sales). The liability account that is related to Sales is Deferred Revenue (sometimes called Unearned Revenue).

Every income statement account is associated with at least one balance sheet account. Some of the more common relationships are presented below.

a. Cost of Goods Sold is related to Inventory and Accounts Payable.

b. Depreciation Expense is related to Fixed Assets, specifically Accumulated Depreciation.

c. Expenses can be related to Prepaid Expenses or Accrued Expenses Payable.

11. Net cash flow from operating activities and net income both provide a measure of the company's operating performance for a period of time. Net cash flows from operating activities provide information about only those operating transactions that affect cash. Net income provides information on all the operating activities that affect any asset or liability account. Thus, net income is a broader measure of performance than net cash

flow from operating activities; net income focuses on all assets and liabilities, not on just one asset (i.e., cash). Because of its focus on all assets and liabilities, net income is more useful than net cash flows from operating activities for assessing a company's earning power. Alternatively, because of its focus on cash, which is used to make interest and principal payments, net cash flow from operating activities is more useful than net income for assessing a company's solvency.

12. The manager has incentives not to let the current ratio drop below 2:1. Consequently, if the manager has the option to report a particular transaction in different ways or to enter into certain transactions, the manager may select the reporting method or transaction that results in the lowest probability that the current ratio requirement will be violated. For example, this current ratio requirement might affect management's decision whether to account for inventory using LIFO (which results in lower reported inventory values, and hence lower current assets in time of rising inventory costs) or FIFO (which results in higher reported inventory values). The current ratio requirement could also alter management's decision regarding when to pay cash for inventory purchases or when to sell marketable securities.

Assume that the owners of a company give senior managers a contract that specifies that the managers will receive a percentage of net income as a bonus. The managers now have incentives to maximize reported net income since higher net income implies higher bonuses. If, instead, the bonus contract had upper and lower boundaries, the managers' incentives would be different. This type of contract would state that the managers would receive no bonus if net income was below a specified level and that the managers would receive no additional bonus once net income reached a certain level. If net income had already reached the upper level, the managers would have incentives to try to defer net income to future periods so that they could maximize the probability of receiving a bonus in a future period. Alternatively, if net income was already below the lower boundary, the managers may want to "take a bath" in order to increase the probability that they would receive bonuses in future years.

13. Financial statements of companies based in different countries vary not only because the countries have disparate accepted accounting methods and procedures, but also because of differences in business environments and culture. The chapter points out, for example, that a person comparing a company based in the United States versus a company based in Japan would expect the companies' debt/total asset ratios to be different—debt has different cultural meanings in the two countries. High levels of debt is considered risky in the United States, while high levels of debt in Japan is considered a sign of confidence by the creditors. In order to evaluate the financial statements of companies based in different countries, financial statement users need to understand the differences across countries in both accepted accounting principles and culture.

CHARACTERISTICS OF END-OF-CHAPTER ASSIGNMENTS

Item	Difficulty	Description

Brief exercises:

Item	Difficulty	Description
BE–1	E	Dividends as a percentage of net income
BE–2	E	Financing assets
BE–3	E	Assessing solvency
BE–4	E	The statement of cash flows across time

Exercises:

Item	Difficulty	Description
E2–1	M	Identifying financing, investing, and operating transactions
E2–2	M	Identifying financing, investing, and operating transactions
E2–3	E	Balance sheet or income statement account?
E2–4	M	Relationships between retained earnings and revenues and expenses across time
E2–5	M	Relationships between retained earnings and revenues and expenses across time
E2–6	M	Using working capital to assess solvency
E2–7	H	The effects of different forms of financing on financial statement numbers and debt covenants
E2–8	M	The statement of cash flows across time
E2–9	M	The statement of cash flows across time
E2–10	H	Preparing a statement of cash flows
E2–11	H	Preparing a statement of cash flows
E2–12	H	Preparing financial statements from simple transactions
E2–13	H	Preparing financial statements from simple transactions

Problems:

Item	Difficulty	Description
P2–1	E	Classifying balance sheet accounts
P2–2	E	Classifying income statement accounts
P2–3	H	Preparing a balance sheet in proper form
P2–4	M	Balance sheet and income statement relationships across five years
P2–5	M	Using financial statements to assess solvency and earning power
P2–6	M	Analyzing financial statements
P2–7	M	Analyzing financial statements
P2–8	H	Balance sheet value and the fair market values of the assets
P2–9	H	Debt covenants can limit investments and dividends

Issues for discussion:

Item	Difficulty	Description
ID2–1	M	Relationships between cash flows, income, and dividends
ID2–2	M	Investing and financing transactions
ID2–3	H	The annual report of NIKE
ID2–4	E	Debt covenants
ID2–5	H	Statement of cash flow patterns across companies
ID2–6	H	Statement of cash flow patterns across time
ID2–7	H	Statement of cash flows—British format

CHAPTER 3 Using Financial Statement Information

SYNOPSIS

In this chapter, the author discusses ways in which information contained within financial statements may be used to evaluate a company. The author discusses how financial statements can be useful in (1) helping investors and creditors influence and monitor the business decisions of a company's managers, and (2) helping to predict a company's future earnings and cash flows.

The discussion on using the financial statements focuses on the elements of financial statement analysis: (1) assessing the business environment; (2) reading and studying the financial statements and footnotes; (3) assessing earnings quality; (4) analyzing the financial statements; and (5) predicting future earnings and/or cash flows.

The author discusses ways to analyze a company's financial statements (through ratio analysis) and emphasizes the importance of comparisons across time and within the industry. Comparisons within the financial statements are covered in detail and include (1) common-size financial statements; (2) profitability ratios; (3) leverage ratios; (4) solvency ratios; (5) asset turnover ratios; and (6) market ratios.

The chapter includes a thorough discussion on the limitations of financial statements and an overview of financial statement analysis in an international setting. Appendix 3A contains a framework designed to help in the analysis of ratios as a package (called the DuPont model). It also describes the basics of cash flow analysis.

The ethics vignette considers a company's use and the auditor's acceptance of aggressive accounting practices that are only barely acceptable.

The Internet research exercise directs the student to earnings forecast information to identify industry groups expected to report rising versus falling earnings.

The following key points are emphasized in Chapter 3:

1. Using financial accounting numbers to influence management decisions and to predict future events.

2. Five steps of financial statement analysis.

3. Assessing the business environment.

4. Assessing earnings quality and persistence.

5. Analyzing financial statements.

6. Difficulties involved in using annual report information to identify mispriced securities.

7. Difficulties involved in using financial statements to compare the performance of companies operating in different countries.

LECTURE/TEXT OUTLINE

Using financial statement information.

I.   Usefulness of financial accounting numbers.

    A.   Influencing and monitoring business decisions of a company's managers.

        1.   Equity investors can influence management's business decisions by basing a large portion of management's compensation on reported profits.

        2.   Debt investors can influence management's business decisions through debt covenants.

    B.   Predicting a company's future earnings and cash flows.

        1.   Equity investors use financial information to predict future earnings and cash flows in their efforts to identify securities that will provide high returns.

        2.   Creditors use financial information to predict whether companies can generate enough cash in the future to cover debt payments.

        3.   Future cash flows are the heart of a company's true value, which is of interest to both investors and creditors. The following three reasons can cause a company's reported book value and true value to differ:

            a)   Business environment.

            b)   Inherent financial statement limitations.

            c)   Management bias.

II. Elements of financial statement analysis.

    A.   Assessing the business environment.

        1.   Learn about the company, its industry, and how these relate to the overall economy.

        2.   Other experts (Moody's, Value Line, Dun & Bradstreet, Standard & Poors, *The Wall Street Journal*) provide ready insight.

B.   Reading and studying the financial statements and footnotes.

1.   The audit report.

2.   Significant transactions.

3.   The financial statements and footnotes.

C.   Assessing earnings quality.

1.   Quality of earnings—the degree to which a company's reported earnings diverge from its "true" operating earnings because management exercised its discretionary influence over reported accounting numbers.

2.   Ways for management to "manage" financial accounting numbers.

a)   Overstating operating performance.

b)   Taking a "bath."

c)   Creating hidden reserves.

d)   Engaging in off-balance-sheet financing.

3.   Assessing earnings quality also includes considering inherent limitations of the financial statements.

a)   The value of human resources (i.e., human capital) is not included in the financial statements.

c)   The value of intangibles in technology-oriented companies is not reported in the financial statements.

d)   Few market values are used in the financial statements.

D.   Analyzing the financial statements.

1.   Comparisons across time.

2.   Comparisons within the industry.

3.   Comparisons within the financial statements: common-size statements and ratio analysis.

E.   Common-size financial statements.

1.   Financial statement numbers are expressed as percentages of other financial statement numbers.

2.   Benefits of common-size financial statements.

a)   Provides relative rather than absolute comparisons.

b)   Helps indicate why changes occur in financial performance and condition.

F.   Financial ratios.

1.   Ratio analysis is based on the comparison of two or more financial statement numbers.

2.   Categories of ratios.

a)   Profitability ratios.

(1)   Profitability ratios are useful in assessing a company's earning power.

(2)   Different profitability ratios.

(a)   Return on equity.

i)   Ratio of net income to average stockholders' equity.

ii)   Measures the efficiency with which a company manages its stockholders' investments.

(b)   Return on assets.

i)   Ratio of the sum of net income and after-tax interest expense to average total assets.

ii)   Measures the efficiency with which a company manages both its stockholders' and its creditors' investments.

(c)   Return on sales (profit margin).

i)   Ratio of the sum of net income and after-tax interest expense to net sales.

ii)   Provides information on a company's ability to generate and market profitable products and control its costs. It reflects the number of cents in profit for every dollar of sales.

   b) Leverage ratios.

       (1) Leverage ratios provide information useful in evaluating a company's capital structure.

       (2) Different leverage ratios.

            (a) Common equity leverage.

                 i)   Ratio of net income to the sum of net income and after-tax interest expense.

                 ii) Compares the return available to the stockholders to the returns available to all capital providers.

            (b) Capital structure leverage.

                 i)   Ratio of average total assets to average stockholders' equity.

                 ii) Measures the extent to which a company relies on borrowings (liabilities).

            (c) Debt/equity ratio.

                 i)   Ratio of average total liabilities to average stockholders' equity.

                 ii) Another way to measure capital structure leverage.

            (d) Long-term debt ratio.

                 i)   Ratio of long-term debt to total assets.

                 ii) Indicates the relative importance of long-term debt as a source of asset financing.

   c) Solvency ratios.

       (1) Solvency ratios are useful in assessing a company's ability to meet its debts.

       (2) Different solvency ratios.

       (a) Current ratio.

          i) Ratio of current assets to current liabilities.

          ii) Provides a measure of a company's ability to cover its current liabilities with current assets.

       (b) Quick ratio.

          i) Ratio of quick assets (i.e., cash, marketable securities, and accounts receivable) to current liabilities.

          ii) Provides a measure of a company's ability to cover its current liabilities with cash-like assets.

       (c) Interest coverage ratio.

          i) Ratio of income before interest and taxes plus tax expense and interest expense to interest expense.

          ii) Measures a company's ability to meet its interest charges through operations.

       (d) Accounts payable turnover.

          i) Ratio of cost of goods sold to average accounts payable.

          ii) Measures how quickly, on average, suppliers are paid off.

          iii) Dividing this ratio into 365 days indicates the number of days, on average, that accounts payable balances remain outstanding.

    d) Asset turnover ratios.

      (1) Asset turnover ratios provide a measure of the speed with which assets move through operations.

      (2) Different asset turnover ratios.

       (a) Receivables turnover.

          i) Ratio of net credit sales to average accounts receivable.

          ii) Indicates the number of times receivables are recorded, collected, and recorded again each year.

       (b) Inventory turnover.

        i)   Ratio of cost of goods sold to average inventory.

        ii)   Indicates the number of times inventory is replaced each year.

(c) Fixed assets turnover.

        i)   Ratio of sales to average fixed assets.

        ii)   Indicates the speed with which fixed assets are used up.

(d) Total asset turnover.

        i)   Ratio of sales to average total assets.

        ii)   Indicates the speed with which all assets are used up in operations, aggregating the turnover measures of the component assets in (a) to (c).

(3) Each turnover ratio can be converted to "days" by dividing it into 365 days.

e) Market ratios.

(1) Market ratios provide measures of returns to common stockholders due to changes in the market price of common stock and the receipt of dividends.

(2) Different market ratios.

(a) Earnings per share.

        i)   Ratio of net income to the average number of common shares outstanding.

        ii)   Standardizes a company's income, which makes it easier to make comparisons across companies. It provides a measure of a company's profitability strictly from the common stockholders' viewpoint.

(b) Price/earnings (P/E) ratio.

        i)   Ratio of market price per share to earnings per share.

        ii)   Indicates the sensitivity of a company's stock price to changes in its earnings.

(c) Dividend yield ratio.

              i)   Ratio of dividends per share to market price per share.

              ii)   Measures the cash return on stockholders' investments.

    (d) Annual return on investment.

              i)   Ratio of the sum of price appreciation per share and dividends per share to market price per share at the beginning of the period.

              ii)   Measures the rate of return on common shares for the period.

IV. Predicting future earnings and/or cash flow.

V. Annual report information and predicting stock prices.

VI. Financial statement analysis in an international setting.

VII. Ethics in the real world.

VIII. Internet research exercise.

IX. Further analytical techniques (Appendix A).

    A.   Analyzing financial ratios (DuPont model).

    B.   Cash flow analysis.

LECTURE TIPS

1. Students must avoid getting bogged down in computing ratios and must understand what the ratios indicate. The purpose of each ratio should be thoroughly discussed and illustrated. Further, it should be stressed that there are no "correct" formulas; the actual formula for a ratio will vary depending upon the needs of the person performing the analysis.

2. Students often try to analyze a company using a single company's ratios at a particular point in time. It should be stressed that analyzing a company only makes sense across time, across companies, or both.

OUTSIDE ASSIGNMENT OPPORTUNITIES

Financial analysis project (longer term assignment)

1. Form groups (3–5 students) and select a "target" public company and a comparable company in the same industry; obtain the annual reports and 10-Ks for both.

    Compute the ratios covered in the text (summarized in Figure 3–3) for both companies for as many periods as possible with the most recent reports. Prepare graphic presentations of selected ratios.

    Obtain and summarize two substantive articles on the target company from the financial press.

    Obtain comparative market statistics for the companies selected, as well as for the entire industry and the market as a whole. A good source is *http://www.Quicken.com.*

    Use the information gathered to evaluate the target company as a candidate for (1) a short-term loan; (2) a bond investment; and (3) an equity investment. Prepare a written report and make an oral presentation to the class.

    Submit the written report for instructor feedback before the final report and presentation. Use the computer for all assignments—the internet to access annual reports, 10-Ks, market data, etc.; programs for word-processing and spreadsheets for text, computations, and graphic presentations.

Article search: "managed" financial statements

2. Search the current financial press (*The Wall Street Journal, Barrons, Fortune, Forbes,* etc.) for an article relating to a company that may have "managed" its financial statements. Report your findings in writing and/or in a brief presentation to the class.

Application of other analytical techniques: bankruptcy prediction model

3. Obtain and read the Altman article on bankruptcy prediction referenced below.[1] Using the financial statements in Appendix A, compute the Z-score (discussed in the referenced article) for NIKE and interpret the result in a written report.

Application of other analytical techniques: cash flow ratios

4. Obtain and read the Giacomino-Mielke article on cash flow ratios referenced below.[2] Using the financial statements in Appendix A, compute the nine ratios (presented in the referenced article) for NIKE on a comparative basis for two years and evaluate the results.

---

[1] E. I. Altman, "Financial Ratios, Discriminant Analysis and the Prediction of Corporate Bankruptcy," *The Journal of Finance,* September 1968, pp. 589–609.

[2] Don E. Giacomino and David E. Mielke, "Cash Flows: Another Approach to Ratio Analysis," *Journal of Accountancy,* March 1993, pp. 55–58.

ANSWERS TO END-OF-CHAPTER QUESTIONS

1. Earning power refers to a company's ability to generate wealth through operating activities and, ultimately, to generate cash; solvency refers to a company's ability to have sufficient cash available to pay its debts as they come due. Both earning power and solvency, therefore, address cash flows. However, earning power focuses more on long-term future cash flows, and solvency focuses more on day-to-day cash inflows and outflows. This different focus implies that equity investors are more interested in assessing a company's earning power while creditors are more interested in assessing a company's solvency. Although these two concepts are distinct, they are nevertheless related. A company cannot generate future cash flows if it does not exist, and a company cannot exist if it is not solvent. Further, most companies rely on operating activities to generate cash used to pay its debts.

2. Stockholders earn their return through dividends and stock appreciation. Dividends are paid out of the cash reserves that are available over a company's life; stock appreciation results from increases in a company's expected future dividends (i.e., future cash reserves). Since cash reserves are generated through operations, equity stockholders prefer companies to maintain high earning power. To induce management to make decisions consistent with maintaining high earning power, stockholders provide management with incentives consistent with this goal. Two common incentive schemes are (1) providing management with incentive compensation based on net income and (2) providing management with ownership shares in the company. In this way, management's wealth is directly tied to those factors that increase stockholders' wealth. Such schemes often require net income to exceed a certain level before the incentive scheme becomes effective. Having a lower boundary on the scheme provides management with incentives to strive for this cutoff, at a minimum.

3. Creditors are interested in a company's ability to meet its interest and principal payments as they come due. By imposing restrictions on a company, creditors can increase the probability that the company will be able to meet its interest and principal payments. For example, by limiting a company's freedom to pay dividends, the company should, theoretically, have more cash available to meet debt payments. Further, requiring a company to maintain a certain level of current assets in relation to its current liabilities increases the probability that the company will have sufficient cash to settle its current liabilities and remain solvent.

4. Audited financial statements are not necessary for most companies. Audited financial statements are legally required only for those companies whose equity securities are publicly traded. Additionally, companies relying on outside debt investors or private equity investors may be required (by the investors) to provide audited financial statements as a condition of the investment agreement. Outside investors have limited knowledge about a company's performance; the auditor's report provides independent assurances to investors that the financial statements distributed by the company fairly represent, in all material respects, its financial position and operations. Hence, small businesses whose stock is not publicly traded would only have to have their financial statements audited if they had outside debt investors or private equity investors who required audited financial statements as a condition of the investment.

5. Financial accounting numbers by themselves do not provide any information. These numbers can only provide information on how well a company is performing by comparing the numbers to other relevant numbers. One such approach is to make comparisons across time. Comparing financial accounting numbers across time helps users identify important trends and turning points in a company's operations. Further, such comparisons may also give users insights into a company's business such as any seasonal or cyclical variations in performance.

    Although comparisons across time can be useful, at least two problems exist with such comparisons. First, financial statements are based on historical data. Trying to predict future events and trends using historical data and trends is dangerous; there is no guarantee that past trends will continue into the future. Second, comparisons across time are only meaningful if the financial accounting numbers were prepared using the same accounting methods. If a company changes its accounting methods, financial statement users must adjust for these changes when evaluating trends in a company's financial accounting numbers.

6. Earnings persistence refers to the extent to which an income number reported in the current period is expected to reflect future income levels. Financial statement users would usually desire high earnings persistence because it makes it easier for them to predict future income levels, which they use to help predict future cash flows. Income statement items can be classified as operating items (i.e., those items that are both usual and frequent); continuing items (i.e., those items that are usual or frequent, but not both); or noncontinuing items (i.e., discontinued operations, extraordinary items, and cumulative effects of changes in accounting principles). Because operating items, by definition, are part of the company's central, ongoing operations, they are expected to continue into the future. Thus, operating items would be expected to have higher earnings persistence than continuing items and noncontinuing items.

7. There are numerous types of significant transactions. Five examples of such transactions are given below.

    a. A company borrows $1,000,000 by issuing bonds. This transaction is important to financial statement users because they will want to know (1) how the company intends to use the $1,000,000; (2) whether the company will be able to invest the money to generate a return for the stockholders; and (3) whether the company will be able to service the interest and principal payments on the debt. In addition, the debt issue will affect certain ratios (either immediately or over the life of the debt) such as the debt/equity ratio, times interest earned, and return on assets.

    b. One of a company's manufacturing facilities was destroyed by a tornado. This event is important because it would affect the company's ability to maintain its current level of production. In addition, financial statement users would want to know whether the company had insurance to cover the loss and whether the company intended to rebuild the manufacturing facility. The answers to these questions are important because they have implications for the company's future operations. Financial statement users would also have to use ratio analysis carefully because the loss of the manufacturing facility (and the resulting drop in inventory and sales) could distort trends in certain key ratios such as return on equity and return on assets.

c. A company purchases two new business lines from another company. An important question from financial statement users is how these new lines of business will affect the future direction of the company. In addition, trend analysis of ratios will be difficult because the company's assets, liabilities, and net income will be affected by the addition of the new business lines.

d. A company decides to discontinue two of its five business segments. Financial statement users will want to know how discontinuing the two business segments will affect the company's future operations. In addition, performing trend analysis of ratios will be more difficult. Financial statement users will also have to decide whether the effect of the discontinued operations on the income statement should be included or ignored when calculating ratios that include net income (such as return on equity, return on assets, times interest earned, and earnings per share).

e. A company issues 250,000 new shares of common stock. Financial statement users will want to know how the company intends to use the cash generated from the stock issue and whether the new shares will affect the amount of dividends per share declared by the company's board of directors. In addition, the stock issue will affect certain ratios (either immediately or over the life of the debt) such as the debt/equity ratio and earnings per share.

8. Credit rating agencies, such as Moody's Investor Service, Dun & Bradstreet, and Standard & Poor's, are a primary source for credit ratings. Credit ratings are important because they provide information about a company's riskiness (which is related to solvency) and future prospects (which is related to both solvency and earning power). These ratings also affect a company's ability to issue debt and the terms of any new debt it issues. The credit rating agencies establish credit ratings by analyzing a company's financial position, operations, and future prospects.

9. Managers can bias financial statements in numerous ways, all of which are acceptable under GAAP. (1) Managers can choose one acceptable accounting policy over another, such as using FIFO rather than LIFO for inventory valuation. (2) Managers can change estimates used in preparing financial statements, such as the estimated useful life used to depreciate fixed assets. (3) Managers can make reporting decisions that "distort" the financial accounting numbers. (4) Managers can make operating decisions designed to bias the financial statements. For example, managers could delay purchasing inventory at the end of the year in an effort to report lower liabilities. (5) Managers may use conservative accounting methods, estimates, and judgments as part of a strategy such as "taking a bath" (e.g., recognize an accounting loss in an already poor year), or creating "hidden reserves" (e.g., recognize an accounting loss in a good year to "smooth" reported earnings over time.)

10. Quality of earnings refers to how well a company's reported earnings reflect its true operating earnings. That is, how well do the company's financial statements reflect the objective and appropriate book values and results of operations? Low-quality earnings would usually not be expected to be very predictive about future earnings because they do not adequately reflect the company's results of operations. This implies that low-quality earnings would not be of much value to financial statement users. Alternatively, high-quality earnings, by definition, reflect the company's results of operations, and

should, therefore, be useful in predicting future cash flows. For these reasons, stock prices should be more responsive to high-quality earnings than to low-quality earnings.

11. Research has indicated that the major security exchanges are efficient with respect to publicly available information. That is, security prices almost instantaneously reflect the information available to the public. Hence, once information becomes publicly available, it is impounded in stock prices and cannot be used to identify undervalued securities.

Financial reports are just one source of information. The information contained within the reports, such as net income, is often disseminated to the public through other channels prior to the release of the financial report. Hence, much of the information contained in financial reports is already publicly available and reflected in security prices. Even if there are no alternative sources of financial information, that information contained in financial reports could not be used to identify undervalued securities. As before stated, once the report is released, the information contained in the report is almost instantaneously impounded in the security prices and it can no longer be used to identify undervalued securities.

Although financial accounting numbers cannot be used to identify undervalued securities, these numbers can be used in several other ways. First, financial statement numbers are often used as the basis of contracts between a company and its equity and debt investors. Second, accounting numbers can be used to assess the risk and return from investing in a particular company. Third, creditors use financial accounting numbers to make loan decisions. Finally, these numbers, along with financial ratios, can be used to predict the probability that a company will go bankrupt or violate its debt covenants.

12. There are several reasons why it is difficult to analyze financial statements provided by companies based in other countries. These reasons include (1) differences in language and terminology across countries; (2) differences in accounting principles and practices across countries; and (3) differences in the acceptable magnitudes of certain ratios. These differences have developed because of the different cultures, which has led to financial accounting having different objectives in different countries.

CHARACTERISTICS OF END-OF-CHAPTER ASSIGNMENTS

Item	Difficulty	Description
Brief exercises:		
BE–1	E	Analyzing financial statements
Exercises:		
E3–1	E	Analyzing financial statements
E3–2	E	Analyzing financial statements
E3–3	M	Analyzing financial statements

Item	**Difficulty**	**Description**
E3–4	H	Computing ratios and preparing common-size financial statements
E3–5	M	Solvency and the role of the activity ratios
E3–6	E	Solvency and the statement of cash flows
E3–7	M	Using solvency and activity ratios together
E3–8	M	Explaining return on equity with inventory turnover
E3–9	H	Using ratios and the statement of cash flows to assess solvency and earning power
E3–10	H	The effects of transactions on financial ratios
E3–11	M	Debt covenants limiting additional debt and dividend payments
E3–12	E	Examining market ratios over time
E3–13	H	Computing ratios and the effect of transactions on return on equity
E3–14	M	Appendix 3A: Interpreting financial statement ratios
E3–15	M	Appendix 3A: Interpreting financial statement ratios

Problems:

P3–1	E	Computing ratios and the role of market values
P3–2	M	Borrow or issue equity: effects on financial ratios
P3–3	M	Percentage changes and common-size financial statements
P3–4	H	Comprehensive ratio analysis
P3–5	M	Analyzing financial statements
P3–6	M	Comparing companies on earning power
P3–7	M	Unusual items and financial ratios
P3–8	H	Preparing the financial statements from financial ratios
P3–9	M	Common-size financial statements
P3–10	M	Comparing ratios to industry averages
P3–11	M	Assessing the loan risk of a potential bank customer
P3–12	H	Issuing debt or equity: effects on ratios and owners
P3–13	H	Preparing financial statement data from financial ratios

Issues for discussion:

ID3–1	H	Linking company characteristics to the financial statements
ID3–2	H	Linking company characteristics to the financial statements
ID3–3	H	Market and book values
ID3–4	E	Meeting earnings projections
ID3–5	H	The importance of economic and industry factors
ID3–6	E	Human capital and the financial statements
ID3–7	M	Financial accounting information in an efficient market
ID3–8	M	Recent trends in earnings quality
ID3–9	M	Leverage, stock prices, and earning power
ID3–10	M	Financial ratios, earning power, solvency, and stock prices
ID3–11	M	Stock price reactions to earnings announcements
ID3–12	H	The annual report of NIKE
ID3–13	H	Appendix 3A: Analyzing the financial statements of Federal Express Corporation
ID3–14	H	Appendix 3A: Cash flow profiles and company life cycles

CHAPTER 4

The Measurement Fundamentals of Financial Accounting

SYNOPSIS

In this chapter, the author discusses the measurement fundamentals of financial accounting which consist of the basic assumptions, valuation issues, principles, and exceptions underlying the financial statements.

An international perspective on the conservatism principle is presented.

The ethics vignette considers the case of an industry leader (Microsoft) which uses and promotes ultra-conservative accounting for revenue recognition that may make it more difficult for smaller players in the industry to compete.

The Internet research exercise examines the criteria that must be met before revenue for sales of software can be recognized.

The following key points are emphasized in Chapter 4:

1. Four basic assumptions of financial accounting.

2. The markets in which business entities operate and the valuation bases used on the balance sheet.

3. The principle of objectivity and how it determines the dollar values that appear on the financial statements.

4. The principles of matching, revenue recognition, and consistency.

5. Two exceptions to the principles of financial accounting measurement: materiality and conservatism.

TEXT/LECTURE OUTLINE

The measurement fundamentals of financial accounting.

    I.   Objective of financial accounting. Financial accounting provides information to current and potential investors.

        A.   Allows investors to evaluate the solvency and earnings potential of the company.

        B.   Allows investors to influence and control the decisions of managers.

II.   Assumptions of financial accounting.

    A.   The assumptions concern the business environment and provide a foundation for creating an accounting system.

    B.   The basic assumptions of financial accounting.

        1.   Economic entity assumption.

            a)   Investors are interested in obtaining information about a particular profit-seeking entity. Consequently, the economic activities of that entity must be able to be identified and separated from the economic activities of its owners and all other entities.

            b)   Economic units versus legal units.

        2.   Fiscal period assumption.

            a)   The life of the entity can be broken into arbitrary time periods (fiscal periods) over which its performance and financial position can be measured.

            b)   This assumption is necessary to provide timely performance measures to investors. However, there is a tradeoff between timely and objective financial information.

        3.   Going concern assumption.

            a)   The life of the economic entity is assumed to extend indefinitely beyond the current fiscal period.

            b)   This assumption allows accountants to adhere to accrual accounting and to record assets and liabilities.

        4.   Stable dollar assumption.

            a)   An entity's performance and financial position is measured in monetary units. The monetary unit is assumed to possess stable purchasing power over time.

            b)   The assumption is inconsistent with the reality of inflation. Consequently, this assumption leads to financial statements that "distort" a company's actual performance.

III.   Valuations on the balance sheet.

    A.   Four valuation bases to use in measuring an entity's performance and financial position.

1. Present value—represents the discounted future cash flows associated with a particular financial statement item.

2. Fair market value—represents the sales value in the output market.

3. Replacement cost—represents the current prices paid in the input market.

4. Original cost—represents the input price paid when originally purchased by the company.

IV. The principles of financial accounting measurement.

    A. Principle of objectivity.

        1. Financial accounting information must be verifiable and reliable. The value of a transaction (and the assets and liabilities arising from that transaction) must be objectively determined; individuals with conflicting incentives would agree on the value of the transaction.

        2. Evaluation of present value, fair market value, and original cost on the dimension of objectivity.

        3. Requirement for objective measures excludes items of value, such as accrued goodwill, from an entity's financial statements.

    B. Matching principle.

        1. Costs are matched against the benefits that result from them.

        2. The first step in applying the matching principle is deciding when to recognize the benefit (i.e., revenue).

    C. Principle of revenue recognition.

        1. Addresses the question of when to recognize revenue.

        2. Criteria for recognizing revenue.

            a) The company must have completed a significant portion of the production and sales effort.

            b) The amount of revenue can be objectively measured.

            c) The major portion of the costs has been incurred and the remaining costs can be reasonably estimated.

            d) The eventual collection of cash is reasonably assured.

    D. Principle of consistency.

1. Consistency refers to the use of the same accounting policies over time.

2. GAAP encourages a company to use the same accounting policies to promote comparability of a company's performance over time.

3. Uniformity refers to the comparability of financial statements across different companies. Uniformity could only be achieved if all companies were required to follow the same accounting policies and methods. However, companies have latitude in the selection of accounting policies and methods.

   a) Each company faces a unique environment.

   b) GAAP is the result of a political process.

V. Two exceptions to the basic principles.

   A. Materiality.

      1. If the cost of providing financial information to investors exceeds the expected benefit they would derive from the information, then the company may record the event in the least costly method. In other words, an event is immaterial if the way in which it is recorded would not affect investors' evaluation and control decisions.

      2. Applying materiality requires a great deal of judgment.

   B. Conservatism.

      1. Conservatism states that, *when in doubt,* financial statements should understate assets, overstate liabilities, accelerate the recognition of losses, and delay the recognition of gains; when there is significant uncertainty about a transaction's value, the conservative alternative should be chosen.

      2. Cost of overstatement errors versus cost of understatement errors.

VI. International perspective.

VII. Ethics in the real world.

VIII. Internet research exercise.

LECTURE TIPS

1. It is important to tie the principles and assumptions back into the objective of financial accounting and to illustrate how the principles and assumptions affect accounting procedures. A highly recommended approach is to have students evaluate different

companies using financial statements based on different assumptions and valuation bases.

2. When discussing conservatism, a discussion of the relative costs of overstatements and understatements from the perspective of both managers and auditors would be appropriate.

3. The use of illustrative cases may make it easier for students to understand the specific principles and assumptions.

OUTSIDE ASSIGNMENT OPPORTUNITIES

Comparative study of annual reports: U.S. companies

1. Obtain a recent annual report for two publicly held companies in the same industry. Read the financial statements and footnotes (particularly the accounting policy footnote) and compare the accounting principles employed by each in terms of the fundamental concepts developed in the chapter. Evaluate which of the two appears most conservative. Report your findings in writing and/or in a brief presentation to the class.

Comparative study of annual reports: a continental European company compared to a U.S. company

2. Obtain a recent annual report for both a continental European company and for a U. S. public company (preferably both in the same industry). Read the financial statements and disclosures and compare the accounting principles employed by each in terms of the fundamental concepts developed in the chapter. Explain the rationale behind differences between the two. Report your findings in writing and/or in a brief presentation to the class.

Research of accounting literature: international standards

3. Form groups (3–5 students) to research current accounting literature for articles explaining the accounting model employed in a country other than the United States. Each group will research a different instructor-selected country. Compare the principles employed with those used in the United States and explain differences in terms of likely socio-economic levels in the country studied. Report the results in a class presentation. Follow up with an overall comparative summary by each group for all the selected countries.

Research of accounting literature: fair value accounting

4. Research current accounting literature for articles covering fair value accounting and its expanding place in our accounting model. Focus on the impact on users of financial statements as well as the economic consequences effect on management decisions. For example, much has been written about the financial services industry, which has especially been affected by recent fair value accounting pronouncements. Prepare a written and oral report of the findings.

ANSWERS TO END-OF-CHAPTER QUESTIONS

1. The financial statements were prepared in accordance with the economic entity assumption. This assumption states that profit-seeking entities are separate and distinct from their owners and other economic entities and that they can be identified and measured.

2. The stable dollar assumption allows accountants to add transactions from different time periods because it ignores changes in purchasing power that result from inflation or deflation. This assumption, however, is usually not valid because almost every company experiences inflation or deflation. Ignoring changes in purchasing power causes financial statements to be misstated, but preparing financial statements that do not follow this assumption would be very costly and less reliable.

3. The fiscal period assumption breaks the life of an entity into shorter time periods, thereby allowing the preparation of financial reports on a more timely basis. Financial statement users, therefore, receive information that is more relevant to their decision-making process. The relevance, though, is at the expense of reliability. As the time periods become shorter, more assumptions and estimates must be made to allocate amounts to particular periods.

4. A fiscal year is a twelve-month period that ends on a date other than December 31. Many companies use a fiscal year rather than a calendar year when their operations are seasonal; using a fiscal year allows an entire season to be reported as part of the same period. The selection of a fiscal year, as opposed to a calendar year, arises from the fiscal period assumption.

5. The going-concern assumption states that the entity is expected to exist indefinitely beyond the current accounting period. This assumption allows accountants to record assets and to follow the process of capitalizing and amortizing cash outflows. Assets are defined as items and rights that are expected to provide future benefits to the economic entity. If the entity is not expected to exist in the future, the entity could not expect to receive any future benefits. Further, capitalizing a cash outflow also assumes that the entity will exist in the future so that the outflow can eventually be amortized. While this assumption is useful, it is not very realistic. No company lasts indefinitely!

6. The input market is the market that provides the inputs (e.g., materials and labor) that a company uses in its operations. The output market is the market in which the company sells its goods and services. Both markets can be used to measure a company's performance and financial position. The input market can be used to determine replacement cost and the output market can be used to determine fair market values.

   The four valuation bases can all be described in terms of input and output markets. As already mentioned, fair market value represents the sales price of the company's assets in the output market, and replacement cost represents the current cost of the company's assets in the input market. Present value represents the discounted future cash flows from the output market. Finally, original cost represents the cost of an asset in the input market on the date that the asset was acquired.

7. The valuation bases used for the different balance sheet accounts are:

   a. Cash and current liabilities are valued at face value.

   b. Marketable securities are valued at fair value.

   c. Inventory is valued at the lower-of-cost-or-market value.

   d. Accounts receivable are valued at net realizable value.

   e. Long-term investments (other than notes receivable and bonds receivable) are valued at original cost.

   f. Prepaid expenses, fixed assets, and intangible assets are valued at net book value—the original cost less the portion of the asset's original cost amortized to date.

   g. Long-term notes receivable and long-term liabilities are valued at the present value of their future cash flows.

8. The principle of objectivity is probably the most pervasive of the different accounting principles. This principle guides the valuation bases used for valuing assets and liabilities. The principle of objectivity states that financial statement information must be verifiable and reliable and that the value of transactions be objectively determined. The only objective valuation base for many assets is original cost. But in those cases where more relevant valuation bases are relatively objective, the principle dictates using these other valuation bases. For example, using present value is acceptable to value long-term liabilities because future cash flows are contractually specified and, hence, objective. Additionally, marketable securities are valued at fair market value because the securities are traded on an exchange, which makes the securities' market values objective.

9. Present value reflects economic value. Under the principle of objectivity, however, this valuation base is usually not acceptable. The future cash flows associated with most assets and liabilities cannot be objectively determined. However, in those cases where the future cash flows are relatively objective, the assets and liabilities are valued at the present value of future cash flows. The most common case in which present value is used is for long-term liabilities and long-term debt investments because the future cash flows are contractually specified and, hence, objectively determined.

10. Measuring performance is based on the matching principle. This principle states that the efforts to generate benefits should be matched against those benefits. Inventories provide benefits to a company when the inventories are sold. Consequently, the cost of inventories should be capitalized until the inventory is sold, at which time the cost of the inventory sold should be expensed. Fixed assets also provide future benefits to a company. Consequently, the cost of the asset should be capitalized initially and then amortized (i.e., expensed) as the asset helps generate a benefit. With fixed assets, the link between the cost and the benefit is usually not clearly defined so assumptions and estimates must be made about how the asset provides benefits.

11. There are four criteria that must be met before a company can recognize revenue. First, the company must have completed a significant portion of the production and sales effort. Second, the amount of revenue must be objectively measurable. Third, the company must have incurred the major portion of the total costs and it must be able to

reasonably estimate any remaining costs. Finally, the company must be reasonably assured that it will eventually realize cash from the transaction.

Under the matching principle, all costs associated with generating a benefit should be matched against the benefit. Hence, the first step in applying the matching principle is deciding when the company has received a benefit. Once the benefit (i.e., revenue) has been generated, all the associated costs (including post-sale costs that are probable and can be reasonably estimated) should be expensed.

An example will help illustrate the link between the revenue recognition principle and the matching principle. Assume that a company purchases $50,000 of inventory. The company expects to sell this merchandise in the future, so the company expects a future benefit. Consequently, the company capitalizes $50,000 as inventory. At some later point in time, the company sells the entire inventory on account for $75,000. The company must first decide whether it is appropriate to recognize any revenue. The company has met the first criterion. The company has acquired the inventory and presumably expended money to provide a building in which to conduct business and to employ salespeople to sell the merchandise. The company has also met the second criterion. The buyer and seller have different incentives and both have agreed that $75,000 is a fair amount for the goods. Whether the company has met the last two criteria is less clear. If there are no remaining potential costs, such as warranty costs, or if the company can reasonably estimate any such costs and the company expects to eventually collect the $75,000, then it should recognize the $75,000 as revenue. Now that the company has received a benefit, it must try to match all the costs that were incurred to generate this benefit. Consequently, the company should match the cost of the inventory sold, $50,000, against the $75,000 in revenues.

12. Materiality is one of the exceptions to the principles of accounting. Materiality states that if a transaction is so small that the method used to account for it would not affect financial statement users' decisions, then the company can account for this transaction in any manner it desires. The company does not have to adhere to the principles of accounting. The justification for materiality is a cost/benefit trade off; the cost of adhering to the accounting principles outweighs the benefits to the financial statement users. Applying materiality requires a great deal of judgment. Managers should consider both the magnitude and the nature of the item when assessing materiality.

13. Conservatism is one of the exceptions to the principles of accounting. Conservatism states that if there is doubt about how to record a transaction or item, understate, rather than overstate the company's financial position. Conservatism is considered to be an exception to the principles of accounting because when accountants apply conservatism, they are using something other than the principles to decide how to value the item.

Assume that a company records a transaction in which there is some uncertainty as to the magnitude of the transaction or how it should be recorded. When the uncertainty is resolved, there are three possible outcomes. First, the transaction could have been correctly recorded. In this case the financial statements are correctly stated. Second, the company's financial health could have been understated, resulting in an error of understatement. Finally, the company's financial health could have been overstated, resulting in an error of overstatement. Errors of understatement and overstatement are not desirable since such errors can cause financial statement users to incur losses. The errors of overstatement are usually associated with out-of-pocket losses that might be quite large. The users can sue the auditors and managers for such losses. Alternatively, errors of understatement tend to be opportunity losses for which a financial statement user cannot sue. Hence, the legal liability of auditors and managers would tend to lead to more errors of understatement than to errors of overstatement. This position is identical to conservatism.

14. Inventories are carried on the balance sheet using the lower-of-cost-or-market rule. This is an example of conservatism. Downward price changes in inventory are recognized immediately while price increases are not recognized until the inventory is sold. This practice is consistent with the concept of conservatism in that profits should not be anticipated, but all possible losses should be recognized.

15. Companies based in countries from the Continental group rely primarily on a few, very large banks for capital. To protect the banks from granting bad loans, the accounting systems in these countries encourage (and in some cases require) companies to intentionally produce conservative financial statements. That is, the companies are encouraged to intentionally understate their assets and net income and overstate their liabilities. This situation is quite different in the United States where conservatism is expected to be applied only when there is doubt about how an item should be valued. It should be noted, however, that the legal environment in the United States is encouraging managers and auditors to become more and more conservative in order to protect themselves from massive legal settlements.

CHARACTERISTICS OF END-OF-CHAPTER ASSIGNMENTS

Item	Difficulty	Description
Brief exercises:		
BE4–1	E	Real data: Accounting assumptions, principles, and exceptions
Exercises:		
E4–1	E	The effects of inflation on holding cash
E4–2	E	The effects of inflation on holding land
E4–3	E	Valuation bases on the balance sheet
E4–4	M	Revenue recognition
E4–5	M	The effects on income of different methods of revenue recognition
E4–6	E	Assets and depreciation—which assumption and principle?
E4–7	E	The concept of materiality
E4–8	H	Changing accounting methods and net income
Problems:		
P4–1	E	The effects of inflation on reported profits
P4–2	E	Inflation and bank loans
P4–3	H	The irrelevance of original cost

Item	Difficulty	Description
P4–4	M	The stable dollar assumption and sales growth
P4–5	M	The economic value of a company vs. its book value
P4–6	H	Economic value and income vs. book value and income
P4–7	H	The differences between present value, book value, and liquidation value
P4–8	H	Three different measures of income
P4–9	M	Different methods of recognizing revenue
P4–10	M	Revenue recognition and net income
P4–11	H	Comparing companies using different accounting methods
P4–12	M	The economics of conservatism

Issues for discussion:

ID4–1	M	Revenue recognition and matching
ID4–2	E	Aggressive revenue recognition
ID4–3	M	Revenue recognition
ID4–4	H	Consistency and uniformity
ID4–5	E	Comparability
ID4–6	M	Conservative reporting?
ID4–7	M	The annual report of NIKE

CHAPTER 5   The Mechanics of Financial Accounting

SYNOPSIS

This chapter covers the mechanics of the preparation of financial statements. The author discusses economic events and the criteria necessary before such events can be reflected in the financial statements. The author describes the fundamental accounting equation and explains its relationship to the economic events that are reflected in the financial statements. The author explains the use of journal entries and T-accounts to capture the effects of economic events on the accounting equation and the financial statements. The author also describes how and why periodic adjustments to financial statements are made to reflect economic events that are not represented by transactions. Financial statement presentation in a multinational environment is presented.

In Appendix 5A, the author provides a more detailed description and a comprehensive example of the accounting cycle, including the preparation of financial statements.

This chapter and Appendix 5A cover the mechanics of the financial accounting process from an economic consequences perspective, emphasizing that managers must understand the mechanics that link their choice of transactions to the financial statements. Appendix 5B further covers the mechanics from a financial statement user's perspective, explaining how managers in their role as users can infer from financial statements the events and transactions that occurred during the accounting period. Appendix 5B covers a mechanical process, called T-account analysis, which can be used to make such inferences.

The ethics vignette addresses the subjectivity involved in decisions to capitalize or expense costs.

The Internet research exercise refers to the "Report of Management" in the annual report of Toys "R" Us, Inc., to consider how the company ensures that transactions are properly recorded.

The following key points are emphasized in Chapter 5:

1. Two criteria necessary for economic events to be reflected in the financial statements.

2. The accounting equation and how it relates to the balance sheet, income statement, statement of retained earnings, and statement of cash flows.

3. Journal entries (and T-accounts) and how they express the effect of economic events on the basic accounting equation and the financial statements.

4. Why managers need to understand how economic events affect the financial statements.

5. Why the financial statements are adjusted periodically to reflect certain economic events.

TEXT/LECTURE OUTLINE

The mechanics of financial accounting.

  I.   Economic events—must be both relevant and objectively measurable to be included in the financial statements.

        A.   Relevant means that the event has economic significance to the company.

        B.   Objectively measurable means that parties with differing incentives reach agreement on the value of the event and that those events are backed by documentary evidence which can be audited.

  II.   The fundamental accounting equation.

        A.   Assets = Liabilities + Stockholders' equity.

        B.   Effect of business transactions on the accounting equation.

        C.   Expanding the accounting equation to include accounts.

        D.   Using the expanded accounting equation to generate financial statements.

  III. The journal entry.

        A.   A journal entry records the economic event in a journal which thereby enters the event in the company's accounting records.

        B.   Accountants follow the double entry system. Under the double entry system, the journal entry to record an economic event affects at least two accounts. The double entry system maintains the equality of the accounting equation by requiring that total debits equal total credits.

             1.   Debit is defined as the left-hand side.

             2.   Credit is defined as the right-hand side.

        C.   All journal entries have three components:

             1.   The accounts affected.

             2.   The direction of the effect.

             3.   The dollar value of the transaction.

        D.   T-accounts are useful for keeping running tallies of balances for each account.

        E.   Financial statements can be prepared directly from the T-accounts.

IV.   Recognizing gains and losses.

V.   Periodic adjustments.

A.   Periodic adjustments are necessary because not all economic events that occur during the accounting period are captured by an exchange transaction in the same accounting period. Accrual accounting requires that all economic events that have occurred during the accounting period be recognized to achieve a proper matching of revenues and expenses.

B.   Periodic adjustments take one of three forms.

1.   Accruals.

a)   Accrue means to build up gradually. Accrual adjustments recognize economic events that have occurred in the current accounting period but have not yet been captured in an exchange transaction.

b)   Accrued expenses.

(1)   Accrued expenses are expenses that have been incurred but not yet paid.

(2)   The appropriate journal entry would be to debit an expense account and credit a liability account.

c)   Accrued revenues.

(1)   Accrued revenues are revenues that have been earned but cash collection has not yet occurred.

(2)   The appropriate journal entry would be to debit a receivable account and credit a revenue account.

2.   Deferrals (or cost expirations).

a)   Cost expiration adjustments write down an already established asset or liability account.

b)   Capitalizing versus expensing an expenditure.

c)   Cost expiration of assets.

(1)   Companies should prepare a cost expiration adjustment for an asset as the company consumes the asset due to the passage of time.

(2)   The appropriate journal entry would be to debit an expense account and credit the appropriate asset account.

d) Expiration of deferred revenues.

    (1) Deferred revenues are payments collected from customers that have not yet been earned.

    (2) The appropriate journal entry would be to debit the liability account and credit a revenue account.

3. Revaluation adjustments.

VI. Financial statement presentation in a multinational environment.

VII. Ethics in the real world.

VIII. Internet research exercise.

IX. Overview of the accounting cycle (Appendix 5A).

A. The accounting cycle is the process through which a company's economic events are transformed into financial statements.

B. The accounting cycle involves 16 steps or components.

1. Identify relevant and measurable economic events.

2. Interpret relevant and measurable events by identifying accounts affected, direction of effect, and dollar value of effect.

3. Prepare journal entry.

4. Enter journal entry in journal.

5. Post journal entry to ledger.

6. Prepare unadjusted trial balance as part of work sheet.

7. Enter adjusting entries on work sheet.

8. Prepare adjusted trial balance as part of work sheet.

9. Enter closing entries on work sheet.

10. Prepare final trial balance as part of work sheet.

11. Record adjusting and closing entries in journal.

12. Post adjusting and closing entries to ledger.

13. Prepare income statement.

14. Prepare statement of retained earnings.

15. Prepare balance sheet.

16. Prepare statement of cash flows.

X.   Mechanics—a user's perspective (Appendix 5B).

A.   The chapter and Appendix 5A cover mechanics from an *economic consequence perspective*.

B.   Many financial statement *users* employ T-account analysis to infer economic events from financial statements.

C.   Steps in T-account analysis.

1.   Identify one or more balance sheet accounts for analysis.

2.   Create T-accounts for each account.

3.   Recreate the activity that explains the change in the T-account balance.

4.   Infer the missing part of the activity in the T-account.

LECTURE TIPS

1.   Particular attention should be given to helping students in deciding whether an economic event has accounting significance and should be recorded. It would be worthwhile to spend some time covering the concepts of relevant and objectively measurable. Further, discussing different economic events that would be recorded (such as purchasing inventory) or would not be recorded (such as signing a new union contract) in a journal entry would be worthwhile.

2.   Often students need extra help understanding how to record economic events. In particular, students need help to understand (1) which accounts have debit and credit balances and (2) how debits and credits affect particular accounts. A useful approach is to break the recording process down into two distinct steps. The first step is to have students record economic events on the accounting equation (similar to Figure 5–2) expanded to include revenue, expense, and dividend accounts. This step prepares them (1) to work with revenue, expense, and dividend accounts, which are difficult for many students to grasp, and (2) to address which accounts are affected and how the accounts are affected without having to worry about debits or credits. The second step is to have students prepare journal entries for the transactions they recorded in the first step. This step allows students to focus exclusively on the debits and credits.

3. Students need help in understanding what each account represents and measures to be able to analyze economic events and prepare the appropriate journal entry. A written assignment or in-class presentation that requires them to explain what a particular account balance represents is recommended.

4. Many introductory students have difficulty differentiating between cash collections and revenue, and between cash disbursements and expenses. It is critical that these differentiations are made when discussing revenues and expenses so that students will be able to correctly analyze economic events and prepare journal entries.

5. Extra effort is often needed to help students understand adjusting entries. The key to this is the students' understanding of the relationship of specific income statement accounts to specific balance sheet accounts. A suggested method for helping students understand how specific accounts on these two statements fit together is to have students create T-accounts for balance sheet and income statement accounts. They should then indicate what the beginning and ending balances in each account represent, what economic events cause various accounts to increase or decrease, and which economic events affect more than one account. It is this last step that should help students better understand the relationships between income statement and balance sheet accounts. This exercise is also very useful in helping students understand which accounts have permanent balances and which ones have temporary balances; why some accounts have permanent balances; and what each account balance represents. Other potential ways to help students understand the relationships between specific income statement and balance sheet accounts are listed below:

    a. Presenting several examples of each type of adjustment.
    b. Discussing the effects on the financial statements of *not* making a required adjusting journal entry.
    c. Converting from accrual accounting amounts to cash accounting amounts or vice versa.

    It is also important for students to understand why adjusting entries are necessary. This understanding comes when students truly comprehend the difference between accrual accounting and cash-basis accounting. Spending time illustrating the differences using examples relevant to the students is strongly recommended.

6. Students need help in grasping the rationale for closing entries. Time should be spent discussing why temporary accounts are used rather than recording events affecting revenues, expenses, and dividends directly in the retained earnings account. A particularly useful approach is to have students record economic events on the accounting equation (similar to Figure 5–2) expanded to include revenue, expense, and dividend accounts. After recording the events, point out that assets do not equal the sum of liabilities and stockholders' equity unless the balances in the temporary accounts are considered.

OUTSIDE ASSIGNMENT OPPORTUNITIES

Additional assignments covering the accounting cycle

1. Develop the understanding of the mechanics of the financial accounting cycle through additional outside self-study and assignments available in supplements which complement the text.

    INTACT, by Dasaratha Rama, is an accounting cycle on-line and/or CD-ROM product that contains tutorials, practice assignments, and student instructions.

    The Accounting System: A Self-Study Primer for Introductory Accounting, by William Ruland, is a self-paced workbook which helps those with little or no prior exposure to the accounting system and accounting mechanics.

    Such outside assignments could be spaced over several weeks following coverage of Chapter 5, and would leave class time free to focus on the conceptual issues without sacrificing an understanding of the mechanics. It also meets the objective of utilizing computer technology.

T-account analysis using actual financial reports

2. Use the process described in Appendix 5B to reconstruct selected past accounting activity from the financial statements and footnotes of an actual public company. Interpret the additional information gained from this process from a user's perspective.

Simulation game

3. Obtain the Albrecht article[1] (referenced below) which describes an accounting and investment simulation game. Play the game and complete the written assignments as instructed therein.

ANSWERS TO END-OF-CHAPTER QUESTIONS

1. The fundamental accounting equation states that the dollar value of assets equals the sum of the dollar values of liabilities and stockholders' equity. The balance sheet is the statement of the accounting equation because the balance sheet lists a company's assets, liabilities, and stockholders' equity as of a point in time. The three other financial statements—income statement, statement of retained earnings, and statement of cash flows—each explain changes in balance sheet accounts. The income statement

---

[1] David W. Albrecht, "A Financial Accounting and Investment Simulation Game," *Issues in Accounting Education,* Spring 1995, pp. 127–141.

explains the change in the company's net assets due to operating activities; this activity is reflected in the company's operating assets and liabilities and in its retained earnings account. The statement of retained earnings explains the change in the balance of retained earnings during the accounting period. Finally, the statement of cash flows explains the change in the company's cash account during the year. In doing so, the statement of cash flows also helps explain changes in other asset and liability accounts.

2. a. Issuing stock for cash increases total assets by the amount of the cash received; it also increases contributed capital (part of stockholders' equity) by the same amount.

    b. Providing a service in exchange for a receivable increases total assets by the amount of the receivable and increases revenue by the same amount. The revenue is closed into retained earnings (part of stockholders' equity) as part of the closing process. Thus, providing a service for a receivable increases both total assets and total stockholders' equity.

    c. Paying cash for an expense decreases total assets by the amount of cash disbursed and increases expenses by the same amount. The expense is closed into retained earnings (part of stockholders' equity) as part of the closing process. Thus, paying cash for an expense decreases both total assets and total stockholders' equity.

    d. Purchasing equipment for cash increases total assets for the equipment acquired and decreases total assets by the same amount for the cash disbursed.

    e. Purchasing equipment in exchange for a note increases total assets for the equipment acquired and increases total liabilities by the same amount.

3. Objectivity is defined as amounts in monetary terms arising from exchange transactions that can be documented. Objectivity is usually assumed to exist when two parties with differing incentives base an exchange on an agreed dollar value. The two factors that ensure that only objective information is contained in the financial statements are the legal liability of auditors and managers to financial statement users and the investors' demand for reliable information.

4. To prepare a journal entry, one must know the accounts to use in the journal entry, whether to increase or decrease each account, and how much to increase or decrease each account. In this particular case, the two accounts affected are equipment and cash. Equipment is increased by $5,000; Cash is decreased by $5,000. The appropriate journal entry would be:

Equipment (+A)	5,000	
Cash (-A)		5,000
Purchased equipment.		

5. (1) Machinery (+A)   5,000

(1) Machinery (+A)	5,000	
Cash (-A)		5,000
Purchased machinery.		
(2) Accounts Payable (-L)	500	
Cash (-A)		500
Made payment to supplier.		

(3) Accounts Receivable (+A)   300
       Fees Earned (R, +SE)   300
    Performed services.

(4) Wages Expense (E, -SE)   800
       Cash (-A)   800
    Incurred and paid wages.

6. The basic accounting equation is Assets = Liabilities + Stockholders' Equity. The four transactions affect the accounting equation as follows:

   (1) Assets are increased $5,000 for the machinery acquired and decreased $5,000 for the cash disbursed.
   (2) Assets are decreased $500 for the cash disbursed, and liabilities are decreased $500 for the settlement of accounts payable.
   (3) Assets are increased $300 for the receipt of accounts receivable, and stockholders' equity is increased $300 for the fees earned.
   (4) Assets are decreased $800 for the cash disbursed, and stockholders' equity is decreased $800 for the wages incurred.

   Completing a service or incurring wages affects the retained earnings account. The four transactions affect the income statement and balance sheet as follows:

   (1) This transaction decreases current assets by $5,000 and increases long-lived assets by $5,000, leaving total assets unchanged. Liabilities and stockholders' equity are not affected.
   (2) This transaction decreases both current assets and total assets by $500. Liabilities also decrease $500 while stockholders' equity is not affected.
   (3) This transaction increases current assets and total assets by $300. Stockholders' equity, through retained earnings, increases by $300; liabilities are not affected.
   (4) This transaction decreases current assets and total assets by $800. Stockholders' equity, through retained earnings, decreases by $800; liabilities are not affected.

7. Permanent accounts are accounts whose balances carry forward from one accounting period to the next. In other words, those accounts represent the company's financial position. Assets, liabilities, and stockholders' equity accounts are considered permanent accounts. Temporary accounts are accounts whose balances do not carry forward to the next period. In other words, those accounts measure performance for a particular period of time. Revenue, expense, and dividend accounts are considered temporary accounts.

   The distinction between permanent and temporary accounts is useful for two reasons. First, the distinction is useful in assessing a company's financial performance during the accounting period versus its financial position. Second, the distinction is important because the accounting equation must remain in balance. The accounting equation (in its most fundamental form) only includes permanent accounts. Since the temporary accounts are not explicitly part of the fundamental accounting equation, the balances in the temporary accounts must be transferred to a permanent account. This process is known as closing.

8. The balance in retained earnings represents the cumulative net income of the company less the cumulative dividends declared by the company. If a company declares larger

dividends than it generates in net income, the company could have a debit balance in retained earnings. However, most states do not allow a company to declare a dividend if the company has a debit balance in retained earnings; it is unlikely that a company would have a debit balance in retained earnings from declaring "excessive" dividends. If a company generates net losses instead of net income, then the company would have a debit balance in retained earnings.

9. A company recognizes gains and losses when the proceeds it receives from disposing of an asset is different from the amount recorded in its financial records for the asset (although more uncommon, it is possible for a company to have a gain or loss associated with disposing, i.e., retiring, a liability). For example, if a company sold some marketable securities for $10,000 and the securities had cost the company $7,000, the company would recognize a gain of $3,000. Alternatively, if the company had sold the securities for $5,000, the company would recognize a loss of $2,000. The proceeds received will increase an asset account, usually cash, and the asset account for the asset disposed of will be decreased. The difference between the proceeds and the asset's book value will be recorded in either a gain or a loss account, which are temporary accounts.

10. Accrual accounting focuses on the inflows and outflows of assets and liabilities from operating activities. That is, a company generates revenue when it experiences an inflow of an asset or an outflow of a liability associated with operating activities; the company incurs an expense when it experiences an outflow of an asset or an inflow of a liability associated with operating activities. Alternatively, cash accounting focuses only on the inflows and outflows of cash from operating activities. Because asset and liability inflows and outflows are usually not the same as cash inflows and outflows, the two systems will usually provide different measures of operating performance in a particular year. The two systems should, however, provide identical measures of operating performance when the operating period is defined as the life of the company. The difference between the two systems is simply one of timing, as illustrated in the following example:

Assume that on December 28, two companies (Company A and Company B) each make a sale on account for $50,000. Both companies collect the $50,000 on January 15. Company A follows accrual accounting. Under this approach, the $50,000 would be included in net income in December because it was earned in December. Collecting the $50,000 in January would not affect net income. Company B follows cash accounting. Under this approach, the company would not include the $50,000 in net income until it was collected in January. Over the two-month period, though, both companies would recognize total revenues of $50,000. Consequently, accrual and cash accounting give rise to the same measures of operating performance over time; just the timing of the income recognition differs across the two approaches.

11. Both accrual and cash accounting provide useful information to financial statement users. Accrual accounting focuses on the inflow and outflow of assets and liabilities; cash accounting focuses only on the inflow and outflow of cash. Since accrual accounting takes a broader focus than does cash accounting, many consider it to be the more useful of the two approaches. One must realize, though, that these two approaches provide different types of information. Consequently, one cannot really conclude that one approach is more useful than the other approach. Accrual accounting provides information that is more useful in evaluating a company's overall financial performance

and long-run profitability. Such information would probably be more valuable to equity investors. Alternatively, cash accounting provides information that is more useful in evaluating a company's solvency position. Such information is probably more useful to debt investors.

12. The matching principle states that the efforts required to generate benefits should be matched to the benefits that the efforts helped generate. Under accrual accounting, revenues are recognized when they are earned and expenses are recognized when they are incurred. Applying the matching principle to accrual accounting implies that expenses are not incurred, and, hence, not recognized, until the expense helps generate revenues. In understanding the matching principle, it is important to differentiate between a cost or expenditure and an expense.

13. Accrual adjusting entries represent revenues or expenses that build up over time but have not yet given rise to cash inflows or outflows. That is, the revenue has been earned but the associated cash has not yet been collected, or the expense has been incurred but the associated cash has not yet been paid. Cost expiration adjusting entries represent revenues or expenses that have occurred for which cash collection had previously taken place. That is, the cash was previously collected and the revenue is just now being earned, or the cash was previously disbursed and the expense is just now being incurred.

14. Capitalizing means that the cash outflow is initially recorded as an asset; expensing means that the cash outflow is initially recorded as an expense. To the extent that no adjusting entry is made in the year that the cash is disbursed, expensing the cost will have a more negative effect on the income statement than will capitalizing the cost. However, capitalizing or expensing the cost will result in the exact same amount of expense being recognized over the "life" of the cost, because all costs are eventually consumed and reported as expenses. If a cost is capitalized, expense recognition is achieved through cost expiration adjusting entries.

15. Under the matching principle, efforts should be recognized as expenses when the effort helps generate benefits. The cost of inventory generates a benefit when the inventory is sold, so that is when it should be expensed. This expense is recognized by debiting Cost of Goods Sold and crediting Inventory. This entry is necessary because expenditures for inventory are traditionally capitalized.

16. The cost of paying salaries is matched against the associated benefit when the salaries help generate the associated benefit. This matching of costs with the associated benefits provides a measure of the firm's performance that allows investors to evaluate the firm. The cost of paying salaries can be recognized as an expense in two different ways. First, the expense can be recognized when the exchange transaction occurs (i.e., when the employees are paid their wages). This approach is appropriate if the timing of the wage payment corresponds to the wages providing a benefit. Second, the expense can be recognized through an adjusting journal entry. This approach is appropriate if the timing of the wage payment does not correspond to the wages providing a benefit. If the wages had been paid prior to the wages providing a benefit, then a cost expiration adjusting entry would be necessary. If the wages had not been paid prior to the wages providing a benefit, then an accrual adjusting entry would be necessary.

17. If Mr. Gizmo wants to maximize net income in the year he acquired the machinery, he will want to minimize that year's expenses. Mr. Gizmo can minimize expenses by allocating the cost of the machinery over a longer period of time. Consequently, Mr. Gizmo would select a ten-year life (as opposed to a five-year life) over which to depreciate the machinery.

The matching principle states that the efforts that help generate benefits should be matched to those benefits. In the case of fixed assets, such as machinery, it is sometimes difficult to link the cost of the fixed asset to specific benefits. Consequently, companies must make assumptions as to how the cost of the fixed assets helps generate benefits. With Mr. Gizmo, it is unclear whether a five-year or a ten-year life is more appropriate for depreciating the machinery.

18. Multinational corporations have five basic approaches for addressing the problem of reporting to different parties who speak different languages (which usually implies both a different currency and different accounting principles). The five approaches are: (1) do nothing; (2) restate the financial statements to reflect the accounting principles of the user's country and translate both the language and the currency used in the financial statements to the user's language and currency; (3) translate both the language and the currency used in the financial statements to the user's language and currency but do not adjust for the different accounting principles; (4) translate only the language; or (5) prepare the financial statements using "world" or "global" accounting principles. The approach a company selects varies depending on in which country the company is based. Most multinational companies based in the United States select the first approach because the majority of their capital is generated in the United States; also, the English language, the U.S. dollar, and U.S. accounting principles are well known throughout the world. The third and fourth approaches are used by many multinational companies based in Europe because the majority of their capital providers are spread throughout Europe. Many Japanese multinationals use the second approach because they list their stocks not only on the Japanese stock markets but also on United States stock markets, which require that all registrants follow U.S. generally accepted accounting principles. A few companies attempt to provide financial statements based on "world" accounting principles. Development of a global set of accounting principles is underway by the International Accounting Standards Committee (IASC).

19. The following sixteen steps comprise the accounting cycle.

a. Identify relevant and measurable economic events.
b. Interpret relevant and measurable events by identifying accounts affected, direction of effect, and dollar value of effect.
c. Prepare journal entry.
d. Enter journal entry in journal.
e. Post journal entry to ledger.
f. Prepare unadjusted trial balance as part of work sheet.
g. Enter adjusting entries on work sheet.
h. Prepare adjusted trial balance as part of work sheet.
i. Enter closing entries on work sheet.
j. Prepare final trial balance as part of work sheet.
k. Record adjusting and closing entries in journal.
l. Post adjusting and closing entries to ledger.

m. Prepare income statement.
n. Prepare statement of retained earnings.
o. Prepare balance sheet.
p. Prepare statement of cash flows.

Journal entries are used for the initial recording of economic events in the accounting cycle. An incorrect entry would carry through the accounting cycle and result in incorrect financial statements. Therefore, it is vital that journal entries be correctly prepared.

20. The journal is a document in which economic events are recorded through journal entries. The ledger is a document in which the journal entries are summarized into accounts. The ledger can be referred to as a "scoreboard" because it shows the position of any account at any point in time.

21. A ledger summarizes economic transactions by account. Economic events are first captured by a journal entry; this information is then posted to the appropriate accounts in the ledger. Hence, the general ledger summarizes journal entries by account. It is useful to conceptualize a ledger as a series of T-accounts because the two sides of the T represent debits and credits; the left side represents debits while the right side represents credits.

Subsidiary ledgers are sub-ledgers that record additional information about a particular account in the general ledger. Two very common subsidiary ledgers are accounts receivable ledgers and accounts payable ledgers. The accounts receivable ledger lists the amounts owed to the company by each individual customer; the accounts payable ledger lists the amounts owed by the company to each individual supplier.

22. Adjusting journal entries come at the end of the accounting period between the unadjusted trial balance and the adjusted trial balance. These entries include relevant economic events not captured by exchange transactions during the accounting period. When the adjusting journal entries are added to the appropriate accounts listed in the unadjusted trial balance, the result is the adjusted trial balance.

23. The closing process is a process through which the balances in the temporary accounts are transferred into the retained earnings account. This process involves the following four steps:

a. Create an income summary account.
b. Transfer the balances of the revenue and expense accounts into the income summary account.
c. Transfer the balance of the income summary account into the retained earnings account.
d. Transfer the balance of the dividend account into the retained earnings account.

24. The income summary account summarizes the account balances used to calculate net income. Consequently, only revenue and expense accounts are transferred into the income summary account. Dividends are neither revenues nor expenses; consequently, the dividend account should not be closed into retained earnings via the income summary account. Instead, the balance in the dividend account is transferred directly into the retained earnings account.

25. T-account analysis is a mechanical process that involves examining the activity in a given T-account to acquire information that is not directly disclosed in the financial statements or footnotes. It is useful to managers in their role as financial statement users because it enables them to infer economic events from the financial statements. The additional information obtained helps managers in their evaluation of solvency, earning power, and management performance of a company.

26. Using T-account analysis, a T-account can be constructed for prepaid rent. The beginning and ending balances of $5,600 and $4,700, respectively, can be taken directly from the 1999 and 2000 balance sheets. The $8,000 rent expense on the income statement represents the expired portion of the prepaid rent and was a reduction in the prepaid account. The increase in the account, therefore, was $7,100, which represents the amount of cash paid for rent during 2000.

Prepaid Rent

Beginning balance 1999	5,600	
		8,000
	7,100	
Ending balance 2000	4,700	

Prepaid Rent (+A) 7,100	Rent Expense (E, -SE) 8,000
Cash (-A) 7,100	Prepaid Rent (-A) 8,000
Entry to record cash payments	*Entry to recognize rent expired*
for rent during 2000.	*during 2000.*

CHARACTERISTICS OF END-OF-CHAPTER ASSIGNMENTS

Item	Difficulty	Description
Brief exercises:		
BE5–1	E	Real data: Effects of transactions on the accounting equation
BE5–2	E	Real data: Effects of transactions on the accounting equation
BE5–3	E	Real data: Effects of transactions on the accounting equation

Exercises:

E5–1	E	Effects of transactions on the accounting equation
E5–2	E	Effects of transactions on accounts
E5–3	E	Preparing the financial statements from the accounts
E5–4	M	Preparing the financial statements
E5–5	E	Which economic events are relevant and objectively measurable?
E5–6	E	Preparing financial statements
E5–7	E	Preparing a statement of cash flows from the cash ledger
E5–8	M	Preparing a statement of cash flows from journal entries
E5–9	M	Preparing statements from transactions
E5–10	M	Preparing the statement of cash flows from the cash T-account
E5–11	M	Classifying adjusting journal entries
E5–12	M	Classifying transactions
E5–13	M	Recognizing accrued wages
E5–14	M	Depreciating a fixed asset
E5–15	H	The difference between accrual and cash accounting
E5–16	M	The difference between net income and net cash flow from operations
E5–17	H	Preparing a statement of cash flows from original transactions
E5–18	H	Cash and accrual accounting: comparison of performance measures
E5–19	H	Assessing economic consequences
E5–20	M	Appendix 5A: Complete a work sheet
E5–21	H	Appendix 5B: T-account analysis

Problems:

P5–1	E	Journal entries and the accounting equation
P5–2	E	T-accounts and the accounting equation
P5–3	M	Journal entries and preparing the four financial statements
P5–4	H	Preparing the four financial statements
P5–5	M	Effects of transactions on the income statement and statement of cash flows
P5–6	M	The effects of adjusting journal entries on the accounting equation
P5–7	M	Preparing adjusting journal entries
P5–8	M	Inferring adjusting journal entries from changes in T-account balances
P5–9	H	Reconciling accrual and cash flow dollar amounts
P5–10	M	Revenue recognition, cost expiration, and cash flows
P5–11	H	The effects of transactions on financial ratios
P5–12	H	Effects of different forms of financing on the financial ratios
P5–13	H	Effects of events on financial ratios
P5–14	H	Effects of events on financial ratios
P5–15	H	Effects of events on financial ratios
P5–16	M	Appendix 5A: Completing the work sheet and preparing the financial statements
P5–17	H	Appendix 5A: Comprehensive problem
P5–18	H	Appendix 5B: T-accounts analysis
P5–19	M	Appendix 5B: T-accounts analysis
P5–20	M	Appendix 5B: T-accounts analysis

Item	Difficulty	Description

CHAPTER 6

The Current Asset Classification, Cash, and Accounts Receivable

SYNOPSIS

In this chapter, the author discusses the uses and limitations of the current asset classification, the measurement and recording of cash and accounts receivables, and the major concerns of financial statement users in accounting for these items. The specific topics covered include the nature of cash, cash controls, cash discounts, and bad debts using the allowance method. Appendix 6A considers the international dimension through a discussion of accounting for receivables and payables expressed in foreign currencies.

The ethics vignette presents the case of a regional bank with admittedly overstated bad debt expense in good periods and understated bad debt expense in poor periods. In this manner, the bank can achieve consistent increases in reported net income across time. The ethical conduct of both the bank executives and the outside auditors is considered.

The Internet research exercise directs the student to access and analyze the activity in the allowance for bad debts account for a major retailer, Sears.

The following key points are emphasized in Chapter 6:

1. Current assets, working capital, current ratio, and quick ratio, and how these measures can be used to assess the solvency position of a company.

2. "Window dressing" and the reporting of current assets, working capital, and the current ratio.

3. Techniques used to account for and control cash.

4. Accounts receivable and how they are valued on the balance sheet.

5. The allowance method for uncollectible receivables.

6. Major concerns of financial statement users in the area of receivables reporting.

TEXT/LECTURE OUTLINE

The current asset classification, cash, and accounts receivable.

I. Current assets.

    A. A current asset is any asset that is intended to be converted into cash within one year or the company's operating cycle, whichever is longer. An operating cycle is the time that it takes a company to begin with cash, convert the cash to inventory, sell the inventory, and collect the cash from the sale.

    B. Usefulness of the current asset classification.

        1. Current assets provide a low-cost measure of a company's ability to generate cash in the short run.

        2. Comparing current assets to current liabilities provides a measure of solvency. Three common comparisons of current assets with current liabilities are given below:

            a) Working capital.

            b) Current ratio.

            c) Quick ratio.

    C. Limitations of the current asset classification.

        1. The measure of current assets is as of a particular point in time (i.e., the measure is static).

        2. Current assets may serve as a poor proxy for future cash inflows. For example, prepaid expenses do not provide any indication of future cash inflows.

        3. Given the difficulty of determining the length of a company's operating cycle, the definition of the time period of current assets is rather arbitrary.

        4. The dichotomy of current versus noncurrent assets provides managers with incentives to "window dress" the financial statements.

II. Cash.

    A. Cash is defined as coin, currency, checking accounts, and negotiable instruments such as personal checks, money orders, certified checks, cashiers' checks, and bank drafts. Postdated checks and IOUs are not considered cash.

    B. Reporting issues.

1. Cash is reported on the balance sheet at face value.

2. Restricted cash.

    a) Access or use of cash is restricted for some special purpose.

    b) Restricted cash usually arises through borrowing arrangements. The creditor(s) may require cash to be held in escrow or as compensating balances. The restricted cash helps ensure a source of funds for future interest and principal payments.

    c) Reporting restricted cash.

        (1) Restricted cash should be reported separately from unrestricted cash.

        (2) If the restricted cash arises from an obligation to be classified as current or will become available within the time period of current assets, then the restricted cash should be classified as current.

        (3) If the restricted cash arises from an obligation to be classified as noncurrent or will not become available within the time period of current assets, then the restricted cash should be classified as noncurrent (typically as a long-term investment).

C. Managers' responsibilities for managing cash.

    1. Having enough cash available to meet the company's day-to-day cash needs. However, idle cash is not desirable since it earns no return and also loses purchasing power during inflationary periods.

        a) Using a cash budget to estimate the company's day-to-day cash needs.

        b) Idle or "excess" cash should be invested in productive assets such as short-term investments.

    2. Establishing controls over cash.

        a) Since cash is almost universally desired, access to cash must be limited.

        b) An effective internal control system encompasses:

            (1) Record control—procedures designed to ensure that the amount reported on the balance sheet for cash reflects the appropriate amount.

            (2) Physical control—procedures designed to safeguard cash from loss or theft.

III.   Accounts receivable.

    A.   An account receivable is an amount owed to a company from selling goods or services to customers on account. The agreement between the company and the customer is usually informal.

    B.   Net realizable value (NRV).

        1.   Net realizable value is the net expected future benefit arising from accounts receivable. NRV represents the amount of cash the company expects to realize from accounts receivable.

        2.   NRV equals the face value of the receivable less adjustments for the following items:

            a)   Cash discounts.

            b)   Bad debts.

            c)   Sales returns.

    C.   Accounting for accounts receivable.

        1.   Since a company records an account receivable when it makes a sale on account, the criteria for recording an account receivable are the same as for recording a sale (i.e., the revenue recognition principle).

            a)   The company must have completed a significant portion of the production and sales effort.

            b)   The amount of revenue can be objectively determined.

            c)   The major portion of the costs has been incurred and the remaining costs can be reasonably estimated.

            d)   The eventual collection of cash is reasonably assured.

        2.   Cash discounts.

            a)   A discount offered by a company to provide incentives to its customers to pay their open accounts promptly.

            b)   Methods to account for cash discounts.

                (1)   Gross method.

(a) The sale and related receivable are recorded at the gross amount of the transaction.

(b) Recognition is given to the discount only if the customer takes the discount. If the customer takes the discount, Cash Discount is debited for the amount of the discount. This account is a contra revenue account to Sales.

(c) The gross method is the most common method because it is the easiest to use.

(2) Net method.

3. Bad debts.

a) Bad debts are amounts sold to customers on account that the company does not expect to convert into cash.

b) Companies would prefer to have no bad debts, but it would be extremely costly to eliminate all bad debts. Hence, from a cost/benefit perspective, some bad debts are inevitable.

c) Bad debts should be recognized in accordance with both the revenue recognition principle (i.e., bad debts provide after-the-fact evidence that cash collection was not reasonably assured) and the matching principle.

d) Allowance method.

(1) Bad debts are estimated and recognized in the period in which the underlying credit sale took place. That is, the allowance method results in an amount being estimated and recognized for both Bad Debt Charge (which is offset against the company's sales) and Allowance for Doubtful Accounts (which is offset against the balance in accounts receivable in the period the underlying credit sale took place).

(a) The allowance account is a contra asset account that offsets Accounts Receivable.

(b) The balance in the allowance account represents the amount reported in Accounts Receivable that the company does not expect to eventually collect.

(c) The balance in Bad Debt Charge represents the amount reported in that period's sales that the company does not expect to eventually collect.

(2)   Approaches to apply the allowance method.

(a)   Percentage-of-credit-sales approach—bad debt charge is estimated as a percentage of the accounting period's credit sales. This approach takes an income statement approach.

(b)   Aging approach.

i)   A company decomposes its accounts receivable balance into different ages and uses this aging to compute the balance necessary in Allowance for Doubtful Accounts.

ii)   Bad Debt Charge represents the change from the unadjusted to the necessarily adjusted balance in the allowance account. This approach takes a balance sheet valuation focus.

iii) Companies will often use the aging approach to verify the accuracy of the balance in the allowance account computed using the percentage-of-credit-sales approach.

(c)   Regardless of the approach used, the balances in both Allowance for Doubtful Accounts and Bad Debt Charge are based on estimates.

i)   With the percentage-of-credit-sales approach, the ending balance for Bad Debt Charge is estimated directly and the ending balance for Allowance for Doubtful Accounts is estimated indirectly.

ii)   With the aging method, the ending balance for Allowance for Doubtful Accounts is estimated directly and the ending balance for Bad Debt Charge is estimated indirectly.

(3)   Write-offs and recoveries of accounts.

(a)   Effect on current assets, total assets, and net income.

(b)   Effect on estimating bad debt charge under the aging and percentage-of-credit sales approaches.

4.   Sales returns.

a)   Sales returns represent merchandise that has been previously sold and is expected to be returned by a customer.

b)   Both Accounts Receivable on the balance sheet and an account on the income statement should be adjusted for estimated sales returns.

5. Accounts receivable from a user's perspective.

   a) Discretion in recognizing a receivable and related revenue can result in manipulation of the financial statements.

   b) Judgment in estimating bad debts and sales returns can result in manipulation of the financial statements.

   c) T-account analysis assists users in more closely analyzing activity in the accounts for sales, accounts receivable, bad debt, and allowance for uncollectible accounts.

   d) The accounts receivable collection period ratio measures how quickly a company's accounts receivable are normally converted into cash.

IV. Ethics in the real world.

V. Internet research exercise.

VI. Accounting for receivables and payables expressed in foreign currencies (Appendix 6A).

   A. Accounting for gains and losses from changes in exchange rates.

      1. Receivables.

      2. Payables.

   B. Hedging.

LECTURE TIPS

1. Students are often puzzled by the computational difference in estimating bad debt expense between the percentage-of-sales and the aging approach. The numerical example below uses the same data set as a basis to demonstrate the alternative approaches. The example can be expanded (Case II) to illustrate the effect of a debit balance in the allowance account before adjustment. The data was constructed so as to produce results that are different but reasonable, reflecting the inherent subjectivity in the estimation process and the appropriateness of alternative approaches. The example emphasizes that the primary difference between the two methods is which balance is being estimated directly and which balance is being estimated indirectly.

Data	
Sales	$1,050,000
Estimated % of sales uncollectible	½ %
Accounts receivable balance	$ 75,000
Estimated % of accounts receivable uncollectible based on an aging analysis	7½ %
Case I—Allowance for doubtful accounts	$250 (Cr.)
Case II—Allowance for doubtful accounts	$250 (Dr.)

Demonstration Examples

Using the percentage-of-sales approach and, alternatively, the aging approach, prepare the entry to record bad debt expense and compute the final balance in Allowance for Doubtful Accounts for each case. Treat each case independently and compare the results.

Check Numbers

	Bad Debt Expense	Allowance Balance
Case I—Percentage-of-sales approach	$5,250	$5,500
Case I—Aging approach	$5,375	$5,625
Case II—Percentage-of-sales approach	$5,250	$5,000
Case II—Aging approach	$5,875	$5,625

OUTSIDE ASSIGNMENT OPPORTUNITIES

Group study of current assets, cash, and receivables both across time and within and across industries (continuing assignment for Chapters 6–14)

1. Form groups (3–5 students) and obtain the most recent annual report of a major public company in one of the four general industry groupings (manufacturing, retailing, general services, and financial services). This report will be used for this assignment and for similar assignments for each succeeding chapter. Depending on class size, each industry group will be represented by several companies. Research the economic characteristics of and current conditions in the industry (e.g., competitive market; capital and labor intensity and other production characteristics; regulatory status; growth profile; and sensitivity to technological, demographic, and macroeconomic trends) and the company's strategy for competing. Prepare a written summary of those background factors. This summary will be used as a framework for understanding and interpreting financial statement information to be studied in these assignments.

Identify or compute the items listed below for the two most recent years. Compare the items across time. Relate your findings to the industry and company background factors. Report findings in a class discussion session in which comparisons will be made both across time and within and across industries.

> Current assets as a percentage of total assets
> Current ratio
> Quick ratio
> Balance sheet caption for cash and equivalents
> Cash as a percentage of total assets and current assets
> Balance sheet caption for receivables and the related allowance for uncollectibles
> Receivables as a percentage of total assets and current assets
> Bad debts as a percentage of outstanding receivables
> Average accounts receivable collection period

Inferring bad debt reporting strategies for a commercial bank

2. Obtain the most recent annual report for a commercial bank. Identify the trend in net income for as many periods as possible. (The 10-year summary may provide enough information for a long-term analysis.) Identify any strategy the bank may be using to report bad debts and support your position with appropriate computations. Explain why the bank's management may be using the strategy you identified.

ANSWERS TO END-OF-CHAPTER QUESTIONS

1. Probably not. Because current assets are defined as assets expected to be converted into cash within one year or the company's operating cycle, whichever is longer, the current asset classification is a function of the company's operating cycle. Companies with operating cycles of different lengths could define the time period of current assets differently. It is likely that a small retailer's operating cycle would run only for a fraction of a year, while a bridge-building company's operating cycle would run for longer than a year. Consequently, a small retailer would probably use a one-year cutoff for classifying assets as current or noncurrent; the bridge-building company would probably use its operating cycle for classifying assets as current or noncurrent.

2. In a borrowing arrangement, the creditor may stipulate that the borrower deposit a certain amount of cash in an escrow account. If the creditor is a bank, the bank may require the borrower to maintain a compensating balance. Amounts held in escrow and compensating balances provide the creditor with a source of funds for protection against the borrower defaulting.

   Amounts reported as cash on the balance sheet should represent amounts that the company owns and can use at its discretion. Any cash that a company owns but cannot use at its discretion should be disclosed separately on the balance sheet. Disclosing restricted cash separately from unrestricted cash (as opposed to reporting the two amounts together) provides financial statement users with more relevant information about the availability of cash. If the debt giving rise to the restricted cash is to be classified as a current liability, then the restricted cash should be classified as a current asset. If the debt giving rise to the restricted cash is to be classified as noncurrent, then the restricted cash should be classified as a noncurrent asset, typically as a long-term investment.

3. In trying to maintain a proper cash balance, managers must consider two issues. First, the manager must make sure that the company has sufficient cash, or near-cash assets, to meet its day-to-day cash needs. Insufficient cash could force the company into bankruptcy. Second, the manager should try to make the company's idle cash productive. Idle cash does not generate a return and also loses purchasing power. By investing idle cash, a manager can make the cash more productive. The manager must trade off these two considerations in deciding exactly how much cash to have available and to invest in other assets.

4. Accounts receivable is linked to the income statement through the sales account. Accounts receivable is recognized only if the company recognizes revenue. Consequently, the criteria for recognizing accounts receivable are identical to the criteria for recognizing revenue as specified in the revenue recognition principle. The criteria are (1) the company must have completed a significant portion of the production and sales effort; (2) the amount of revenue can be objectively determined; (3) the major portion of the costs have been incurred and the remaining costs can be reasonably estimated; and (4) the eventual collection of cash is reasonably assured.

Net accounts receivable is also linked to the income statement through the bad debt expense account. As the company increases bad debt expense, the net realizable value of accounts receivable is decreased through Allowance for Doubtful Accounts.

5. Window dressing occurs when a manager reports an economic event or transaction in a way that makes the financial position of the company appear more favorable than it would otherwise appear. The following are three examples of window dressing:

(1) Selecting a revenue recognition policy to influence the timing of revenue (and related accounts receivable) recognition. If a company recognizes revenue when it bills its customers rather than when it ships the merchandise, it can alter its financial position.

(2) Selecting the cutoff for revenue recognition on transactions near the fiscal year end. Delaying or accelerating revenue (and the related accounts receivable) for transactions near the end of the accounting period can alter a company's financial position.

(3) Selecting a policy for computing bad debts expense (such as choosing a low percentage of credit sales as being uncollectible) that will bolster the company's financial position.

Although window dressing may make the financial statements appear more attractive and to thus benefit management and the stockholders, the practice is not really in the best interest of either group, especially in the long-term. Attempts to manipulate financial statements involve the risk that the credibility of the statements is diminished, which in turn may negatively affect the company's ability to access the credit and equity markets.

6. Companies are often evaluated based on financial ratios by investors and creditors. These ratios are, in turn, often based on current assets and net income. If a company can report higher current assets, higher revenues, or lower expenses, the company may be perceived as more financially sound. One way a manager could achieve these objectives is to record revenue before it is earned. Such a practice would increase revenues and current assets (through accounts receivable). Consequently, auditors have to be concerned with whether sales on account were recorded in the proper accounting period. Another way that a manager could achieve these objectives is to record an insufficient amount for bad debt expense. Estimating bad debt expense requires a great deal of judgment, which allows the manager more discretion. Consequently, an auditor must be concerned that the client records a sufficient provision for bad debts.

7. Net realizable value equals the amount of cash that a company expects to collect from open accounts receivable. It is computed as the face value of the sale on account adjusted for cash discounts, bad debts, and sales returns.

8. Cash (sales) discounts are discounts offered to credit customers to prompt them to pay their open accounts on a timely basis. Quantity discounts are discounts offered to customers for purchasing a certain quantity of merchandise. Typically, the discount increases as the quantity purchased increases. Trade discounts are reductions in the sales price offered to customers.

   Quantity discounts and trade discounts are not explicitly reflected in the financial statements for two reasons. First, these discounts are incorporated into the amount recorded as revenue so additional explicit recognition of the discounts is not necessary. Second, no future economic event is associated with these two types of discounts. In the case of cash discounts, the customer will either take the discount or not take the discount. Consequently, this future event must be captured in the financial statements.

9. Companies offer cash (sales) discounts to encourage their credit customers to make prompt payment on open accounts receivables. Due to the time value of money, a dollar collected today is worth more than a dollar collected a month from now. By encouraging prompt payment, the company is, therefore, receiving something of greater value than it would if the open accounts were not paid promptly. Further, the longer an account is outstanding, holding everything else constant, it is less likely that the customer will pay the account. Consequently, the longer an account is outstanding, the more likely the company is apt to incur collection costs. Offering a cash discount decreases the probability that the account will be outstanding for an excessive period of time. So by offering a cash discount, a company receives something of greater value than it otherwise would and reduces its collection costs. To receive these benefits, the company must incur the cost of the cash discount. For a cash discount to make economic sense, the cost of the discount should not exceed its benefits.

10. Companies can undertake various activities to reduce uncollectible accounts receivables. The company could (1) expend more resources checking the credit worthiness of its customers; (2) expend more resources collecting open accounts; and (3) as a final measure, stop extending credit to its customers. However, each of these actions has a cost, either explicit or implicit, that must be considered. If the benefits derived from

undertaking these actions do not exceed the costs of the actions, then the company should not take the actions. In many cases, it is simply less costly for the company to incur the uncollectible accounts receivables than institute measures to prevent bad debts.

11. With the percentage-of-credit-sales approach, bad debts are estimated by multiplying credit sales by an estimated uncollectible percentage. The estimated uncollectible percentage is usually based on the company's collection history. If the company's collection history is insufficient to adequately estimate the uncollectible percentage, the company could use the industry average or hire a consultant.

12. An aging of accounts receivable is an approach to estimate bad debts. With this approach, the accounts receivable balance is decomposed into classifications based on how long the account has been outstanding. This decomposition is, in turn, used to compute the portion of the accounts receivable balance that the company does not expect to eventually collect (i.e., the ending balance that should be in Allowance for Doubtful Accounts). Bad Debt Expense is the difference between the unadjusted balance in Allowance for Doubtful Accounts and the estimated uncollectible amount per the aging.

An aging indicates the dollar amount currently in accounts receivable that the company does not expect to eventually collect. Since this amount is the most the company can expect to collect if it undertakes new collection activities, the aging indicates the most a company should be willing to expend for any new collection activities. One possible collection activity is offering cash discounts; companies offer cash discounts to encourage their customers to pay promptly. An aging would indicate the maximum amount that a company would be willing to forego for cash discounts.

Preparing an aging requires detailed records of accounts receivable. A company must have access to the date of the sale and the outstanding balance of each sale. Without computers, it was very costly to compile this information. However, with computers, almost any company can gain access to this information, so companies are more likely to perform an aging analysis.

13. Under the allowance method, the entry to record estimated bad debts results in a debit to Bad Debt Charge and a credit to Allowance for Doubtful Accounts. Since the allowance account is a contra asset account, it is a permanent account and carries over from one accounting period to the next. If the balance in the allowance account is growing from year to year (in relation to the balance in accounts receivable), it would indicate that the accounts deemed to be uncollectible and, hence, written off, are less than the estimated uncollectible accounts. Thus, an increasing balance in the allowance account would indicate an overestimate of bad debts.

Alternatively, if the balance in the allowance account is decreasing from year to year (in relation to the balance in accounts receivable), it could indicate that the accounts being written off as uncollectible exceed the amount estimated for bad debts. Thus, a decreasing balance in the allowance account could indicate an underestimate of bad debts. A decreasing balance in the allowance account could also result if the company has improved its collections from customers, thereby resulting in lower estimated non-collections.

14. An exchange rate is the value of one currency in terms of another currency. Holding receivables or payables expressed in terms of a foreign currency can result in economic gains and losses. Increasing the value of a foreign currency relative to the U.S. dollar implies that a company would receive (pay) more U.S. dollars when the receivable (payable) expressed in the foreign currency is settled. Alternatively, decreasing the value of the foreign currency relative to the U.S. dollar implies that a company would receive (pay) fewer U.S. dollars when the receivable (payable) expressed in the foreign currency is settled. These changes in the dollar amounts expected to be received or paid are economic gains and losses.

15. Hedging is a technique to reduce variations in income due to fluctuating exchange rates. Holding receivables or payables expressed in a foreign currency results in economic gains and losses if the value of the foreign currency (relative to the U.S. dollar) changes. The globalization of business has increased companies' exposure to these gains and losses. Consequently, hedging is practiced by a significant number of companies.

With hedging, a company basically plays both sides of the potential outcomes. The company puts itself in a position so that increases or decreases in the exchange rate result in the company realizing offsetting economic gains and losses. For example, if a company had a receivable expressed in Japanese yen, the company would hedge its position by acquiring a payable expressed in Japanese yen in an amount equal to the receivable. In this way, the company neither realizes any economic gains from fluctuating exchange rates, nor incurs any economic losses.

CHARACTERISTICS OF END-OF-CHAPTER ASSIGNMENTS

Item	Difficulty	Description
Brief exercises:		
BE6–1	E	Real data: Analysis of accounts receivable
BE6–2	E	Real data: Uncollectible accounts expense
BE6–3	E	Real data: Uncollectible accounts expense
Exercises:		
E6–1	E	Classifying cash on the balance sheet
E6–2	E	Classifying cash on the balance sheet
E6–3	E	Accounting for cash discounts
E6–4	E	Accounting for cash discounts
E6–5	M	Bad debts under the allowance method
E6–6	M	Accounting for uncollectibles
E6–7	M	Accounting for doubtful accounts: the allowance method
E6–8	H	Inferring bad debt write-offs and reconstructing related journal entries
E6–9	M	Preparing an aging schedule
E6–10	M	Appendix 6A: Exchange gains/losses on outstanding receivables
E6–11	M	Appendix 6A: Hedging to reduce the risk of currency fluctuations

Item	Difficulty	Description

Problems:

P6–1	M	Classifying cash on the balance sheet
P6–2	E	Cash discounts
P6–3	M	Bad debts over time
P6–4	M	Accounting for uncollectibles over two periods
P6–5	H	Ignoring potential bad debts can lead to serious overstatements
P6–6	H	Estimating uncollectibles, financial ratios, and loan agreements
P6–7	M	Uncollectibles: ignoring an allowance
P6–8	H	Accounting for uncollectibles and the aging estimate
P6–9	M	Inferring reporting strategies
P6–10	M	Appendix 6A: Exchange gains and losses
P6–11	M	Appendix 6A: Fluctuating exchange rates, debt covenants, and hedging

Issues for discussion:

ID6–1	M	Restricted cash and solvency ratios
ID6–2	E	Revenue recognition, ethics, and reputation
ID6–3	M	Working capital, debt covenants, and restrictions on management decisions
ID6–4	M	Analyzing the allowance account
ID6–5	M	Using the bad debt estimate to manage earnings
ID6–6	H	International banks and bad debt expense
ID6–7	H	Bad debt rates over time
ID6–8	H	Boosting earnings with bad debt estimates
ID6–9	H	Appendix 6A: The annual report of NIKE
ID6–10	E	Appendix 6A: Accounting for foreign currencies—an economic consequence

CHAPTER 7   Merchandise Inventory

SYNOPSIS

In this chapter, the author discusses the economic consequences faced by managers in accounting for inventory. Specifically discussed are the effects of inventory accounting on (1) financial statement users; (2) existing contracts; (3) income taxes; (4) bookkeeping costs; and (5) the usefulness of resulting information. The author also presents the conceptual and practical issues in accounting for inventory, including (1) the acquisition of inventory, covering which units to include as part of inventory and what costs to capitalize as part of inventory; (2) the two potential methods to account for inventory, periodic and perpetual; (3) the potential cost flow assumptions for allocating inventory costs to cost of goods sold, FIFO, LIFO, and averaging; and (4) the lower-of-cost-or-market rule, as it applies to inventory.

The ethics vignette considers the pressure on auditors to cut hours spent auditing such critical areas such as inventories due to competition.

The Internet research exercise explores the inventory policies of Ann Taylor Stores and its competitors.

The following key points are emphasized in Chapter 7:

1. Inventory and how it affects the financial statements.

2. Four issues that must be addressed when accounting for inventory.

3. General rules for including items in inventory and attaching costs to these items.

4. Differences between the perpetual and periodic methods and trade-offs involved in choosing between them.

5. The three cost flow assumptions—average, FIFO, and LIFO.

6. The lower-of-cost-or-market rule.

TEXT/LECTURE OUTLINE

Merchandise inventory.

I.   Merchandise inventory refers to items held for sale in the ordinary course of business.

    A.   Stockholders, creditors, managers, and auditors are all interested in a company's inventory.

    B.   The value and marketability of inventory can also provide an indication of a company's ability to continue as a going concern.

II.   The relative size of inventories.

III.   Accounting for inventory: four important issues.

    A.   Acquiring inventory: what costs to capitalize.

        1.   Items to include in inventory.

            a)   As a general rule, items held for sale and for which the company has complete and unrestricted ownership should be included in inventory. Purchases should be recorded when legal title to the items passes from the seller to the buyer.

            b)   Sometimes it is more difficult to determine the appropriate number of inventory units.

                (1)   Goods on consignment.

                    (a)   Items owned by one party (the consignor), but physically held for sale by another party (the consignee).

                    (b)   Goods on consignment should be included in the inventory of the consignor, not the consignee, since the consignor retains legal title to the goods.

                (2)   Goods in transit.

                    (a)   Inventory items not in the physical possession of either the buyer or the seller as of a point in time because the goods are in transit from the seller to the buyer.

                    (b)   Ownership is determined by the shipping terms.

                        i)   FOB shipping point—legal title to the inventory items passes from the seller to the buyer when the seller delivers the goods to the shipping point.

ii)   FOB destination—legal title to the inventory items passes from the seller to the buyer when the goods reach their destination.

2.   Costs to attach to inventory items.

   a)   As a general rule, all costs associated with manufacturing, acquiring, storing, or preparing inventory items should be capitalized as inventory.

   b)   Cash discounts.

      (1)   A discount offered by suppliers for prompt payment on purchases made on account.

      (2)   Cash discounts are accounted for using the gross method.

   c)   Potential costs that could be capitalized for manufacturing companies.

      (1)   Direct costs (such as direct labor and raw materials) should be capitalized as part of inventory.

      (2)   Overhead (such as indirect materials, indirect labor, utility costs, depreciation, and so forth) must be allocated to inventory. Allocating overhead to inventory is subjective and allows for potential management manipulation of financial statements.

B.   Carrying inventory: the perpetual or periodic method?

1.   Perpetual method.

   a)   The inventory account is directly increased for every inflow of inventory.

   b)   The inventory account is directly decreased for every outflow of inventory.

2.   Periodic method.

   a)   Inflows of inventory are debited to the inventory account, while outflows of inventory are not recorded until the end of the accounting period.

   b)   An entry at the end of the accounting period updates the inventory account and recognizes cost of goods sold for the period.

3.   Tradeoffs between the two methods.

   a)   The perpetual method provides information throughout the accounting period on the inventory levels that should be on hand. The periodic method does not provide this information.

b) With the perpetual method, comparing the balance in the inventory account to the total of a physical inventory count reveals inventory shrinkage. Since inventory is not tracked during the period under the periodic method, it is not possible to determine inventory shrinkage; shrinkage is buried in cost of goods sold.

c) The perpetual method requires an entry to record cost of goods sold every time inventory is sold, while the periodic method only requires an entry to record cost of goods sold at the end of the accounting period. The additional journal entries under the perpetual method increase bookkeeping costs.

C. Errors in the inventory count.

1. Inventory counts are made under both the perpetual and periodic methods and sometimes may be in error.

a) An overstatement of inventory overstates net income by the same amount; an understatement of inventory understates net income by the same amount.

b) Net income for the next period is misstated by the same amount in the opposite direction.

2. Inventory errors are not unusual, often quite significant, and sometimes made intentionally by management to manipulate reported income.

D. Selling inventory: which cost flow assumption?

1. Specific identification.

a) The cost of the actual inventory item sold is allocated to cost of goods sold.

b) Only practical for companies that sell large-ticket, easily-tracked items.

c) Allows manipulation of net income and inventory.

2. Three inventory cost flow assumptions.

a) A cost flow assumption is used to determine the inventory cost allocated to cost of goods sold and inventory. The cost flow assumption does not refer to the physical flow of inventory.

b) Averaging assumption.

(1) A weighted average cost of all inventory units available is used to allocate inventory costs.

          (2)   May be applied using either the periodic or the perpetual method (i.e., moving average).

    c) First-in, First-out (FIFO) assumption.

        (1)   The oldest inventory costs are assumed to be the first inventory costs sold.

        (2)   May be applied using either the periodic method or the perpetual method; both methods result in identical amounts for ending inventory and cost of goods sold.

    d) Last-in, First-out (LIFO) assumption.

        (1)   The most recent inventory costs are assumed to be the first inventory costs sold.

        (2)   May be applied using either the periodic method or the perpetual method.

3.   Inventory assumptions: effects on the financial statements.

4.   Inventory assumptions: effects on federal income taxes.

5.   Tradeoffs among the cost flow assumptions.

    a) Income and asset measurement tradeoffs.

        (1)   LIFO matches the most current inventory costs to current revenues, whereas FIFO matches older inventory costs to current revenues. Consequently, LIFO provides "better" matching than FIFO. The averaging assumption falls between LIFO and FIFO.

        (2)   FIFO reports the most current inventory costs as ending inventory, whereas LIFO reports older inventory costs as ending inventory. LIFO can report an inventory balance that is grossly out-of-date. The averaging assumption falls between LIFO and FIFO.

    b) Economic tradeoffs.

        (1)   Income taxes and liquidity.

            (a) LIFO conformity rule.

            (b) In times of rising prices, LIFO results in lower net income than does FIFO. This lower net income results in lower current taxes. The tax effect has cash flow implications and can also have liquidity implications.

(2) LIFO requires more detailed accounting records so bookkeeping costs are higher under LIFO than FIFO.

(3) Unexpected increases in sales or unexpected decreases in purchases or production can deplete LIFO inventory layers. LIFO liquidations can give rise to substantially increased taxes (with rising prices) and poor inventory purchasing practices.

(4) If debt covenants specify a minimum debt/equity ratio or a minimum working capital requirement, management can minimize the probability of violating the covenant by maximizing inventory and net income via FIFO. Further, if management is compensated, at least partially, with a bonus contract, management can maximize the value of its bonus by maximizing net income via FIFO.

(5) If managers believe that investors cannot "see through" accounting methods but, rather, focus on net income, then managers may prefer to use FIFO to increase income. Research in accounting and finance generally supports the view that investors "see through" accounting methods and value a company on the basis of its underlying cash flows.

(6) Financial statements of companies using LIFO include footnote disclosure of "LIFO reserves," which reflect the difference between inventories computed using LIFO and FIFO. This disclosure is helpful to financial statement users in assessing the tax and income effects of using LIFO versus FIFO, and for making more valid comparisons with other companies that use FIFO.

IV. Ending inventory: applying the lower-of-cost-or-market rule.

A. Determine the original cost of the inventory based on the inventory method and the cost flow assumption selected.

B. Compare the original cost to market value.

1. If the market value is less than the original cost, adjust the original cost down to the market value, thereby resulting in an unrealized loss.

2. If the market value exceeds the original cost, then no adjustment is necessary.

V. The lower-of-cost-or-market rule and hidden reserves.

A. Conceptually, the lower-of-cost-or-market-value (LCM) rule is inconsistent, since decreases, but not increases, in value are recognized.

B. Although this inconsistent treatment can create hidden reserves that managers can use to manipulate income, the LCM rule makes economic sense due to conservatism.

VI.   International perspective.

VII. Ethics in the real world.

VIII. Internet research exercise.

LECTURE TIPS

1.   Students often have difficulty understanding goods in transit, particularly (1) deciding on in whose books goods in transit should be recorded, and (2) how to adjust the books if they have already been adjusted to the physical count and goods in transit are then detected. End-of-chapter exercise 7–1 is useful to demonstrate how to account for goods in transit. The exercise can be extended to illustrate the correcting entries required and how not correcting the errors affects the current and following period.

2.   A comprehensive demonstration problem that compares the financial statement and income tax effects of the alternative cost flow assumptions under both the periodic and perpetual systems is shown below. The problem could be extended to illustrate how the specific identification method could be used to manipulate reported profits.

	Data	
Inventory:		
7/01/00	Beg. inventory	2,000 units @ $10 per unit
7/11/00	Purchase	400 units @ $16 per unit
7/17/00	Sale	1,000 units @ $24 per unit
7/21/00	Purchase	600 units @ $12 per unit
7/31/00	End. inventory	2,000 units

Operating expenses for July were $8,000. The income tax rate is 40%.

Demonstration Examples

Compute ending inventory using the FIFO, LIFO, and average cost flow assumptions under both the periodic and perpetual systems. Prepare an income statement for each for July 2000. Compute the cash tax savings of the LIFO and average methods as compared to FIFO.

Check Numbers

Ending inventory:

Periodic		*Perpetual*	
LIFO	$20,000	LIFO	$21,200
Weighted average	22,400	Moving average	22,600
FIFO	23,600	FIFO	23,600

Cash tax savings over FIFO:

Periodic		*Perpetual*	
LIFO	$1,440	LIFO	$960
Weighted average	480	Moving average	400

OUTSIDE ASSIGNMENT OPPORTUNITIES

Group study of inventories both across time and within and across industries (continuing assignment for Chapters 6–14)

1. Using the most recent annual report of a major public company in one of the four general industry groupings, identify or compute the items listed below for the two most recent years. Compare the items across time. Relate your findings to the economic characteristics and the current conditions in the industry and the company's strategy for competing. Prepare a written summary of your findings. Report findings in a class discussion session in which comparisons will be made both across time and within and across industries.

    Captions used for inventories
    Inventories as a percentage of total assets and total current assets
    Cost flow assumption(s) used
    Cost of goods sold as a percentage of total revenues

Article search: inventory fraud

2. Search the recent financial press (*The Wall Street Journal, Barrons, Fortune, Forbes*, etc.) for an article reporting inventory fraud. Evaluate the situation in terms of valuation principles violated, methods used, management's motivation, the auditor's role, and ethical considerations. Present your findings in writing and in a class discussion.

ANSWERS TO END-OF-CHAPTER QUESTIONS

1. Inventory is linked to the income statement through cost of goods sold. This account represents the cost of the inventory sold during the current period. Ending inventory in one period becomes the beginning inventory for the next period. Consequently, inventory is used to compute cost of goods sold in two different accounting periods—in the first period as ending inventory and in the second period as beginning inventory. Inventory is allocated to the two periods in accordance with the matching principle.

2. Four issues must be addressed when accounting for inventory. First, managers must decide which units to include in inventory and what costs to capitalize as part of inventory. Only those units to which the company has legal title should be included in inventory. Second, managers must decide whether to use the periodic or the perpetual method to account for inventory. The method selected dictates how the company records inflows and outflows of inventory. With the perpetual method, inventory is adjusted for every inflow and outflow of inventory; with the periodic method, inflows of inventory are recorded as purchases and outflows of inventory are not recorded until the end of the accounting period. Third, managers must decide how to allocate inventory costs between inventory and cost of goods sold. They can select the specific identification method or some cost flow assumption. The dollar amounts allocated to inventory and to cost of goods sold are a function of the method used to account for inventory (periodic or perpetual) and the cost flow assumption used. Finally, the manager must adjust the inventory to reflect the lower-of-cost-or-market value.

3. If Rawlers Corporation includes the goods held on consignment in its physical count and, hence, in its inventory, then its ending inventory will be overstated. However, because Rawlers never recorded the acquisition of this inventory its cost of goods available for sale will be correct. Since cost of goods available for sale is allocated between ending inventory and cost of goods sold, and since ending inventory is overstated, it follows that cost of goods sold will be understated. Consequently, for Rawlers Corporation, both net income and inventory will be overstated.

4. Legal title determines on whose books inventory should be carried. For goods in transit at the end of the accounting period, managers and auditors must decide which company, the buyer or the seller, has legal title to the goods. Legal title for goods in transit is determined by the shipping terms.

5. Manufacturing companies must include all manufacturing costs as part of inventory. Such costs would include raw materials, direct labor, and overhead. Overhead, such as the supervisors' salaries and depreciation on plant equipment, must be allocated to inventory even though a clear relation between the overhead and a particular unit of inventory may not be evident. On the other hand, retailers basically purchase finished goods and distribute these goods to consumers. The costs associated with such acquisitions are more direct and are primarily the cost (including any freight charges) incurred to acquire the inventory.

6. The perpetual method requires a company to track every inflow and outflow of inventory, which can be quite costly and time consuming. Computers have decreased both the cost and the time requirements of using the perpetual method. The perpetual method offers one significant advantage over the periodic method—it provides information to managers on inventory shrinkage. With the perpetual method, the balance in inventory indicates the value of inventory that should be on hand. Any excess of the balance in inventory over the value of inventory on hand per a physical count represents inventory shrinkage. Because the company does not have any record of the value of inventory that should be on hand with the periodic method, it is not possible to determine inventory shrinkage; it is simply buried in cost of goods sold.

7. With specific identification, the actual cost of a unit of inventory is assigned to that unit. As long as that particular unit is on hand, the actual cost of that unit remains in inventory; when that particular unit is sold, the actual cost of that unit is allocated to cost of goods sold. The specific identification method, therefore, does not require an assumption about the flow of inventory costs. However, this method has limited applicability. To be cost effective, and hence useful, a company must be able to identify the costs associated with particular units of inventory. Consequently, specific identification can only be used by companies that sell large, big-ticket items such as cars, furs, major appliances, and so forth. The specific identification method also allows managers to manipulate cost of goods sold, net income, and inventory, as well as any ratios based on these amounts. If a company possesses identical units of inventory purchased at different prices, the customer will be indifferent about which unit he or she receives while the manager can sell the unit that provides him or her with the greatest benefit.

8. The basic difference between the FIFO and LIFO cost flow assumptions concerns the assumption regarding the flow of inventory costs through the company. FIFO assumes that the first inventory costs to flow into the company are the first inventory costs to flow out of the company; LIFO assumes that the most recent inventory costs to flow into the company are the first inventory costs to flow out of the company. During times of changing prices, these two cost flow assumptions will result in different values being assigned to ending inventory and cost of goods sold because the most recent inventory costs will not equal the oldest inventory costs. During times of stable prices, however, these two cost-flow assumptions will result in the assignment of equal values because the most recent inventory costs and the oldest inventory costs will be the same.

9. The LIFO conformity rule states that a company that selects LIFO for federal income tax purposes must also use LIFO for financial reporting purposes. If a company faces rising inventory costs and the manager desires to minimize the company's tax liability by using LIFO, then the manager must also select LIFO for financial reporting purposes.

10. The tradeoffs between FIFO and LIFO can be classified as measurement issues and economic tradeoffs. First, the two cost flow assumptions result in different measures of inventory and cost of goods sold. With LIFO, the most recent inventory costs are disclosed on the income statement as part of cost of goods sold, and the older inventory costs are disclosed on the balance sheet as part of inventory. Thus, LIFO discloses current inventory costs on the income statement and provides a better matching of current costs against current revenues. With FIFO, the most recent inventory costs are disclosed on the balance sheet as part of inventory, and the older inventory costs are disclosed on the income statement as part of cost of goods sold. Thus, FIFO discloses

current inventory costs on the balance sheet and provides a more relevant inventory measure. Hence, a company must decide whether to focus on the income statement or the balance sheet.

Second, the two cost flow assumptions can result in different cash flows. During times of rising prices (as is usually the case), LIFO results in higher cost of goods sold and, hence, lower net income than FIFO. Lower net income, in turn, results in a lower tax liability and lower cash outflows for taxes. However, if a company is unable to replenish its inventory, due to either a strike or to losing a supplier, the company may sell off much of its inventory, and under LIFO the old, outdated inventory costs will have to flow through to cost of goods sold. Having these old inventory costs flow through to cost of goods sold will significantly increase the company's net income and, therefore, its tax liability. Managers will often try to avoid liquidating old LIFO inventory layers by engaging in poor inventory purchasing habits.

Managers must also consider the cash flow effects from bookkeeping costs and from existing contracts. LIFO requires more extensive financial records to track the older inventory costs that are carried on the books as part of Inventory. Further, existing debt covenants or incentive contracts might be based on current assets or net income. The choice of LIFO or FIFO will affect these contracts.

11. During inflation, FIFO results in a higher amount being reported for net income and inventory. However, managers should consider all relevant costs in deciding whether reporting higher income and inventory is desirable. Managers should consider the effect on (1) taxes, (2) bookkeeping costs, (3) debt covenants, and (3) firm value (as measured by the stock market).

It is often assumed that higher net income is valued by the stock market. However, the stock market only uses net income to predict a company's future cash flows. Research has generally indicated that the stock market "sees through" accounting methods to the underlying cash flows. Hence, the stock market will not be fooled by paper profits reported under FIFO. In fact, the stock market may even view the paper profits negatively since the company could have used LIFO and saved on taxes.

12. Under LIFO, old layers of inventory costs accumulate and are carried from one accounting period to the next. These layers contain the older inventory costs allocated to inventory. If the number of inventory units sold during the year exceed the number of inventory units produced or purchased, then a company will have to dip into these layers in allocating costs to cost of goods sold. The company is, in essence, liquidating its LIFO layers. Since these layers contain old, lower costs, net income will be inflated, resulting in higher taxes.

13. Companies using LIFO include footnote disclosure of "LIFO reserves," which reflects the difference between inventories computed using LIFO and FIFO. This disclosure is useful for assessing the tax and income effects of using LIFO, and for making more valid comparisons with other companies that use FIFO.

14. In the lower-of-cost-or-market (LCM) rule, inventory is reported on the balance sheet at its cost or its market value, whichever is lower. The LCM rule is often criticized as being inconsistent because the rule allows decreases in value to be recognized but not

Managers and auditors face legal liability associated with the financial statements. Since the cost of errors of overstatement tend to be larger than the cost of errors of understatement, managers and auditors would prefer to be conservative and report inventory at its lower-of-cost-or-market value.

15. Inventory turnover is a ratio that indicates the speed with which inventories move through a company. It is calculated by dividing cost of goods sold by the average inventory balance during the period. A low inventory turnover can indicate either low demand for the inventory or excessive levels of inventory. In either case, a low turnover may indicate future obsolete inventory. A high inventory turnover can indicate that the company is maintaining too little inventory. Low inventory levels imply that the company may not be able to meet demand for its goods in the future.

16. Many of the company groups in Japan consist of both manufacturers and their suppliers. Through the company group, a manufacturer and its suppliers can coordinate their activities so that each company knows how much inventory is needed by the other companies on specific dates. In this way, the companies can produce the inventory just as it is needed, thereby eliminating the need to have large stocks of inventory on hand. With this approach, the vast majority of products produced in a particular year are sold during that year. This means that the choice of a cost flow assumption is not very important because there are virtually no costs to assign to ending inventory.

CHARACTERISTICS OF END-OF-CHAPTER ASSIGNMENTS

Item	Difficulty	Description
Brief exercises:		
BE7–1	E	Real data: Inventory
BE7–2	E	Real data: Inventories
BE7–3	E	Real data: FIFO vs. LIFO
Exercises:		
E7–1	M	Goods in transit as of the end of the accounting period
E7–2	E	Accounting for inventory purchases
E7–3	E	Accounting for inventory purchases
E7–4	E	Compute the missing values
E7–5	M	Carrying inventories: perpetual and periodic methods
E7–6	M	The financial statement effects of inventory errors
E7–7	M	Income manipulation under specific identification
E7–8	M	Inventory assumptions and manipulating income under specific identification
E7–9	M	Inventory cost flow assumptions
E7–10	M	Inventory flow assumptions over several periods and income taxes
E7–11	H	Using the LIFO reserve
E7–12	H	The lower-of-cost-or-market rule and hidden reserves

Item	Difficulty	Description
Problems:		
P7–1	E	Purchases and cash discounts
P7–2	E	The gross method and partial payments
P7–3	M	The financial effects of inventory errors
P7–4	H	The financial statement and income tax effects of averaging, FIFO, and LIFO
P7–5	M	The gross method, the periodic method, and the LIFO and FIFO cost flow assumptions
P7–6	H	Using LIFO and saving tax dollars
P7–7	M	LIFO liquidations, income tax implications, and year-end purchases
P7–8	H	Using the LIFO reserve
P7–9	M	Avoiding LIFO liquidations
Issues for discussion:		
ID7–1	M	Choosing FIFO or LIFO
ID7–2	M	LIFO reporting
ID7–3	E	The annual report of NIKE
ID7–4	E	LIFO liquidation and hidden reserves
ID7–5	M	The lower-of-cost-or-market rule and the recognition of loss/income
ID7–6	M	Inventory write-down
ID7–7	M	Auditing risky clients
ID7–8	M	Inventory footnotes
ID7–9	M	Just-in-time inventory

CHAPTER 8   Investments in Equity Securities

SYNOPSIS

In this chapter, the author discusses investments in equity securities. The discussion is divided into equity securities classified as current and long-term investments. The specific topics associated with investments in equity securities are (1) the criteria for equity investments to be classified as current; (2) accounting for investments in trading and available-for-sale securities, including the mark-to-market rule; and (3) selected economic and theoretical issues. The specific topics associated with long-term equity investments are (1) accounting for long-term equity investments under the cost method, the mark-to-market method, the equity method, and consolidations, and (2) the economic consequences associated with the different methods. The author provides a discussion of the detailed accounting procedures for consolidating financial statements in Appendix 8A.

The ethics vignette examines the liberal accounting rules for recognition and amortization of goodwill in countries outside the United States. It then considers whether it is ethical for the government or standard-setting body in a particular country to set accounting standards that are designed to provide international economic advantages enjoyed solely by the companies and capital markets in that country.

The Internet research exercise examines the accounting for short and long-term investments by PepsiCo.

The following key points are emphasized in Chapter 8:

1. Criteria that must be met before a security can be listed in the current assets section of the balance sheet.

2. Trading and available-for-sale securities and how the mark-to-market rule is used to account for them.

3. Why companies make long-term investments in equity securities.

4. The mark-to-market method, the cost method, and the equity method of accounting for long-term equity investments, and the conditions under which each method is used.

5. Consolidated financial statements, when they are prepared, and how they differ from financial statements that account for equity investments using the equity method.

6. Why goodwill accounting is controversial.

LECTURE/TEXT OUTLINE

Investments in equity securities.

I.   Equity investments are an investment in the equity securities of other companies. These investments are made (1) to earn investment income through dividends and stock appreciation, and (2) to exert influence or control over the board of directors and management of the investee company.

II.   Equity securities classified as current.

    A.   Short-term investments in equity securities are reported as current assets.

    B.   Criteria to be classified as current.

        1.   The securities must be readily marketable. This criterion implies that the security can be sold and converted into cash at will.

        2.   Management must intend to convert the investment to cash within the time period of current assets.

            a)   Management's incentives to "window dress" current assets through the classification of equity securities.

            b)   Auditors can examine the company's past practices and the nature and size of the investment to determine management's intentions.

        3.   If neither criterion is met, the investment must be included in the long-term investment section.

III. Trading and available-for-sale securities.

    A.   Accounting for readily marketable equity securities is governed by *SFAS No. 115*, "Accounting for Certain Investments in Debt and Equity Securities."

    B.   Investments in readily marketable equity securities are classified into one of two categories.

        1.   Trading securities—securities bought and held principally for the purpose of selling them in the near future with the objective of generating profit on short-term price changes. These securities are always listed in the current section of the balance sheet.

        2.   Available-for-sale securities—those investments not classified as trading securities. These securities are listed on the balance sheet as current or long-term, depending on management's intention.

    C.   Events related to accounting for trading and available-for-sale securities.

1. Purchase of securities.

    a) Equity securities are always recorded at cost when they are acquired.

    b) Cost includes any incidental acquisition costs such as brokerage commissions and taxes.

2. Declaration and receipt of cash dividends.

    a) On the date the dividend is declared, dividend income and the corresponding dividend receivable are recorded.

    b) When the cash from the dividend is received, Cash is debited and Dividend Receivable is credited. Receiving the dividend is simply an exchange of assets.

3. Sale of securities.

    a) The balance sheet value of the securities is removed from the books.

    b) The difference between the balance sheet value of the securities and the proceeds of the sale is recognized as either a realized gain or a realized loss.

4. Price changes of securities.

    a) The FASB mandated in *SFAS No. 115* that readily marketable equity securities be carried on the balance sheet at current market value.

    b) The mark-to-market rule gives rise to unrealized (or holding) gains or losses.

    c) End of period adjustments to reflect current market values differ for trading securities and available-for-sale securities.

        (1) For trading securities, holding gains or losses are considered temporary accounts. They appear in the income statement and are reflected in retained earnings.

        (2) For available-for-sale securities, the unrealized price changes are considered permanent accounts and are carried in the stockholders' equity section of the balance sheet.

5. Reclassifications and permanent market value declines.

    a) When management changes the classification of investments from trading to available-for-sale, or vice versa, unrealized holding gains or losses should be recognized immediately in the income statement.

b)   When permanent market value declines (i.e., the price declines and is not expected to recover) the security should be written down to its market value and a realized loss should be recognized immediately.

6.   Mark-to-market accounting and comprehensive income.

a)   While unrealized price changes in available-for-sale securities are not reflected in net income, the FASB now requires that such changes be reported on a statement of comprehensive income.

b)   No specific form is required, but the statement of comprehensive income must be displayed with the same prominence as the other financial statements.

c)   Comprehensive income provides the statement user with an estimate of the overall change in a company's wealth during the period.

7.   Practical and theoretical issues associated with the mark-to-market rule.

a)   Current market values provide more useful information about the wealth of the firm.

b)   Market value accounting, in general, is criticized because market values are subjective and can result in large fluctuations from period to period (which are not necessarily relevant). Mark-to-market accounting for investments in equity securities avoids these criticisms.

(1)   The rule applies only to readily marketable equity securities, i.e., those that have readily determinable and objective market prices.

(2)   Market value changes of only those securities that are intended to be sold in the very near future (trading securities) are reflected in current income. Unrealized price changes related to securities classified as available-for-sale are not included in the income statement.

c)   Management's subjective judgment may influence the reported dollar amount of net income because the classification of securities as trading or available-for-sale relies heavily on management's intention.

III.   Long-term equity investments.

A.   The accounting treatment used for long-term equity investments depends upon the investor's potential to influence the investee company.

1.   If the investor has little potential to influence the investee company (defined as owning less than 20 percent of the investee's outstanding stock), then the marketability of the investee's stock determines the appropriate accounting treatment.

a) If the investee's stock is not readily marketable, then the cost method is used to account for the equity investment.

   (1) The investment is initially recorded at cost, which includes any incidental costs like brokerage fees.

   (2) Dividends declared by the investee are recognized as revenue.

   (3) The investment is carried on the books at cost until it is sold or until it suffers a permanent impairment in value.

b) If the investee's stock is readily marketable, then the securities are classified as available-for-sale and the mark-to-market rule is applied. The investment is accounted for as outlined in [II.–C.] above.

2. If the investor can exert significant influence over the investee company (defined as owning between 20 percent and 50 percent of the investee's outstanding stock), then the investment, regardless of whether the investee's stock is marketable, should be accounted for using the equity method.

   a) The investment is initially recorded at cost, which includes any incidental costs like brokerage fees.

   b) The amount reported for the investment is adjusted for changes in the investor's proportionate share of the investee's net assets.

      (1) The carrying value of the investment is adjusted for the investor's proportionate share of the investee's net income or loss.

         (a) Net income increases the investment, and the investor's share of the investee's net income flows through to the investor's income statement. That is, the investment account is debited, and an investment income account is credited for the investor's proportionate share of the investee's net income.

         (b) Net loss decreases the investment, and the investor's share of the investee's net loss flows through to the investor's income statement. That is, the investment account is credited, and an investment loss account is debited for the investor's proportionate share of the investee's net loss.

      (2) The carrying value of the investment is adjusted for the investor's proportionate share of dividends declared by the investee.

         (a) Dividends declared by the investee decrease the investor's investment and do not flow through to the investor's income statement. That is, Cash is debited and the investment account is credited for the investor's proportionate share of dividends declared by the investee.

        (b) Dividends declared by the investee are simply an exchange of one asset (the investment) for another asset (cash).

    3. Incentives to account for equity investments using the equity method versus consolidations.

IV.   International perspective.

V.   Ethics in the real world.

VI.   Internet research exercise.

VII. Consolidated financial statements. (Appendix 8A)

    A. If the investor controls the investee company (defined as the investor owning at least 50 percent of the investee's outstanding stock), then consolidated financial statements are prepared.

        1. The purpose of consolidated financial statements is to report the combined accounts of the investor and investee companies.

        2. Two types of investments.

            a) Business acquisitions—the investor and investee combine for accounting purposes, but continue as separate legal entities.

            b) Business combinations or mergers—the investor and investee combine to form one legal entity.

    B. The two potential methods to account for consolidations are the purchase method and the pooling-of-interests method. Of these two methods, the purchase method is the most common.

        1. With the purchase method, the parent is assumed to be purchasing the subsidiary's assets and liabilities. The assets and liabilities should be valued at their fair market values.

        2. The pooling-of-interests method is only acceptable if at least 90 percent of the investor's payment is in the form of the investor's common stock. With this method, the investor and investee are considered to be combining their resources.

        3. Accounting for consolidations using the purchase method.

            a) Record the acquisition of the subsidiary at cost, which reflects the fair market value of the subsidiary's net assets by debiting the investment in subsidiary account.

            b) Eliminations and adjustments necessary to combine the balance sheets of the parent and subsidiary.

(1)   Eliminate the investment in subsidiary account.

(2)   Record subsidiary's assets and liabilities at their fair market values.

(3)   Record goodwill, if appropriate. Goodwill equals the excess paid over the parent's share of the fair market value of the subsidiary's net assets. Goodwill should be amortized over a period not to exceed 40 years.

(4)   Record minority interest, if appropriate. Minority interest arises when the parent purchases less than 100 percent of the subsidiary's outstanding voting stock. Minority interest represents the claims of the minority stockholders (i.e., stockholders other than the parent) on the fair market value of the subsidiary's net assets. Minority interest is calculated by multiplying the fair market value of the subsidiary's net assets by the percentage of outstanding voting stock owned by minority stockholders. Minority interest is usually reported on the balance sheet between long-term liabilities and stockholders' equity.

(5)   Eliminate intercompany receivables and payables, if appropriate.

(6)   Eliminate the investee's stockholders' equity.

c)   Eliminations and adjustments necessary to combine the income statements of the parent and subsidiary.

(1)   The consolidated income statement should only reflect consolidated income earned subsequent to the acquisition date.

(2)   Intercompany revenues and expenses must be eliminated.

LECTURE TIPS

1.   Understanding the need for the very different methods used to account for equity securities is aided by a general discussion of the nature of equity securities and the variety of reasons for companies to invest in them. It is important for students to understand the economic motivations and expectations behind each level of investment in order to understand the rationale for the accounting method. Figure 8–8 from the text (which summarizes the conditions under which the different methods are used) and end-of-chapter exercise 8–7 provide a vehicle to develop this understanding.

2.   Several end-of-chapter problems are particularly useful for demonstrating the different accounting methods for equity securities, especially through comparison with other methods. Problem 8–5 emphasizes trading versus available-for-sale classifications; problem 8–7 compares the mark-to-market method with the equity method; and problem 8–8 compares the equity method to consolidated financial statements.

OUTSIDE ASSIGNMENT OPPORTUNITIES

Group study of investments in equity securities both across time and within and across industries (continuing assignment for Chapters 6–14)

1. Using the most recent annual report of a major public company in one of the four general industry groupings, identify or compute the items listed below for the two most recent years. Compare the items across time. Relate your findings to the economic characteristics and current conditions in the industry and the company's strategy for competing. Prepare a written summary of your findings. Report findings in a class discussion session in which comparisons will be made both across time and within and across industries.

> Summary of the accounting policies relative to equity investments
> Captions and amounts reported for equity investments
> Percentage of each to total assets
> Income from equity investments (to the extent separately identifiable)
> Effect of market adjustments on net income, comprehensive income, and
>   stockholder's equity
> Major types of consolidated subsidiaries
> Amount of minority interest in income and net assets
> Footnote disclosures relating specifically to investments

Statement study on the impact of consolidation versus the equity method

2. Obtain a recent annual report and/or Form 10–K of a bank holding company such as BankAmerica Corporation. In conjunction with its consolidated financial statements, bank holding companies are required to present "parent-only" financial statements. The parent-only statements use the equity method to account for investments in the operating bank subsidiaries. Compare amounts for the following financial statement captions from the consolidated financial statements (for the most recent two years) to the amounts reported for the same captions in the parent-only statements. Explain the nature and significance of the differences.

> Total assets
> Total stockholders' equity
> Total income
> Net income

Also, on the parent-only statement of cash flows, compare cash flow from operations to net income for the two most recent years, and explain the differences.

Note to instructor: Total stockholders' equity and net income will be identical for each. Total assets and income on a consolidated basis will be many times greater than on the parent-only financials, because the bank subsidiaries actually collect the deposits and make most of the loans and investments. Cash flow from operations on the parent-only financials will usually be significantly less than net income, because only a portion of earnings of the bank subsidiaries are distributed to the parent in the form of cash dividends.

Research of accounting literature: accounting for goodwill in other countries

3.   Research current accounting literature for articles that cover accounting standards for goodwill in one or more countries outside the United States. Compare those standards to U.S. standards. Consider the impact of differences noted on decision-making by both users and management. Prepare a written and oral report of the findings.

ANSWERS TO END-OF-CHAPTER QUESTIONS

1.   To classify an investment in a security as current, (1) the investment must be readily marketable and (2) management must intend to convert the investment into cash within the time frame of current assets. The latter criterion is extremely difficult for auditors to ascertain. In an effort to inflate the company's working capital, current ratio, or quick ratio, a manager may desire to classify a long-term investment as current. Thus, a manager may state that he or she intends to convert the investment to cash within the time frame of current assets. Since the manager may have incentives to "window dress" the financial statements, auditors should not rely exclusively on management's representations. The auditor should examine the company's past practices and the nature and size of the investment in determining management's intention to convert an investment security.

2.   A realized gain arises from the sale of an asset in which the proceeds from the sale exceed the balance sheet value of the asset; a realized loss arises when the proceeds are less than the balance sheet value. A recognized gain/loss arises when a gain/loss is recorded in the books of a company. All realized gains and losses are recognized (i.e., recorded).   Further, an end-of-accounting-period adjustment is required to reflect unrealized holding gains and losses that arise from price changes.

3.   Investments in readily marketable equity securities are classified as either trading securities or available-for-sale securities. Trading securities are those which are bought and held principally for the purpose of selling them in the near future with the objective of generating profit on short-term price changes. Investments not classified as trading securities are considered available-for-sale securities. Trading securities are always listed in the current assets section of the balance sheet; available-for-sale securities are listed as current or long-term depending on management's intention. Both trading and available-for-sale securities are adjusted to current market value at the end of each accounting period. With trading securities, the related unrealized holding gain or loss arising from price changes is reflected directly in income; with available-for-sale securities, the related unrealized price change is reflected in stockholders' equity.

4.   Under the mark-to-market rule, investments in readily marketable equity securities are carried at current market value in the financial statements. This provides more useful information about the wealth of the firm, especially considering that the market value of an equity security often differs greatly from its historical cost. Market value accounting, in general, is criticized because market values are subjective and can result in large fluctuations from period to period (which are not necessarily relevant). Mark-to-market

accounting for investments in equity securities avoids these criticisms. The rule applies only to readily marketable equity securities, i.e., those that have readily determinable and objective market prices. Also, the market value changes of only those securities intended to be sold in the very near future (trading securities) are reflected in current income. Unrealized price changes related to securities classified as available-for-sale are not included in the income statement, but are reported on the statement of comprehensive income. Management's subjective judgment may influence the reported dollar amount of net income because the classification of securities as trading or available-for-sale relies heavily on management's intention.

5. Comprehensive income is a broader concept than net income, and is reported on a statement of comprehensive income. It includes all changes (not related to the owner) in stockholders' equity that do not appear on the income statement and are not reflected in the balance of retained earnings. Several items fall into this category, including adjustments to stockholders' equity for the holding gains and losses associated with available-for-sale securities.

6. The percentage ownership determines the accounting method that should be used to account for a long-term equity investment because the ownership percentage indicates the amount of influence that the investor can exert over the investee. As the percentage ownership increases, the two companies are viewed as becoming less independent, and the accounting treatment should reflect this decreased independence. If the investor owns less than 20 percent of the investee's outstanding shares, then the investment should be accounted for using either the cost method or the mark-to-market value method, depending upon whether the security is readily marketable. If the investor owns between 20 percent and 50 percent of the investee's outstanding shares, then the investment should be accounted for using the equity method. Finally, if the investor owns more than 50 percent of the investee's outstanding shares, the investment should be accounted for as a consolidation.

7. With the equity method, the investment is carried on the investor's books at an amount equal to the cost of the investment, adjusted for the investor's portion of changes in the investee's net assets. When the investee declares a dividend, the investee records a liability. Because an increase in the investee's liabilities decreases the investee's net assets, the value of the investor's investment has decreased. This decrease in the value of the investment is recognized by reducing the long-term equity investment account. In effect, the investor is exchanging assets. The investor is exchanging a portion of its long-term equity investment for dividends receivable. The investor will eventually exchange the dividend receivable for cash.

8. Users should be cautious when analyzing the financial statements of a company that uses the equity method because of several features of the method. First, the cash dividend received by the investor rarely amounts to as much as the income recognized from the investee company. The operating section of the cash flow statement of the investor company reveals the impact of this difference. Second, the equity method ignores market value changes in the affiliate's equity securities. Price changes are not recognized in the investor's financial statements, but may be determined if the investee's shares are publicly traded. Third, the equity method is used where the percentage of ownership is 20–50 percent, at which level significant influence is presumed. This presumption is not always valid. Fourth, the equity method can be used as a method of

off-balance sheet financing which does not reflect liabilities of the investee company on the balance sheet of the investor company. The footnotes to the investor's financial statements should disclose summary information of the investee, including the amount of liabilities.

9. A business acquisition refers to the acquisition by one company of a controlling interest in another company. A controlling interest is defined as owning at least 50 percent of the investee's voting shares. The two companies remain separate legal entities and only combine for accounting purposes. A merger refers to two or more companies combining to form a single legal entity.

10. Assume that Company A purchases 50 percent of the outstanding common shares of Company B for $500,000. If Company A uses the equity method to account for this investment, Company A would both increase its investment account and decrease its cash account by $500,000. Alternatively, if Company A prepares consolidated financial statements, it would decrease its cash account by $500,000, and then increase individual asset and liability accounts for the fair market values of the individual assets and liabilities acquired. In addition, Company A would have to report goodwill if the $500,000 is greater than the sum of the fair market values of the individual net assets it acquired.

The different accounting treatments illustrated in the example imply why a company might prefer to use the equity method to consolidated statements to account for a long-term equity investment. First, using the equity method does not require Company A to record any liabilities; Company A would be required to include its proportionate share of Company's B liabilities on its balance sheet with consolidation. Thus, the equity method would result in a lower debt/equity ratio, holding everything else constant. Because the debt/equity ratio is commonly included in debt covenants and is used to set credit ratings, this difference in debt/equity ratios could be important.

Second, Company A may have to recognize goodwill if it prepares consolidated financial statements, but goodwill would not have to be recognized under the equity method. Because goodwill is amortized over future periods, and thereby decreases net income, using consolidated financial statements would result in Company A reporting lower net income in future periods than if it used the equity method, holding everything else constant. Because net income affects stockholders' equity (which is used in the debt/equity ratio), and because management incentive compensation is often based on net income, the income effects arising from goodwill could be important.

11. Goodwill accounting is controversial for two reasons. First, under generally accepted accounting principles, companies are required to amortize (i.e., expense) goodwill over a period not to exceed 40 years. This means that a company that recognizes goodwill when it purchases another company will be required to reduce the amount of net income it reports in future periods as it amortizes the goodwill. Companies usually do not like to reduce their reported earnings.

Second, some people have claimed that requiring goodwill amortization puts U.S. companies at a competitive disadvantage to foreign companies in a company acquisition. The logic underlying this alleged disadvantage is that a U.S. company is unwilling to pay as much as a foreign company because the goodwill the U.S. company will have to eventually reduce its net income through the amortization of the goodwill. Foreign companies, such as companies based in Britain, are not required to amortize goodwill. Another reason for the alleged disadvantage is the deductibility of goodwill for tax purposes in the United States relative to other countries. That is, goodwill is not deductible for tax purposes in the United States, but it is deductible in Japan and Germany. This means that the effective cost of goodwill is less in Japan and Germany, which, in turn, implies that Japanese and German companies can offer to pay more for a company than can a U.S. company.

12. Goodwill is only recognized on a parent company's balance sheet if the price paid for the parent's proportion of the subsidiary's net assets exceeds the fair market value of the individual net assets purchased. Because goodwill is an intangible asset that should be amortized over a period not exceeding 40 years, it implies lower future net income.

13. Minority interest is only recognized on a parent's financial statements if the parent does not acquire 100 percent of the subsidiary's outstanding voting stock. Minority interest represents the claims of minority stockholders (i.e., stockholders other than the parent) on the fair market value of the subsidiary's net assets. Minority interest is similar to a liability in that it represents the claims of outsiders on the company's net assets; it is similar to stockholders' equity in that it represents equity interests held by outsiders. Consequently, minority interest is reported on the balance sheet between long-term liabilities and stockholders' equity.

14. In certain restrictive cases, a company can account for the acquisition of another company by use of the pooling-of-interests method. Unlike the purchase method, the pooling-of-interests method does not fully reflect the value of the exchange—it does not revalue assets of the acquired company (e.g., inventories and depreciable assets), and it avoids the recognition of goodwill. Therefore, under pooling, future income tends to be greater through lower amounts of cost of goods sold, depreciation expense, and goodwill amortization. Pooling also increases the recorded amount in retained earnings. These characteristics make the pooling-of-interests method very controversial.

CHARACTERISTICS OF END-OF-CHAPTER ASSIGNMENTS

Item	Difficulty	Description
Brief exercises:		
BE8–1	M	Real data: Short-term investments
BE8–2	M	Real data: Long-term equity investments
BE8–3	E	Real data: Goodwill
BE8–4	M	Real data: Long-term equity investments
Exercises:		
E8–1	E	Accounting for short-term equity securities
E8–2	M	Mark-to-market accounting
E8–3	M	Mark-to-market accounting

Item	Difficulty	Description
E8–4	M	Activity in the short-term investment account across time periods
E8–5	M	Reporting problems with mark-to-market accounting as applied to available-for-sale securities
E8–6	E	Classifying and accounting for equity investments
E8–7	E	The cost method
E8–8	M	Applying the mark-to-market rule
E8–9	E	The equity method
E8–10	E	Inferring information about the equity method from the financial statements
E8–11	E	Recording an acquisition under the purchase method
E8–12	E	Appendix 8A: 100 percent purchases in excess of the net market value of the assets and liabilities
E8–13	M	Appendix 8A: Per-share book and market value—purchase vs. pooling
E8–14	E	Appendix 8A: Computing goodwill and minority interest
E8–15	M	Appendix 8A: Completing a consolidated worksheet

Problems:

Item	Difficulty	Description
P8–1	E	Applying the mark-to-market rule to investments in equity securities
P8–2	M	Trading securities: purchases, sales, dividends, and end-of-period adjustments
P8–3	M	Changing security investment classifications
P8–4	M	Window dressing and the mark-to-market rule
P8–5	M	Trading versus available-for-sale classifications
P8–6	M	Inferring from balance sheet disclosures
P8–7	H	Long-term equity investments: the mark-to-market method versus the equity method
P8–8	M	The equity method versus consolidated financial statements
P8–9	H	Inferring information from the financial statements
P8–10	M	Appendix 8A: 100 percent purchase and the recognition of goodwill
P8–11	M	Appendix 8A: Minority interest and no goodwill
P8–12	M	Appendix 8A: Minority interest and goodwill
P8–13	M	Appendix 8A: Purchase vs. pooling
P8–14	M	Appendix 8A: Allocating the excess purchase price among tangible assets and goodwill
P8–15	M	Appendix 8A: Minority interest and goodwill
P8–16	M	Appendix 8A: Consolidated statements, the equity method, and debt covenants

Issues for discussion:

Item	Difficulty	Description
ID8–1	M	Equity adjustments for marketable securities
ID8–2	M	Available-for-sale securities
ID8–3	M	Equity method
ID8–4	E	Evaluating the equity method
ID8–5	E	Consolidating a finance subsidiary's financial statement: economic consequences
ID8–6	E	Accounting rules and foreign investment in the United States
ID8–7	M	International mergers
ID8–8	E	1998 annual report of NIKE

CHAPTER 9 Long-Lived Assets

SYNOPSIS

In this chapter, the author discusses (1) accounting for the acquisition, use, and disposal of long-lived assets, and (2) management's incentives for selecting accounting procedures associated with long-lived assets. The specific issues discussed in accounting for long-lived assets include the costs to capitalize when the asset is acquired, the treatment of postacquisition costs, cost allocation, and the disposal of long-lived assets. The discussion of cost allocation focuses on the alternative depreciation methods for fixed assets and the activity method for natural resources. The author discusses intangible assets and deferred costs in Appendix 9A.

The ethics vignette considers a case where management's methods of accounting for long-lived assets may be within the guidelines of GAAP but still leave the statement reader with vague and insufficient information.

The Internet research exercise examines the FASB's recent financial accounting standard for asset impairments.

The following key points are emphasized in Chapter 9:

1. How the matching principle underlies the methods used to account for long-lived assets.

2. Major questions that are addressed when accounting for long-lived assets and how the financial statements are affected.

3. Major economic consequences associated with the methods used to account for long-lived assets.

4. Costs that should be included in the capitalized cost of a long-lived asset.

5. Accounting treatment of postacquisition expenditures.

6. How the cost of a long-lived asset is allocated over its useful life and the alternative allocation methods.

7. Disposition of long-lived assets.

TEXT/LECTURE OUTLINE

Long-lived assets.

I.   Assets used in the operations of a business (not for resale) that provide benefits to the company extending beyond the current operating period. Long-lived assets include the following:

    A.   Land.

    B.   Fixed assets (i.e., buildings, machinery, and equipment).

    C.   Natural resource costs.

    D.   Intangible assets.

    E.   Deferred costs.

II.   The relative size of long-lived assets.

III. Long-lived asset accounting: general issues and financial statement effects.

    A.   Three basic questions when accounting for long-lived assets.

        1.   What dollar amount should be included in the capitalized cost of the long-lived asset?

        2.   Over what time period should the cost be amortized?

        3.   At what rate should the cost be amortized?

    B.   An overview of long-lived asset accounting—acquisition, use, and disposal.

IV. Acquisition: what costs to capitalize?

    A.   As a general rule, all costs necessary to get the asset in a serviceable and usable condition and location should be capitalized. The allowable costs of capitalization vary across long-lived assets.

    B.   The capitalized cost of land should include:

        1.   Purchase price of the land, including closing costs (such as title, legal, and recording fees).

        2.   Costs incurred to prepare the land for its intended use such as razing old buildings, grading, filling, and so forth. Any proceeds received from preparing the land for its intended use (such as the sale of scrap from a demolished old building) reduce the capitalized cost of land.

3. Permanent land improvements such as landscaping, sewers, drainage systems, and so forth.

C. Lump sum purchases.

1. As a general rule, allocate the purchase price to the assets based on their relative fair market values. This method requires that the fair market value of each asset acquired be known.

2. Because fair market values are somewhat subjective, using fair market values to allocate the purchase price among the individual assets acquired gives management discretion about how much to report for each asset. This discretion, in turn, can affect the timing of expense recognition and certain key ratios.

D. Construction of long-lived assets.

V. Post-acquisition expenditures: betterments or maintenance?

A. Betterments—costs incurred to improve an asset.

1. To be considered a betterment, an expenditure must provide one of the following:

a) An increase in the asset's useful life.

b) An improvement in the quality of the asset's output.

c) An increase in the quantity of the asset's output.

d) A reduction in the costs associated with operating the asset.

2. Betterments should be capitalized as part of the long-lived asset and amortized over the asset's remaining useful life.

B. Maintenance expenditures—costs incurred to repair or maintain an asset's current level of productivity. Maintenance expenditures are considered period expenses.

VI. Cost allocation: amortizing capitalized costs.

A. The purpose of cost allocation is to match the costs of long-lived assets against the benefits the assets helped generate.

B. Amortization terms.

1. Depreciation—the amortization of fixed assets.

2. Depletion—the amortization of natural resource costs.

3.   Amortization—the allocation of intangible assets and deferred costs.

C.   Steps in the allocation process.

    1.   Determine over what period of time the long-lived asset will help generate benefits. This step requires the company to estimate the asset's useful life. Estimating an asset's useful life is very subjective and is complicated by technological advances.

    2.   Determine the dollar amount of the asset's capitalized cost that the company expects to consume over the asset's estimated useful life.

        a)   This step requires the company to estimate the asset's salvage value. Estimating an asset's salvage value is extremely difficult. In practice, many managers simply assign a salvage value of zero to assets because of the difficulty in estimating a reasonable salvage value.

        b)   The dollar amount of the asset's capitalized cost that the company expects to consume over the asset's estimated useful life is called the asset's depreciation base (for fixed assets). The depreciation base equals the capitalized cost of the asset less its estimated salvage value.

    3.   Select a cost allocation method.

        a)   The choice of cost allocation methods does not affect the dollar amount amortized over a long-lived asset's estimated useful life. The dollar amount that is amortized over the asset's life is always its depreciation base.

        b)   A cost allocation method determines the rate at which an asset's capitalized cost will be amortized to future periods. That is, the total amount amortized over an asset's life is the same across allocation methods, but the timing of the allocations will differ.

D.   Cost allocation (depreciation) methods.

    1.   Straight-line method.

        a)   Allocates an equal amount of the depreciation base to each period.

        b)   Depreciation expense equals:
(Capitalized cost - Salvage value) ÷ Estimated life in years.

    2.   Double-declining-balance method.

        a)   Allocates larger amounts of an asset's depreciation base to the earlier periods of the asset's life than to the later periods.

b) Salvage value is not used to calculate depreciation expense, but the asset's book value cannot be reduced below its salvage value.

c) Depreciation expense = (Book value x 2) ÷ N, where N = the entire estimated useful life.

3. Activity method (units-of-production).

a) Allocates an equal amount of the cost to each unit of output. This method is most commonly used to deplete natural resource costs.

b) Expense = [(Capitalized cost – Salvage value) ÷ Estimated life in units of production] x Number of units produced.

E. Economic effects of cost allocation methods.

1. Effects of cost allocation methods on contracts.

2. Effects of cost allocation methods on perceptions of company's long-run earning power and solvency position.

3. Income tax effects.

VII. Disposal: retirements, sales, and trade-ins.

A. General rules for accounting for the disposal of fixed assets.

1. Depreciate the asset up to the date of disposal.

2. Remove the cost and related accumulated depreciation (for fixed assets) from the books.

3. Record the receipt or payment of cash (or other assets) involved in the disposal.

4. Recognize any gains or losses on the disposal. Gains and losses are computed as the difference between the disposed asset's book value and the net value of assets received.

B. Methods to dispose of fixed assets.

1. Retirements—discontinue using the long-lived asset.

2. Sale—exchange a long-lived asset for cash or a receivable.

3. Trade-ins—an exchange for dissimilar assets.

a) Exchanging a long-lived asset (and often cash) for a different type of long-lived asset.

      b)   It is often difficult to determine the value of the new asset, which, in turn, affects the magnitude of any gains or losses on the transaction.

          (1)   As a general rule, value the new asset at the fair market value of the assets given up or at the fair market value of the assets received, whichever is clearly more evident and objectively determined.

          (2)   Accounting for trade-ins is governed by *APB No. 29*, "Accounting for Nonmonetary Transactions."

VIII. International perspective.

IX.   Ethics in the real world.

X.   Internet research exercise.

XI.   Intangible assets and deferred costs (Appendix 9A).

    A.   Assets characterized by rights, privileges, and benefits of possession rather than by physical existence.

    B.   Intangible assets and deferred costs should be amortized over the shorter of the asset's legal life, the asset's useful life, or 40 years.

    C.   The preferred method to amortize intangible assets is the straight-line method.

    D.   Types of intangible assets.

        1.   Copyrights—exclusive rights over musical or artistic works. The legal life is the life of the creator plus an additional 50 years.

        2.   Patents—provide the holder exclusive rights to use, manufacture, or sell a product or process. The legal life is 10 years.

        3.   Trademarks (or trade name)—a word, phrase, or symbol that identifies an enterprise or product. The legal life is 20 years but the exclusive right can be renewed indefinitely.

        4.   Computer software development costs.

        5.   Goodwill.

          a)   Goodwill represents the excess amount paid for another company over the fair market value of the purchased company's net assets (i.e., assets less liabilities).

        b)   Recent changes in the law allow a tax deduction for amortizing goodwill, thus making corporate acquisitions more attractive from an economic standpoint.

   E.   Deferred costs.

       1.   Prepaid expenses extending beyond the current accounting period.

       2.   Organizational costs—costs incurred prior to the start of a company's operations that are necessary to allow the company to begin operations. Such costs typically include legal and accounting services, licenses, underwriting fees, titles, and so forth.

   F.   Research and development costs.

       1.   Governed by *SFAS No. 2*, "Accounting for Research and Development Costs."

       2.   Conceptually, some R&D costs provide future benefits and should be capitalized as an asset and amortized as the R&D provides benefits. However, given the difficulty of matching specific expenditures with associated benefits, the FASB mandated that all R&D costs should be treated as period costs.

LECTURE TIPS

1.   Students often have difficulty in deciding which costs should be capitalized as part of a long-lived asset (such as the cost of demolishing an old building on land just acquired) and which costs should be expensed. It should be stressed that for some costs, a great deal of judgment is involved. However, if the cost is necessary to get the asset into a useable condition, the cost should be capitalized. End-of-chapter exercise 9–3 and problem 9–1 are helpful in addressing which costs to capitalize.

2.   The straight-line method is usually easily understood. However, the double-declining-balance (DDB) method often poses more problems to students. The primary problems are (1) computing the appropriate multiplication factor to multiply against the asset's book value, and (2) depreciating the asset below its salvage value. End-of-chapter exercises 9–9 and 9–10 can be used to illustrate the computations for each method.

3.   Distinguishing between betterment and maintenance expenditures is also a difficult area. It should be pointed out that even practicing accountants face this problem because a great deal of judgment is involved in classifying postacquisition costs. End-of-chapter exercise 9–4 provides several situations to illustrate the concepts involved.

4. Distinguishing between depreciation expense and accumulated depreciation sometimes poses difficulty. It should be stressed that depreciation expense represents the cost of the fixed asset allocated to expenses for a particular accounting period; accumulated depreciation represents the total depreciation expense taken on a fixed asset since that fixed asset was acquired. Recording the entries in end-of-chapter exercise 9–10 in T-accounts will help the student distinguish between the two.

OUTSIDE ASSIGNMENT OPPORTUNITIES

Group study of long-lived assets both across time and within and across industries (continuing assignment for Chapters 6–14)

1. Using the most recent annual report of a major public company in one of the four general industry groupings, identify or compute the items listed below for the two most recent years. Compare the items across time. Relate your findings to the economic characteristics and current conditions in the industry and the company's strategy for competing. Prepare a written summary of your findings. Report findings in a class discussion session in which comparisons will be made both across time and within and across industries.

> Summary of the accounting policies for long-lived assets, including
>   depreciation, depletion, and amortization methods and rates
> Property, plant, and equipment (net) as a percentage of total assets
> Identifiable intangibles as a percentage of total assets
> Goodwill as a percentage of total assets
> R&D expense as a percentage of total revenues
> Depreciation, depletion, and amortization expenses as a percentage
>   of total revenues
> Summary of any impairment losses recognized

Article search: application of accounting standards for impairment of long-lived assets

2. Search the financial press (*The Wall Street Journal, Barrons, Fortune, Forbes,* etc.) for an article reporting on a company that applied the accounting standards issued in 1995 for impairment of long-lived assets. Consider the impact on its current and future financial statements, both from a user orientation and an economic consequences perspective, and present your findings in writing and/or orally to the class.

ANSWERS TO END-OF-CHAPTER QUESTIONS

1. A company must address three primary issues when accounting for long-lived assets. First, the company must decide what dollar amount to capitalize for the cost of a long-lived asset when it is acquired. Second, the company must decide over what time period to amortize an asset's capitalized cost. Finally, a company must decide at what rate to amortize an asset's capitalized cost.

    These three issues are related to the matching principle. Under the matching principle, costs are matched to the benefits that the costs helped generate. In the case of long-lived assets, the acquisition cost will help generate benefits in future periods, so the cost should initially be capitalized. Over time, as the asset helps generate benefits, the cost should then be matched against these benefits. The allocation process, consequently, allows a company to adhere to the matching principle.

2. Over the life of a long-lived asset, the asset's entire estimated unrecoverable cost will be expensed. By deciding how much of the cost to initially capitalize versus expense, and how rapidly to allocate the capitalized cost to future periods, a manager can alter the amounts reported for assets and net income. For example, assume that a company purchases equipment for $20,000. The manager could immediately capitalize the entire $20,000, immediately expense the entire $20,000, or capitalize a portion of the $20,000 and immediately expense the rest. The amount that the company will report for fixed assets and as net income is a direct consequence of how much of the cost the manager decides to capitalize and expense. In addition, managers can affect net income through their decisions as to how long to amortize the portion of a long-lived asset that is initially capitalized.

3. When a long-lived asset is acquired, the manager must decide what costs should be capitalized for the asset. In general, the manager should capitalize all the costs associated with getting the long-lived asset into a serviceable and usable condition and location.

    While the long-lived asset is being used, a manager faces two accounting issues. First, the manager must decide how to account for any postacquisition costs associated with the long-lived asset. If the expenditure increases the asset's useful life, improves the quality of the asset's output, increases the quantity of the asset's output, or reduces the asset's operating costs, then the expenditure is considered to be a betterment. Such expenditures should be capitalized as part of the long-lived asset. If the expenditure simply maintains the asset's current productivity level, then the expenditure is considered maintenance. Such costs should be expensed immediately. Second, the manager must decide how to allocate the capitalized cost to future periods. The manager must decide

(1) how much of the capitalized cost to allocate to future periods by determining the asset's depreciation base; (2) over what periods to allocate the amount to be amortized by estimating the asset's useful life; and (3) at what rate to amortize the asset by selecting an amortization method.

When a manager decides to dispose of a long-lived asset, the manager must decide which method to use to dispose of the asset. The manager can retire the asset, sell the asset, or trade-in the asset. Each disposal method has costs and benefits. The manager should weigh the costs against the benefits and select the appropriate disposal method.

4. A long-lived asset should be capitalized at its acquisition cost, which is determined by either (1) the fair market value of the acquired asset or (2) the fair market value of what was given up to acquire the asset, whichever is more readily determinable. In most cases, the fair market value of what was given up is used because cash (which by definition is at fair market value) is normally given up in such exchanges. In deciding what costs to capitalize when a long-lived asset is acquired, the general rule is that all costs that are required to get the long-lived asset into a serviceable and usable condition and location should be capitalized. The capitalized cost should include the purchase price plus any other necessary costs. These other necessary costs vary across the different types of long-lived assets. Some examples of capitalizable costs are freight, installation, taxes, and title fees.

5. Relative fair market values are used to allocate the cost of a lump-sum purchase among the individual assets acquired. If a company purchases inventory, land, and equipment in a lump-sum purchase, the allocation of the costs to the component items is extremely important for two reasons. First, inventory is classified as a current asset, and land and equipment are classified as noncurrent assets. The current asset classification is used in several ratios for assessing short-term solvency and in many debt covenants.

Second, the costs allocated to inventory, land, and equipment flow through to the income statement differently. The cost of inventory flows through to the income statement as cost of goods sold when the company sells the inventory. The cost of equipment flows through to the income statement as depreciation expense based on the company's choice of a depreciation method and the asset's estimated useful life. Land has an indefinite life, so it remains on the balance sheet and does not flow through to the income statement. Hence, misallocating a lump-sum purchase can affect a company's net income.

6. Postacquisition expenditures are the costs a company incurs to maintain or improve an asset subsequent to acquiring the long-lived asset. There are two general categories of postacquisition costs: betterment expenditures and maintenance expenditures. To be considered a betterment, the expenditure must (1) increase the asset's useful life; (2) improve the quality of the asset's output; (3) increase the quantity of the asset's output; or (4) reduce the asset's operating costs. Betterments should be capitalized as part of the long-lived asset, and then amortized over the asset's remaining useful life.

7. The three steps necessary to allocate the cost of a long-lived asset over its useful life are (1) determine the asset's salvage value, (2) determine the asset's useful life, and (3) select an amortization method. The first item determines how much of the capitalized

cost will eventually be expensed. The second item determines the time period over which the long-lived asset will be amortized. The last item determines the rate at which the capitalized cost will be amortized. All three items jointly affect the amount that a company reports for long-lived assets at any point in time and the amount that a company will report for the expense associated with long-lived assets.

8. Assume that a company has a debt covenant that stipulates a maximum debt/equity ratio. The manager can increase the probability that the company will not violate this requirement either by decreasing total long-term liabilities or by increasing total stockholders' equity. Since net income flows into stockholders' equity through the retained earnings account, one way to increase stockholders' equity is to increase net income. Consequently, the manager might select a depreciation method that gives rise to the smallest depreciation expense in the current period.

9. Research has generally indicated that investors "see through" accounting methods to the underlying cash flows. If a company switches from an accelerated depreciation method to a less conservative method, such as the straight-line method, investors and creditors may view the switch as an attempt by management to hide poor performance. Such an interpretation by investors and creditors may make it difficult for companies to raise capital, thereby affecting the managerial labor market's evaluation of management.

10. The activity method allocates the cost of a long-lived asset (usually a natural resource cost) based on the asset's activity. An equal amount of the cost is allocated to each unit of activity expected to be produced over the asset's life. In the case of natural resources, the cost of the resource is allocated through depletion to each unit of the natural resource expected to be produced.

The cost allocation per unit is considered a product cost so the cost allocation attaches to the inventory produced from the natural resource. The depletion is, therefore, capitalized as part of inventory. The depletion is matched to revenues when the inventory is sold, at which time the depletion flows through to the income statement as part of cost of goods sold.

11. Tax law dictates that fixed assets be classified into one of eight categories. Each category has a specific life and depreciation method.

To the extent that managers have a choice in the depreciation method used for tax purposes, managers will often use one method for financial reporting purposes and a different method for tax purposes. Over an asset's life, all depreciation methods result in equal amounts of depreciation being charged to income. However, the different depreciation methods result in timing differences in depreciation charges. These timing differences can provide benefits to companies.

Companies often use straight-line depreciation for financial reporting purposes because it results in the highest present value of net income. Higher net income is desirable to managers if existing contracts, such as incentive contracts and debt covenants, are written in terms of net income. On the other hand, managers often use accelerated depreciation methods for tax purposes because they result in the lowest present value of taxable income. In turn, the company realizes the lowest present value of tax payments and cash outflows. A manager can also reduce the present value of taxable income and, consequently, tax payments, by selecting a shorter useful life for an asset.

12. Under generally accepted accounting principles, a long-lived asset should be written down when the asset has suffered a "permanent impairment" in value. Because the professional literature is very vague about what constitutes a permanent impairment, managers have considerable discretion. This discretion, in turn, allows them to "manage" reported earnings.

13. When an asset is acquired in exchange for a dissimilar asset and cash, the new asset should be valued at either the fair market value of the assets given up or the fair market value of the assets received, whichever is more clearly evident and objectively determinable.

14. The Netherlands, the United Kingdom, France, and Australia are countries that allow companies to report their fixed assets at current values. This adjustment is achieved by increasing fixed assets and increasing stockholders' equity. Because current values are rather subjective, management has some discretion in determining to what amount to adjust the company's fixed assets. It is through this discretion that management can influence the amounts reported in the company's financial statements.

15. The ability of foreign companies to revalue long-lived assets has not helped them raise capital in U.S. markets, but rather has made it more difficult. When their financial statements are restated to U.S. GAAP (which is required by the major U.S. exchanges) their earnings numbers often fall.

16. Goodwill represents the excess of the value of a company taken as a whole over the sum of the values of its individual assets less its liabilities. In essence, goodwill represents those intangible qualities that make a company a company. Items that lead to a company having goodwill include name recognition, customer loyalty, and employee loyalty. Because it is extremely subjective to determine the value of a company taken as a whole, companies are not allowed to record goodwill on themselves.

However, when a company is purchased by an unrelated party, the value of the purchased company is determined through an arm's-length transaction. In such cases, the goodwill associated with the purchased company can be established, and the purchasing company can record this goodwill on its balance sheet. Thus, a company only reports goodwill if the company purchased another company. Goodwill is amortized over a period not to exceed 40 years. Many factors affect the period over which goodwill is amortized, such as regulatory restrictions, demand, competition, and obsolescence. Most companies use the straight-line method to amortize goodwill.

17. Under the matching principle, costs should be matched to the revenues that the costs helped generate. If a cost will help generate revenues in a future period, the cost should be capitalized and carried as an asset until it helps generate revenue. At that time, the cost should flow through to the income statement and be matched with the associated revenue.

The FASB has mandated that all R&D costs be expensed as incurred. Consequently, any R&D costs that are expected to provide future benefits are expensed in the period incurred rather than in the period in which the costs help to generate revenue. The FASB requires immediate expensing of R&D costs because of the difficulty of determining whether a particular R&D expenditure would actually provide future benefits. At the time R&D activities are undertaken, it is virtually impossible to determine whether these activities will provide benefits down the road. This situation is similar to a contingency. An event (i.e., R&D activity) has taken place but has not yet been resolved. At some point in the future, the uncertainty surrounding the event will be resolved and the company will know whether the R&D activity was successful. Until the uncertainty is resolved, too much doubt exists as to whether the company will ever receive a benefit. Consequently, recording a benefit before knowing there is actually a benefit is not an acceptable accounting practice. The current accounting treatment of R&D costs is the most conservative treatment possible.

CHARACTERISTICS OF END-OF-CHAPTER ASSIGNMENTS

Item	Difficulty	Description
Brief exercises:		
BE9–1	E	Real data: Change in depreciation method
BE9–2	M	Real data: Effect of depreciation on financial statements
BE9–3	M	Real data: Acquisition of fixed assets
Exercises:		
E9–1	E	Determining the capitalized cost and depreciation base
E9–2	E	Allocating cost on the basis of relative market value
E9–3	M	Which costs are subject to depreciation?
E9–4	E	Betterments or maintenance?
E9–5	M	How the matching principle affects the timing of income recognition
E9–6	M	The effect of estimated useful life on income and dividends
E9–7	M	Revising the estimated life
E9–8	E	Different amortization methods achieve different objectives
E9–9	M	Computing depreciation and choosing a depreciation method
E9–10	M	Depreciation calculations and journal entries
E9–11	M	The activity method of depreciation
E9–12	M	Depletion and matching
E9–13	H	An error in recording the acquisition of a fixed asset
E9–14	M	Fixed asset sales
E9–15	M	Retiring, selling, and trading in a fixed asset
E9–16	H	Reverse T-account analysis
E9–17	H	Reverse T-account analysis
E9–18	M	Appendix 9A: Intangible assets: expense or capitalize and amortize?
E9–19	M	Appendix 9A: The capitalized cost of a patent

Item	**Difficulty**	**Description**

Problems:

Item	Difficulty	Description
P9–1	E	Determining capitalized cost and the depreciation base
P9–2	M	Lump-sum purchases and cost allocations
P9–3	M	Determining capitalized cost and depreciation
P9–4	H	Expensing what should be capitalized can misstate net income
P9–5	M	Accounting for betterments and maintenance costs
P9–6	M	Accounting for betterments
P9–7	M	Revising the estimated useful life
P9–8	H	Why is double-declining-balance preferred for tax purposes?
P9–9	M	The effect of depreciation on taxes, bonuses, and dividends
P9–10	M	Natural resources: different methods of cost allocation depending on the nature of the asset
P9–11	M	Selling and trading in fixed assets
P9–12	M	Appendix 9A: Recognizing and amortizing goodwill

Issues for discussion:

Item	Difficulty	Description
ID9–1	M	Lump-sum sales and purchase
ID9–2	M	Capitalizing marketing costs
ID9–3	M	Betterments or maintenance and subsequent depreciation
ID9–4	M	Write-downs due to impairments
ID9–5	M	Recognizing depreciation and economic consequences
ID9–6	E	Fair market value accounting for museums?
ID9–7	M	Corporate restructuring
ID9–8	E	Current values?
ID9–9	M	NIKE's annual report (including questions relating to Appendix 9A)
ID9–10	M	Appendix 9A: Goodwill accounting
ID9–11	M	Appendix 9A: Goodwill write-offs

CHAPTER 10

Introduction to Liabilities: Economic Consequences, Current Liabilities, and Contingencies

SYNOPSIS

In this chapter, the author discusses (1) the economic consequences of liabilities in general and of current liabilities in particular; (2) measuring and reporting current liabilities; and (3) accounting for contingencies. The discussion on current liabilities includes accounts payable, short-term notes payable, current maturities of long-term debt, dividends payable, deferred revenues, third-party collections, and accrued liabilities. Accrued liabilities cover both determinable liabilities and conditional liabilities such as bonuses. The discussion of contingencies outlines the alternative approaches to accounting for contingencies as specified in *SFAS No. 5*, "Accounting for Contingencies" and the costs and benefits associated with the various alternatives. The specific types of contingencies discussed are lawsuits, environmental costs, and warranties.

The author discusses pensions and postretirement health care and insurance costs in Appendix 10A and deferred income taxes in Appendix 10B.

The ethics vignette considers companies that have cut health care coverage for retired workers in response to a new accounting standard (*SFAC No. 106,* which requires accrual of the cost of those benefits) when there is no formal contract requiring the companies to cover such costs.

The Internet research exercise examines *SFAS No. 5* and how it applies to accounting for environmental costs at Waste Management, Inc.

The following key points are emphasized in Chapter 10:

1. Definition of a liability.

2. Economic consequences associated with reporting liabilities on the financial statements.

3. Determinable and contingent liabilities.

4. Current liabilities.

5. Bonus systems and profit-sharing arrangements and the reporting incentives they create.

6. Methods used to account for contingencies.

TEXT/LECTURE OUTLINE

Introduction to liabilities: economic consequences, current liabilities, and contingencies.

I.   Liabilities—defined by the FASB as "probable future sacrifices of economic benefits from present obligations of a particular entity to transfer assets or provide services to other entities in the future as a result of past transactions or events." Liabilities possess the following three characteristics:

    A.   Liabilities should be present obligations that will require probable future transfers or uses of cash, goods, or services.

    B.   Liabilities should be unavoidable obligations.

    C.   Liabilities must arise from a transaction or an economic event that has already taken place.

II.   Reporting liabilities on the balance sheet: economic consequences.

    A.   Stockholders are affected by liabilities through:

        1.   Seniority of interest payments over dividend payments.

        2.   Debt covenants that influence investing, financing, and operating activities that a company may undertake.

        3.   Seniority of creditors' claims on assets over stockholders' claims in the event of liquidation.

    B.   Creditors are concerned with:

        1.   The seniority of liabilities.

        2.   The presence of sufficient assets to cover liabilities.

        3.   The protection of their investments through debt covenants.

    C.   Managers are concerned with liabilities because:

        1.   Liabilities are an important source of capital for operating, investing, and financing activities.

        2.   The amount of debt a company has and the ability to manage this debt affects a company's credit rating.

        3.   Debt covenants may restrict investing, financing, and operating decisions that the managers may make.

4.   The relation of liabilities to off-balance-sheet financing, taking a bath, and creating hidden reserves.

D.   Auditors are concerned with ascertaining that liabilities are not materially understated. Materially understated liabilities could result in the auditor being sued.

E.   Attempts by managers to minimize the amount reported as liabilities may lead to innovative financing arrangements resulting in off-balance-sheet financing.

III.   Current liabilities.

A.   Obligations expected to require the use of current assets or the creation of other current liabilities.

B.   Since current liabilities are short-term, the time value of money is ignored and current liabilities are carried at face value.

C.   Determinable current liabilities.

1.   Liabilities that can be precisely measured; the amount of cash necessary to satisfy the obligation and the payment date are reasonably certain.

2.   Classifications.

a)   Accounts payable.

(1)   The amounts owed to other entities for goods, supplies, and services purchased on open account.

(2)   Measurement issues are accounting for purchase cutoffs at the end of the accounting period and accounting for sales discounts.

b)   Short-term debts.

(1)   Short-term notes—usually carried at their face value less any discount. The discount represents interest on the note and is generally amortized (for short-term notes) using the straight-line method.

(2)   Current maturities of long-term debts—the portion of long-term debt that matures within the time frame of current assets (i.e., will be settled using current assets) should be reported as a current liability.

    c)   Dividend payable—the liability for dividends arises on the date the board of directors declares the dividend (See Chapter 12).

    d)   Unearned revenues.

    e)   Third-party collections.

       (1)   Sales taxes.

       (2)   Payroll withholdings.

    f)   Accrued liabilities.

       (1)   Normal accrued liabilities.

       (2)   Conditional liabilities.

          (a)   Liabilities for which the amount of the obligation is conditional upon net income. Hence, the amount of the liability cannot be measured until the end of the accounting period.

          (b)   Income tax liability—the actual amount owed for local, state, and federal income taxes.

          (c)   Incentive compensation.

             i)   Incentive plans are one device that stockholders can use to try to align the manager's goals with their own goals.

             ii)   Executive compensation and U.S. business in the global marketplace.

D.   Contingencies and contingent liabilities.

    1.   Contingencies are defined by the FASB as "an existing condition, situation, or set of circumstances involving uncertainty as to possible gain or loss to an enterprise that will ultimately be resolved when one or more future events occurs or fails to occur." That is, an event has taken place as of the balance sheet date that may or may not have an economic effect on the company, but the actual effect on the company will not be known until sometime in the future.

    2.   Accounting for contingencies.

       a)   Contingencies are governed by *SFAS No. 5*, "Accounting for Contingencies."

      b)   Gain contingencies.

          (1)   A contingency whose resolution could be financially advantageous to the company (i.e., result in an increase in assets or a decrease in liabilities).

          (2)   Gain contingencies are never accrued for in the financial statements. Under conservatism, gains are not recognized until the gain is realized. Gain contingencies may, if both reasonably estimable and probable, be disclosed in the footnotes.

      c)   Loss contingencies.

          (1)   A contingency whose resolution could be financially disadvantageous to the company (i.e., result in a decrease in assets or an increase in liabilities).

          (2)   General accounting treatment for loss contingencies.

              (a)   If an adverse resolution to the uncertainty is remote, then the contingency may be ignored for financial statement purposes.

              (b)   If an adverse resolution to the uncertainty is reasonably possible, then the contingency, and all relevant information, should be disclosed in a footnote.

              (c)   If an adverse resolution to the uncertainty is probable but the amount of the loss is not reasonably estimable, then the contingency, and all relevant information, should be disclosed in a footnote.

              (d)   If an adverse resolution to the uncertainty is probable and the amount of the loss is reasonably estimable, then a loss should be accrued in the financial statements.

   3.   Types of loss contingencies.

      a)   Lawsuits.

      b)   Environmental costs.

      c)   Post-sale costs.

          (1)   Bad debts (see Chapter 6).

        (2)   Warranties—the post-sale costs under the terms of the warranty should be estimated and then recognized as an expense and contingent liability in the period that the underlying sale took place.

IV.   International perspective.

V.   Ethics in the real world.

VI.   Internet research exercise.

VII.   Retirement costs: pensions and postretirement health care and insurance (Appendix 10A).

    A.   Pensions.

        1.   Money paid to a retired or disabled employee, the amount of which is usually determined by the employee's years of service.

        2.   Pension plans are usually administered by someone outside the company.

        3.   Types of pension plans.

            a)   Defined contribution plan—the company promises to make periodic payments into the pension fund. The company only guarantees the contributions into the plan, not the benefits to be disbursed to employees.

            b)   Defined benefit plan—the company guarantees a specified payout upon the employee's retirement.

        4.   In accordance with the matching principle, pension expenses should be recorded in the accounting period in which the employees earn the rights to the future benefits.

        5.   A company's pension liability represents the difference between the company's contribution to the plan to date and the estimated amount necessary to meet the guaranteed employee benefits.

    B.   Postretirement health care and insurance costs.

VIII.   Deferred income taxes (Appendix 10B).

    A.   An account to reconcile the difference between a company's income tax expense and income tax liability. This difference arises due to differences in measuring net income under GAAP and the Internal Revenue Code.

        1.   Tax liability is based on the company's tax rate and the company's net income using the Internal Revenue Code.

    2.   Income tax expense is based on the company's tax rate and the company's net income using GAAP.

B.   Theoretically, the amount reported as deferred income taxes will eventually be paid as income taxes as the income differences between GAAP and the Internal Revenue Code reverse.

    1.   Managers may make certain investing and/or operating decisions that effectively postpone the reversal period, thereby indefinitely postponing paying these taxes.

    2.   Changes in the statutory tax rates result in restatement of the balance in the deferred income tax account, thereby giving rise to recognized gains or losses.

C.   The conservatism ratio provides a quick way to assess how conservative management's reporting choices have been in a particular year. It measures the extent to which reported income before taxes differs from taxable income.

LECTURE TIPS

1.   The need for companies to be concerned with contingencies even though the company may not be affected should be discussed in the context of the objective of financial accounting (i.e., providing information to investors regarding a company's investment potential and credit worthiness). The diagram in figure 10–5 in the text is useful for an overview of accounting for contingencies. It should be emphasized that the event must first have occurred. It should also be pointed out that contingent losses can be booked as asset valuation accounts (e.g., allowance for bad debts) as well as liabilities. It is helpful to summarize typical types of loss contingencies into categories:

	Usually Accrued	*Not Accrued*	*Maybe Accrued**
Potential loss from:			
Uncollectible receivables	X		
Product warranties	X		
Risk of loss from fire, flood, or other hazards		X	
General business risks		X	
Environmental costs			X
Lawsuits			X

*based on probable and estimable criteria

2. Students' views often vary widely on numerical values for the degrees of probability expressed in accounting for contingencies. An interesting class exercise is to poll the class as to their numerical assignment of probabilities to the "remote," "reasonably possible," and "probable" expressions. A study** examined the differences among key groups of audit opinion users and professional auditors concerning the meaning of the term "substantial doubt" used in the audit literature for the going concern issue. The study employed a survey in which subjects were asked to assign probability values to the term "substantial doubt," and also, especially of interest here, to "possible" and "probable." Significant differences were noted among participants concerning "substantial doubt," but not for the "possible" and "probable" expressions. The mean response for auditors was 0.4067 for "possible" and 0.7296 for "probable."

**Lawrence A. Ponemon and K. Raghunandan, "What is 'Substantial Doubt'?" *Accounting Horizons,* June 1994, pp. 44–54.

OUTSIDE ASSIGNMENT OPPORTUNITIES

Group study of current liabilities both across time and within and across industries (continuing assignment for Chapters 6–14)

1. Using the most recent annual report of a major public company in one of the four general industry groupings, identify or compute the items listed below for the two most recent years. Compare the items across time. Relate your findings to the economic characteristics and current conditions in the industry and the company's strategy for competing. Prepare a written summary of your findings. Report findings in a class discussion session in which comparisons will be made both across time and within and across industries.

> Total liabilities as a percentage of total assets
> Current liabilities as a percentage of total liabilities
> Captions used to report current liabilities
> Summary of accounting policies relating to current liabilities
> Summary of types of employee benefit plans and related
>   accounting policies (Appendix 10A)
> Liabilities for pensions and postretirement health care and insurance
>   benefits as a percentage of total liabilities (Appendix 10A)
> Summary of nature of items giving rise to deferred
>   income taxes (Appendix 10B)
> Deferred income taxes as a percentage of total liabilities (Appendix 10B)
> Conservatism ratio (Appendix 10B)

Group study of contingencies both across time and within and across industries (continuing assignment for Chapters 6–14)

2. Using the most recent annual report of a major public company in one of the four general industry groupings, discuss (1) its disclosure and accounting for the years presented for three categories of contingencies: warranties, environmental costs, lawsuits, and others; and (2) the associated potential economic consequences. Relate your discussion to the economic characteristics of and current conditions in the industry and the company's strategy for competing. Prepare a written summary of your findings. Report findings in a class discussion session in which comparisons will be made both across time and within and across industries.

Research of current accounting literature on a topic relating to liabilities and contingencies

3. Research current accounting literature for articles covering a current topic relating to liabilities and contingencies, e.g., employee postretirement benefit plans, executive compensation, or environmental costs. Focus on the impact of the issue on users of financial statements as well as its economic consequences effect on management decisions. Prepare a written and oral report of the findings.

Classroom game on executive incentive compensation

4. Obtain the Elitzur article (referenced below[1]) which describes a game on the subject of executive incentive compensation schemes. Play the game as a classroom exercise.

ANSWERS TO END-OF-CHAPTER QUESTIONS

1. A liability represents probable future sacrifices of economic benefits arising from the present obligations of a company to transfer assets or provide services to other entities at some time in the future as a result of past transactions or events. All liabilities should (1) be present obligations that entail settlement by probable future transfers or uses of cash, goods, or services; (2) be unavoidable obligations; and (3) have arisen from a transaction or event that has already happened.

2. High levels of debt can make a company appear risky, thereby making it difficult to attract capital. Further, many debt covenants specify minimum or maximum ratios based on liabilities such as the current ratio and the debt/equity ratio. If a

---

[1] R. Ramy Elitzur, "A Classroom Exercise on Executive Incentive Compensation Schemes," *Managerial & Decision Economics,* November/December 1995, pp. 649–652.

manager can understate liabilities, the manager effectively decreases the probability the company will violate the debt covenant and incur costly violation costs. While managers may wish to understate liabilities, such practices are usually not very effective. The trend by the FASB has been to require more and more disclosure. Hence, off-balance-sheet financing arrangements are increasingly disclosed in the footnotes to the financial statements and can be used by creditors to evaluate a company or to calculate ratios specified in debt covenants. Further, financial statement users may place less reliance on financial statements issued by managers who understate liabilities. This decreased reliance, in turn, makes it more difficult for the managers to attract capital, which may have been the very reason managers wanted to understate liabilities in the first place.

Managers may prefer to accrue additional liabilities if such accruals are expected to provide future benefits, namely, higher future profits. If the company has performed poorly, managers will sometimes record significant liabilities, and associated losses, in hopes of setting a foundation for improved future performance. Such cases are referred to as "taking a bath." Managers' incentive compensation schemes may also provide incentives to overstate liabilities. Such compensation plans often have an upper bound. That is, managers receive a portion of net income until net income reaches a certain amount; any income generated over the upper bound yields no additional compensation for the managers. Therefore, once net income has reached the compensation scheme's upper bound, managers have incentives to defer income to future periods, thereby maximizing the present value of their incentive compensation.

3. Current liabilities are obligations that are expected to be settled through (1) the use of current assets, or (2) the creation of additional current liabilities. Current assets represent those assets that are most readily convertible into cash or to be consumed within the longer of one year or one operating cycle. Defining current liabilities in terms of current assets makes it easier for financial statement users to assess a company's short-term solvency.

4. Current assets represent a company's assets that are most readily convertible into cash; current liabilities are obligations a company expected to settle by using current assets or by creating additional current liabilities. So financial ratios based on comparing current assets to current liabilities, such as the current ratio, provide investors and creditors a means to assess a company's short-term solvency. By stipulating a minimum current ratio, creditors prevent managers from taking excessively risky actions that might jeopardize the creditors' chances of collecting their principal and interest payments.

To decrease the probability of violating a debt covenant, a manager may make operating and/or reporting decisions that result in higher current assets or lower current liabilities. For example, the manager may decide to alter the company's inventory purchasing activity (an operating activity) or change the classification of assets and/or liabilities (a reporting activity) in order to increase the company's current ratio.

5. Determinable current liabilities represent current liabilities that can be precisely measured with the amount of economic benefits necessary to satisfy the obligation and the date of payment also reasonably certain. These types of liabilities include accounts payable, dividends payable, short-term debt (such as short-term notes payable) deferred revenues, and third-party collections. Conditional current liabilities are a subset of determinable liabilities. Conditional liabilities are liabilities that cannot be determined until the end of the accounting period because the amount of the obligation is based on net income. Income taxes and incentive compensation are the most common types of conditional current liabilities.

   Contingent liabilities represent potential liabilities that have arisen from past events. When the event happened, uncertainty existed as to whether a liability actually existed. The uncertainty will be resolved in the future, at which time it will be known with certainty whether or not a liability existed. At that time, the liability becomes a determinable liability. Examples of contingent liabilities are potential warranty costs from merchandise sold and civil lawsuits in which the company is the defendant.

6. Accounts payable are dollar amounts owed to another entity for goods, services, or supplies purchased on an open account. In most cases, accounts payable represent the extension of credit by the supplier to the company without a specific, formal contract. A company will often incur a liability prior to its year-end but not receive the corresponding bill until after year-end. If the goods received prior to year-end are included as an asset but the corresponding liability is not recorded, the company's financial position would be overstated. Since the auditor could be held liable for any losses incurred by financial statement users due to understated liabilities, the auditor has incentives to pay special attention to inventory purchases near year-end.

7. When a company receives a returnable deposit or payment in advance, the company often cannot determine exactly when it will settle the obligation, or whether it will be settled with current assets. Because the company faces doubt about how to report the obligation, the company should apply conservatism. Conservatism means that, when in doubt about how to report or disclose a transaction or event, report the transaction or event in the least favorable way. Since reporting an obligation as a current liability would make the company appear to be less financially secure than reporting the obligation as a long-term liability, the company should report returnable deposits and advance collections as current liabilities.

8. Liabilities based on net income, which is not known until year-end, are called conditional liabilities. A company can estimate its net income throughout the year, but does not know its exact net income until year-end. Consequently, the actual amount of a liability based on net income cannot be accurately determined until net income is determined. Common examples of conditional liabilities are income taxes and incentive compensation.

9. Companies compensate their employees through bonus agreements and profit-sharing plans to try to align the employees' goals with the company's goals.

Companies generally wish to increase net income and/or the price of the company's stock. To induce employees to exert effort and to try to increase net income or stock price, companies link employees' compensation to the level of net income and/or stock prices. Since reported earnings are often used as the basis of bonus agreements and profit-sharing plans, managers can increase their compensation by increasing net income. Ideally, such compensation schemes will induce managers to make operating decisions that actually improve a company's financial position. However, managers may benefit even if the increase in net income is purely cosmetic (i.e., not supported by expected cash inflows). For example, a manager may switch from double-declining-balance to the straight-line method of depreciation because such a switch reduces the present value of expenses, thereby increasing the present value of net income. Therefore, incentive compensation schemes may influence both the operating and reporting decisions of management.

10. Responding to much public concern about the level of executive compensation in many corporations as well as the apparent weak linkage between performance and pay, the SEC adopted new rules that require that corporations make detailed disclosures of executive compensation and of company performance. Salary and stock options for the highest paid executives must be disclosed in the proxy statement, as well as total return to shareholders in terms of stock price and dividends, related to the market rate of return as a whole. Shareholders can use this information to compare executive pay with shareholder return. The desired consequence is that the linkage between pay-and-performance will become closer, thus, the wealth of managers will be linked to the wealth of the shareholders for whom they work.

11. A loss contingency is an event involving uncertainty about a potential loss in which the uncertainty will not be resolved until sometime in the future. The appropriate accounting treatment for loss contingencies depends upon (1) whether the amount of the loss is reasonably estimable, and (2) the probability of an adverse outcome. Assume that the amount of the loss is reasonably estimable. If an adverse outcome is considered to be remote, the loss contingency should be ignored for financial accounting purposes. If an adverse outcome is considered to be reasonably possible, the loss contingency should be disclosed in the footnotes to the financial statements. If an adverse outcome is probable, the loss contingency should be accrued on the books. Now assume that the amount of the loss is not reasonably estimable. If an adverse outcome is either reasonably possible or probable, the loss contingency should be disclosed in the footnotes to the financial statements; otherwise, it should be ignored for financial accounting purposes.

Managers and auditors consider the costs and benefits of the potential accounting methods for loss contingencies. If a loss contingency is not disclosed and the outcome proves to be adverse, financial statement users could sue the manager and auditors. If the company accrues the loss, potential providers of capital may withhold their capital, thereby making it more difficult for the company to operate. If the manager does not want to accrue the loss, but the auditor insists, the manager may fire the auditor. The auditor's position is especially vulnerable if the eventual outcome does not result in a loss to the company.

12. Under the concept of conservatism, gains should not be recognized until realized. Consequently, in most cases, the appropriate accounting treatment for gain contingencies is to simply ignore the contingency. However, if the amount of the contingency can be reasonably estimated, and if it is probable that the contingency will be resolved in the company's favor, it is acceptable to disclose the contingency in the footnotes to the financial statements.

Conservatism states that when in doubt, understate rather than overstate. Since doubt exists as to the resolution of a contingency, conservatism governs accounting for contingencies. For a loss contingency, the company could potentially be put in a worse financial position; consequently, the contingency should be disclosed to understate the financial statements. For a gain contingency, the company could potentially be put in a better financial position; consequently, the contingency should be ignored.

13. Product warranties represent potential future claims of customers. These claims can only arise if the product proves to be defective. Consequently, uncertainty exists at the time of sale whether the company will actually incur a cost in the future to repair the product. By definition, a contingency is a past event or transaction involving uncertainty that will not be resolved until sometime in the future. Product warranties meet this definition.

Costs associated with product warranties are only accrued if it is probable that the company will incur warranty costs and if such costs can be reasonably estimated. If neither of these conditions are present, the costs associated with the warranties should not be accrued. However, the nature of the warranties should be disclosed in the footnotes to the financial statements.

The first step in accounting for product warranties is to estimate the costs expected to be incurred in the future under the warranty. Companies usually rely on historical data to make these estimates. Once the estimates have been made, the estimated amount is recorded as an expense and as a liability. As products are returned for service under the warranty, the actual costs incurred to repair the product are debited to the liability account.

14. The philosophy in the United States is that a corporation's primary responsibility is to its stockholders. In applying this philosophy to executive compensation plans, U.S. companies provide compensation plans to executives with incentives to take actions and make decisions that will maximize stockholder wealth. In Japan, alternatively, the philosophy is that a corporation is more responsible to its customers, employees, and suppliers than to its owners. This philosophy is evident in executive compensation plans for executives of Japanese companies in that their plans do not emphasize the needs of the owners. This difference in philosophies between the two countries is highlighted by the pay differential between the average worker and executives in the two countries. In the United States, executives are paid approximately 90 times more than the average worker; Japanese executives are paid only 10 to 20 times more than the average worker.

15. A pension plan is a plan to provide money to employees if they become disabled or when they retire. In many cases, an entity independent of the company manages the pension plan and is responsible for the plan. The assets of the pension plan actually belong to the employees since the cash has been set aside exclusively for their use. Consequently, companies do not report any assets on their books for pension plans. If the dollar amount contributed by the company to the pension plan is insufficient to cover the total estimated amount needed to maintain the fund, then the company is liable for the difference. The company should report this difference on the balance sheet as a liability.

16. Under a defined contribution pension plan, the employer only promises to contribute a specified amount to the pension plan; under a defined benefit pension plan, the employer promises a specified benefit amount upon the employees' retirement. Therefore, the difference between the two types of pension plans is that the defined contribution plan focuses on inputs into the pension plan, while the defined benefit plan focuses on outputs of the pension plan. Defined contribution plans are becoming more popular because they are considered much less expensive than defined benefit plans.

There are two problems in accounting for a defined benefit plan. First, it is difficult to determine the dollar amount to use in preparing the periodic accrual entry to record pension expense and liability. Second, it is difficult to determine how much cash to contribute to the pension fund to cover the promised benefit. These problems are intertwined since the amount of the expense and liability depends upon the amount of the eventual benefit. Companies usually rely on actuaries to estimate the future pension costs and to determine how to allocate these costs to accounting periods.

17. Postretirement health care costs are costs incurred by a company to provide health care benefits to its retired employees. The FASB requires that these costs be matched against the benefits generated from the costs. Because retired employees earn the rights to these health care benefits by working for the company, and the employees provided a benefit to the company while they were working, the FASB's requirement implies that these health costs should be recognized as expenses when the employees earn the rights to the health care benefits. Hence, companies would have to record a large loss, and an associated liability, to record the postretirement health care benefits already earned by its current and former employees.

18. Companies are interested in minimizing the present value of cash outflows for taxes. One way to minimize such outflows is to accelerate expense recognition. A common area in which companies accelerate expense recognition is depreciating fixed assets. Using accelerated depreciation methods (such as the sum-of-the-years'-digits method, the double-declining-balance method, or the Modified Accelerated Cost Recovery System method) rather than the straight-line depreciation method for tax purposes results in a lower present value of taxable income, thereby reducing the present value of cash outflows for taxes.

Although companies usually use an accelerated depreciation method for tax purposes, they usually use the straight-line depreciation method for financial reporting purposes. A company's tax liability is a function of its tax rate and income calculated using the Internal Revenue Code, while a company's tax expense is a function of its tax rate and income calculated using GAAP. By using accelerated depreciation methods for tax purposes and the straight-line depreciation method for financial reporting purposes, a company's tax liability is less than its tax expense in the early years of the assets' useful lives. The excess of the income tax expense over the income tax liability represents deferred income taxes that, theoretically, will be paid in the future when the difference between taxable and book income reverses. Hence, the deferred income taxes should be reported as a liability.

19. The conservatism ratio provides a quick way to assess how conservative management's reporting choices have been in a particular year. It measures the extent to which reported income before taxes differs from taxable income. It is calculated using information available in the annual report, as follows:

Conservatism ratio = Reported income before taxes ÷ Taxable income

Taxable income is computed indirectly:

Taxable income = Annual tax liability ÷ Effective income tax rate

The effective income tax rate is found in the footnotes and the annual tax liability can be computed by reconstructing the journal entry to record tax expense.

Companies generally try to minimize taxes, thus, taxable income (the denominator of the ratio) reflects a very conservative measure of a company's income. The extent to which reported income before taxes (the numerator of the ratio) differs from taxable income indicates how conservative reported income is. Ratios of 1.0 or less indicate relatively conservative levels. As reported income becomes increasingly less conservative, the ratio grows larger than 1.0.

CHARACTERISTICS OF END-OF-CHAPTER ASSIGNMENTS

Item	Difficulty	Description
Brief exercises:		
BE10–1	E	Real data: Cash flow and accruals
BE10–2	E	Real data: Inferring financial information
BE10–3	E	Real data: Cash payments for environmental cleanup
Exercises:		
E10–1	M	Why are current liabilities carried at face value instead of present value?
E10–2	M	Financing with long-term debt, contract terms, and the current ratio
E10–3	M	Accruals, the current ratio, and net income

Item	Difficulty	Description
E10–4	E	Short-term notes payable and the actual rate of interest
E10–5	E	Current maturities and debt covenants
E10–6	E	Gift certificates and unearned revenue
E10–7	E	Gain and loss contingencies
E10–8	M	Bonus plans and contingent losses
E10–9	M	Warranty costs: contingent losses or expense as incurred?
E10–10	E	Appendix 10A: Pension contributions and unfunded pension liability
E10–11	H	Appendix 10B: Deferred taxes and the tax rate
E10–12	H	Appendix 10B: Conservatism ratio
E10–13	H	Appendix 10B: Conservatism ratio

Problems:

Item	Difficulty	Description
P10–1	E	Distinguishing current liabilities from long-term liabilities
P10–2	M	Recognizing current liabilities can restrict dividend payments
P10–3	H	Recognizing current liabilities and violating debt covenants
P10–4	M	Issues surrounding the recognition of a contingent liability
P10–5	M	Accruing warranty costs before they are incurred
P10–6	M	Advertising campaigns can give rise to contingent liabilities
P10–7	M	Appendix 10A: Accruing and funding pension liabilities
P10–8	H	Appendix 10B: Deferred income taxes, changes in tax rates, and investment in long-lived assets
P10–9	M	Appendix 10B: Conservatism ratio

Issues for discussion:

Item	Difficulty	Description
ID10–1	M	Debt covenants and reporting current liabilities
ID10–2	E	Receipts in advance: measurement theory and financial statement effects
ID10–3	E	Lawsuits and contingent liabilities
ID10–4	M	Unreported assets
ID10–5	E	The economic consequences of a technical default
ID10–6	E	Reclassifying short-term notes as long-term debt
ID10–7	E	Using executive compensation disclosures
ID10–8	M	"Taking a bath" during bankruptcy proceedings
ID10–9	E	Replacing currently maturing debt with a long-term note
ID10–10	H	Reversing contingent losses
ID10–11	H	The annual report of NIKE, Inc. (includes questions relating to Appendices 10A and 10B)
ID10–12	E	Appendix 10A: Economic consequences and accounting for postretirement health care and insurance costs
ID10–13	E	Appendix 10A: Postretirement costs
ID10–14	E	Appendix 10B: Changes in expected tax rates and net income

CHAPTER 11

Long-Term Liabilities: Notes, Bonds, and Leases

SYNOPSIS

In this chapter, the author discusses accounting issues surrounding long-term liabilities. The specific issues discussed are (1) accounting for long-term notes payable; (2) accounting for bonds payable; (3) the differences between, and accounting for, operating and capital leases; (4) financial instruments and off-balance-sheet risks; and (5) the economic consequences faced by managers whose companies have long-term debt. The author discusses factors affecting bond prices in Appendix 11A.

The ethics vignette considers a company which structures its leasing contracts in a manner that allows it to avoid reporting debt when some might consider the lease to be debt.

The Internet research exercise examines current financial reports for Imation, looking at how it has managed since 1997 when it almost tripled its debt and encountered problems with certain restrictions in debt agreements.

The following key points are emphasized in Chapter 11:

1. Long-term notes payable, bonds payable, and leasehold obligations, and how companies use these instruments as important sources of financing.

2. Economic consequences created by borrowing.

3. Different forms of contractual obligations.

4. The effective interest rate and how it is determined for contractual obligations.

5. The effective interest method.

6. How changes in market interest rates can lead to misstated balance sheet values for long-term liabilities.

7. Operating leases, capital leases, and off-balance-sheet financing.

TEXT/LECTURE OUTLINE

Long-term liabilities: notes, bonds, and leases.

I.   Long-term liabilities are probable future sacrifices of economic benefits from present obligations of a particular entity to transfer assets or to provide services to other entities in the future as a result of past transactions or events. The obligation will require the disbursement of assets outside the time frame of current assets.

II.   Economic consequences of reporting long-term liabilities.

   A.   Credit ratings.

   B.   Debt covenants.

      1.   Debt covenants can limit a company's operating, investing, and financing activities.

      2.   If a company violates a debt covenant, the borrower can require one of the following:

         a)   The immediate repayment of the debt.

         b)   Renegotiation of the debt at terms that are more costly to the borrower (i.e., higher interest rate or additional collateral).

   C.   Effects of "merger mania."

III. Overview of long-term liabilities.

   A.   Notes, bonds, and leases are supported by contracts.

      1.   The timing and magnitude of future cash outflows are specified in the contracts.

      2.   Types of contractual forms.

         a)   Interest-bearing obligations require the following:

            (1)   Periodic cash payments (interest) calculated as a stated percentage of the obligation's face value (principal or maturity value). The stated percentage is given in the debt contract, and the stated percentage is called the stated interest rate.

            (2)   Payment of the face value at the end of the contract period.

        b) Non-interest-bearing obligations do not require periodic interest payments. Instead, they require only the payment of the face value at the end of the contract period.

        c) Installment obligations require periodic payments throughout the obligation's life, and the periodic payments include both principal and interest.

    3. The contracts may specify the following:

        a) Collateral.

        b) Restrictions (i.e., debt covenants).

  B. Types of long-term liabilities.

    1. Long-term notes payable.

    2. Bonds payable.

        a) Bonds are issued to raise large amounts of capital (usually from multiple creditors) to finance long-term projects.

        b) Secured bonds versus debentures.

        c) Interest is usually paid semiannually on bonds.

    3. Leases.

IV. Issuing notes and bonds.

  A. Long-term debt is accounted for using the present value of future cash flows. Present value is acceptable under GAAP for long-term debt because the future cash flows are contractually specified, which means that the future cash flows can be objectively determined.

  B. Effective interest rate.

    1. The effective interest rate is the interest rate that a company actually incurs on an obligation.

    2. The effective interest rate is the rate that equates the undiscounted future cash flows of an obligation (e.g., periodic interest payments and the face value for interest-bearing obligations) with the present value of the obligation. That is, the effective interest rate is the rate used to discount the future cash flows of an obligation so that the present value of the future cash flows equals the fair market value of that which is received in the exchange.

3.   Relation of stated and effective interest rate for notes and bonds.

   a)   Stated rate equals effective rate. The present value of future cash flows equals the face value of the debt; the note or bond is issued at face value.

   b)   Effective rate exceeds stated rate. The present value of future cash flows is less than the face value, thereby resulting in a discount; the note or bond is issued for less than its face value. Discounts represent future interest expense.

   c)   Stated rate exceeds effective rate. The present value of future cash flows is greater than the face value, thereby resulting in a premium; the note or bond is issued for more than its face value.

V.   Amortizing discounts and premiums on notes and bonds.

A.   Discounts (the excess of the face value of a note or bond over its present value) and premiums (the excess of the present value of a note or bond over its face value) should be amortized over the period that the debt is expected to be outstanding.

B.   Effective interest method of amortization.

1.   The effective interest method results in a constant percentage of the carrying value being charged to interest expense over the life of the debt and is the preferred amortization method.

2.   Relationships under the effective interest method.

   a)   Book value (or carrying value) of the debt equals the debt's face value plus associated premium balance or it equals the debt's face value less associated discount balance.

   b)   Interest expense equals debt's book value at the start of the period times the effective interest rate.

   c)   Periodic interest payments equal debt's face value times the stated interest rate.

   d)   The amount of the discount amortized equals interest expense less the interest payment.

   e)   The amount of the premium amortized equals the interest payment less interest expense.

3. Journal entries need to be prepared to record interest expense incurred and discount/premium amortized on every interest payment date and at the end of the accounting period (i.e., an adjusting journal entry) if an interest payment date does not fall on the last day of the accounting period.

VI. Retiring bonds.

A. At maturity.

B. Before maturity.

1. Call provisions grant the issuing company the right to repurchase bonds prior to the maturity date.

2. Calling bonds normally gives rise to gains or losses. If the gain or loss is material, it should be reported on the income statement as an extraordinary item.

VII. Leases.

A. A contract granting use or occupation of property during a specified period of time in exchange for rent payments. Leases allow companies to use or occupy property without many of the associated costs and risks of ownership.

B. Types of leases.

1. Operating leases.

a) The lessor (i.e., the owner) temporarily transfers the right to use the property to the lessee for a specified period of time in exchange for periodic payments. The lessor is normally responsible for the normal maintenance of the property over the life of the lease. The right to use the property reverts to the lessor at the end of the lease.

b) The property is reported as an asset on the lessor's books. The periodic rental payments are reported on the lessor's books as Rent Revenue; the periodic rental payments are reported on the lessee's books as Rent Expense.

2. Capital leases.

a) Leases that, in substance, transfer the rights and risks of ownership to the lessee.

        b)   Criteria for a lease to be classified as a capital lease—if a lease meets one of the following criteria, the property is considered purchased rather than leased.

            (1)   The leased property's fair market value approximately equals the present value of the lease payments.

            (2)   The term of the lease is 75 percent or more of the leased property's useful life.

            (3)   The lessee has the right to purchase the property from the lessor for less than what the property is actually worth, called a bargain purchase price.

            (4)   Ownership is transferred to the lessee by the end of the lease term.

        c)   Accounting for capital leases on the lessee's books.

            (1)   At the inception of the lease agreement, the lessee records an asset and a liability equal to the present value of the future lease payments.

            (2)   The asset should be depreciated, if appropriate, over its useful life.

            (3)   The periodic rental payments serve to reduce the lease liability and to recognize interest expense. Interest expense is computed using the effective interest method.

VIII.   Financial instruments and off-balance-sheet risks.

     A.   Disclosure of market values required for certain financial instruments, whether or not they are recognized in the financial statements.

        1.   Short-term investments in equity securities (Chapter 8).

        2.   Notes receivable and investments in debt securities.

        3.   For long-term debts, the market value approximates the present value of future cash outflows associated with the debt, discounted at the current market rate of interest for similar obligations.

        4.   Other financial instruments not listed on the balance sheet, such as guarantees of the credit of third parties, commitments to provide financing, and derivatives.

IX.   International perspective.

X.   Ethics in the real world.

XI.   Internet research exercise.

XII. The determination of bond prices (Appendix 11A).

     A.   Risk-free return—the annual return that an individual would earn by investing in a riskless security such as a Treasury note. Factors increasing the risk-free rate tend to decrease bond prices, while factors decreasing the risk-free rate tend to increase bond prices.

     B.   Risk premium—the interest rate over and above the risk-free rate to cover the issuing company's default risk. Factors increasing a company's riskiness tend to decrease bond prices, while factors decreasing a company's riskiness tend to increase bond prices.

LECTURE TIPS

1.   The concept of effective interest rates is sometimes troublesome, especially in cases where these rates are imputed for notes (i.e., when no market exists to establish the effective interest rate). Further, many students do not understand how the effective and stated interest rates could be different. It should be stressed that the stated interest rate is simply a device to structure the future cash flows; it does not have to approximate the rate that a company should actually be paying.

    In addition, discounts or premiums are often viewed as something inherently positive or negative. An approach that may help address this problem is to offer students the opportunity to "invest" in several different notes or bonds—all with the same effective interest rates, the same present values and maturity dates, but with different face values and stated rates. This should drive home the point that discounts and premiums arise because of the way the future cash flows are structured.

    Many students find time lines showing the future cash flows and the change in the debt's carrying value over the life of the debt to be useful in understanding the relation between discounts/premiums and interest expense.

    Figures 11–7 and 11–11, end-of-chapter exercises 11–3 through 11–8, and problem 11–5 are all useful for demonstrating the points involved.

2.   Calculating the present value of the future cash flows, particularly for bonds, is sometimes troublesome. The most common mistake is not adjusting the annual effective and stated interest rates to semiannual interest rates. It should be stressed that present value techniques rely on the compounding period. Since bonds usually pay interest every six months, the appropriate compounding period is six months. End-of-chapter exercise 11–2 emphasizes the concept of compounding.

3. End-of-chapter problems 11–13 and 11–14 and issues for discussion 11–3 and 11–6 are useful for considering the financial statement effects of accounting for leases. The economic differences between capital and operating leases should be discussed as the basis for accounting for each. The lease agreement's economic substance should be stressed over its legal form.

OUTSIDE ASSIGNMENT OPPORTUNITIES

Group study of long-term debt and off-balance-sheet risks both across time and within and across industries (continuing assignment for Chapters 6–14)

1. Using the most recent annual report of a major public company in one of the four general industry groupings, identify or compute the items listed below for the two most recent years. Compare the items across time. Relate your findings to the economic characteristics and current conditions in the industry and the company's strategy for competing. Prepare a written summary of your findings. Report findings in a class discussion session in which comparisons will be made both across time and within and across industries.

>   Captions and amounts for components of long-term liabilities:
>   long-term debt, including capitalized lease obligations,
>   employee benefits, deferred income taxes, and others
>   Footnote disclosures for long-term liabilities
>   Total long-term liabilities as a percentage of total assets
>   Total long-term liabilities as a percentage of total liabilities
>   Total long-term liabilities as a percentage of stockholders' equity
>   Nature of and aggregate commitments for operating leases
>   Disclosures of off-balance-sheet commitments and their associated risks,
>   such as commitments to extend credit, guarantees of debt, interest
>   rate agreements, and foreign exchange contracts

Recalculation of ratios based on constructive capitalization of operating leases

2. Obtain the most recent annual report for a company in an industry likely to have significant operating leases (such as Toys "R" Us) in the retail field. Calculate key financial ratios, especially those for return on assets and debt/equity. Obtain and read the Imhoff article (referenced below[1]) on constructive capitalization of operating leases. Use the method discussed in the article to constructively capitalize the selected company's operating lease commitments. Recalculate key financial statement ratios. Evaluate the results.

---

[1] Eugene A. Imhoff Jr., Robert C. Lipe, and David W. Wright, "Operating Leases: Impact of Constructive Capitalization," *Accounting Horizons,* March 1991, pp. 51–63.

ANSWERS TO END-OF-CHAPTER QUESTIONS

1. Debt covenants can have economic consequences for managers, creditors, and investors. Such covenants can significantly restrict management's operating and investing activities. Restricting management's actions can cause future earnings and cash flows to drop, which may adversely affect the company's stock value and the manager's human capital, as well as increase the probability that the company will go bankrupt. Further, debt covenants often restrict the payment of dividends, which can directly affect stockholders' wealth. In the worst case, a company that violates its debt covenants may be forced to repay the debt, leading to insolvency.

2. Reporting debt on the balance sheet can have at least two negative consequences. First, increasing reported debt can decrease a company's credit rating, thereby making it more difficult and more expensive for that company to acquire capital. Second, many debt covenants are written in terms of a company's debt. For example, a debt covenant may specify a company's maximum debt/equity ratio. Reporting higher amounts of debt increases the probability that the company will violate such debt covenants.

    Managers may want to accelerate debt recognition, and the associated losses, if the company is performing exceptionally poorly (or well). If the company is performing poorly, management may "take a bath" in hopes of setting a solid foundation for future profitability. If a company is performing well, management may want to smooth income to avoid wide fluctuations in performance and, hence, their evaluation and compensation.

3. The effective interest rate on an obligation is calculated by finding the interest rate that equates the present value of the obligation with the future cash outflows, where the benefit received in the exchange equals the present value of the future cash outflows.

4. Long-lived liabilities are carried on the balance sheet at estimated present value in accordance with the principle of objectivity. To report an item on the balance sheet at present value, the company must be able to objectively determine the future cash flows the item will generate and a discount rate. For long-term liabilities, the future cash flows are usually specified in a contract, so there is little doubt about the timing and magnitude of future cash flows. Further, by comparing the present value of the future cash flows, which is the market price of the bond, with the cash flows specified in the contract, a discount rate can be inferred.

5. The stated interest rate is the rate stated in the debt agreement. Interest payments are calculated by multiplying this rate by the debt's face value. The effective interest rate represents the actual interest rate paid by the company; it equals the rate that equates the present value of future cash flows with the undiscounted future cash flows.

6. The basic rule of the effective interest method is that the interest expense recognized during each period of the liability's life is equal to the effective interest rate multiplied by the balance sheet value of the liability at the beginning of the period.

7. The stated interest rate determines the timing and magnitude of future periodic cash outflows associated with a note or bond. Assume that a company wishes to borrow a specific amount of money. The company can structure the terms of a note in various ways so that the present value of the future cash payments will be the same (i.e., the specific amount it wishes to borrow). For example, a company could make periodic interest payments over the life of the note and make a small lump-sum payment on the maturity date. Alternatively, the company could structure the note so that the company simply makes one large lump-sum payment on the maturity date. The latter case would be a non-interest-bearing note.

    If a company thinks that it may have insufficient cash to meet periodic interest payments, or if the company thinks that it will receive a cash windfall several periods in the future, the company may prefer not to make periodic payments; it may instead choose to make a lump-sum payment at the end of the note's life. Structuring the note as a non-interest-bearing note simply allows the company to better match its expected availability of cash with its cash needs.

8. Amortizing a discount on a long-term note or bond payable involves three steps under the effective interest method. First, interest expense is calculated as the effective interest rate times the book value of the liability at the beginning of the accounting period. Second, the interest payment is calculated as the stated interest rate times the face value of the liability. Finally, the amount of the discount amortized is calculated as the difference between the interest expense and the interest payment. In short, the company incurred interest expense, and it pays part of its interest obligation in cash (i.e., the amount of the periodic payment) and gives a promise to the creditor to pay the remaining interest later (i.e., the amount of the discount amortized).

9. Bonds are popular forms of financing because they allow companies to raise large amounts of capital. If a company wanted to raise $750 million, it is doubtful that a single creditor could supply that amount of money. However, by issuing bonds, a company can simultaneously borrow money from many different creditors.

10. The important features of a bond contract are:

    a. Life—time period from bond issuance date to maturity date.

    b. Maturity date—date the face value and final interest payment are due to the bondholders.

    c. Face value—dollar amount written on the bond certificate, usually $1,000. This amount is also referred to as the principal, par value, or maturity value.

    d. Interest payment—amount paid to the bondholders periodically throughout the life of the bond. The amount is calculated as the stated interest rate times the bond's face value.

    e. Proceeds at issuance—dollar amount received when the bonds are issued. The proceeds equal the present value of the future cash flows discounted at an appropriate interest rate, net of any issuance fees.

    f. Effective interest rate—actual interest rate paid on the bonds. The effective rate equals the rate used to discount the future cash flows to determine the proceeds.

    g. Restrictions—listed in the debt agreement limiting the company's operating or investing activities in order to protect the creditors' rights to interest and principal payments.

    h. Security—any collateral provided to satisfy the claims of the bondholders in the case of default. Unsecured bonds are called debentures.

    i. Call provision—a clause in the bond agreement that specifies that the issuing company has the right to buy back the bonds at a specified price after a certain date. The call price is usually greater than the face value.

11. Debentures are unsecured bonds. In other words, they are bonds not backed by assets of the issuing company. Investing in debentures is generally riskier than investing in secured bonds because the investors do not have claims to specific assets if the issuing company defaults. Small companies are more likely to be risky, and hence more likely to go bankrupt, than large, well-established companies. Thus, small, unknown companies, such as Jones Airlines, Inc., would have more trouble issuing debentures than large, well-known companies such as DuPont or IBM.

12. A debt covenant is part of the debt agreement that lists restrictions placed by the creditor(s) on the issuing company's operating or investing activities. The purpose of these restrictions is to increase the probability that the creditors will receive their interest and principal payments. Debt covenants serve to protect the creditors' rights, so the presence of a debt covenant should make an investment less risky, holding everything else constant. Because the issue price of a bond is a function of how risky the bond is, anything that affects the riskiness of the bond should affect the bond's price. Reducing the riskiness of a bond by including a debt covenant should reduce the effective interest rate, and thereby increase the price of the bond. Thus, one reason a company would allow a debt covenant to be written into a bond is that the company should be able to raise more capital per bond than it would if the bond did not include the covenant.

13. If a bond is issued at a discount, the stated interest rate is less attractive to investors than the effective interest rate. Consequently, the stated rate is less than the effective rate. The opposite holds for bonds issued at a premium. The stated interest rate is more attractive to investors than the effective interest rate, so the stated rate is greater than the effective rate.

14. Under the effective interest method, bonds are carried on the issuing company's books at an amount equal to the remaining future cash flows (specified in the bond agreement) discounted using the effective interest rate on the date the bonds were issued. Thus, in one sense, the effective interest method does result in bonds being reported on the balance sheet at their present value.

   However, the present value reported on the balance sheet for bonds is not the same as the bonds' economic value, which is the value that present value is usually supposed to represent. The economic value of bonds equals the bonds' remaining future cash flows discounted using the current effective interest rate (i.e., the interest rate that equates the future cash flows with the bond's market value at that particular point in time). Hence, the effective interest method does not report long-term bonds at their economic value. The use of different discount rates is consistent with the principle of objectivity. The effective interest rate on the date the bonds are issued can be inferred from an arm's length transaction and is, therefore, objective. Using the effective interest rate of any other point in time is not as objective because it assumes that the company intends to retire the bonds prior to their maturity.

15. Companies may wish to retire their bonds prior to maturity because of changes in economic conditions. For example, if interest rates drop, companies may wish to buy back their bonds and issue new bonds that have lower stated rates. Such a move could dramatically reduce a company's periodic cash payments for interest.

16. Several forms of financing are not reflected in the balance sheet. In addition to operating leases (covered in questions 21–24), a company may carry financial instruments not listed on the balance sheet, many of which involve significant risks. Examples include commitments to guarantee the credit of third parties; commitments to provide financing to customers who purchase certain inventory items; and other financing arrangements often designed to reduce the risks associated with fluctuations in interest rates and the value of foreign currencies relative to the U.S. dollar. Users can assess these risks from required financial statement disclosures that contain extensive descriptions of these instruments.

17. Off-balance-sheet financing refers to future obligations faced by a company that are not disclosed on the balance sheet as liabilities. When a lease is classified as an operating lease, the lessee does not report an asset or liability on its balance sheet; when a lease is classified as a capital lease, the lessee reports both an asset and a liability. If the company has existing debt covenants, recording a liability under a capital lease might cause the company to violate a debt covenant that specifies a maximum debt/equity ratio. Thus, the company may prefer to structure a lease as an operating lease to avoid violating a debt covenant.

18. Generally accepted accounting principles require that companies disclose in the footnotes the future cash payments associated with both their operating and their capital leases. Financial statement users can use this information to ascertain the extent to which the financial statements are affected by the lease accounting

method. To make all companies comparable, the user could reconstruct the financial statements as if all leases had been accounted for as capital leases by computing the present value of the cash flow payments associated with the company's operating leases, and including that dollar amount as both a liability and an asset on the balance sheet.

19. The relative importance, as well as the form, of debt financing varies across countries. For example, debt financing is extremely important in Japan, but there is very little reliance on bonds (or stocks). Instead, Japanese companies acquire their debt financing from banks. The same is true of companies in Germany and Switzerland.

The differences in the importance and form of debt financing have resulted in differences in accounting disclosure requirements across countries. For example, disclosure requirements in foreign countries are usually less comprehensive than the requirements in the United States. These differences arise because U.S. companies have to provide information to a much broader spectrum of investors, whereas companies in other countries (such as Japan, Germany, and Switzerland) only have to provide information to a few large banks that have many personal contacts with the companies. In addition, other countries have developed regulations designed to protect creditors or to help assess solvency, as opposed to the regulations in the United States that are designed to generate general-purpose (i.e., multi-purpose) financial statements.

20. An investor's required rate of return is the sum of the risk-free return and a risk premium. The risk premium represents the return required to compensate the investor for the probability that the issuing company will default on the bonds. A change in a company's credit rating usually indicates a change in the probability of the company defaulting on its bonds. A reduction in a company's credit rating indicates an increased chance of default, so the risk premium on this company would increase. The increase in the risk premium indicates that the effective rate associated with these bonds should increase, thereby reducing the present value of the bond's future cash flows. Therefore, a reduction in a company's credit rating implies that the price of the company's bonds should decrease.

21. If you plan to hold the bonds until they mature, you will be indifferent about changes in the interest rate. You will receive the same amount of money whether interest rates decrease, increase, or remain unchanged. However, if you plan to sell the bonds prior to their maturity, then you should be concerned about changes in interest rates. Changes in interest rates cause changes in the effective rate currently being used by the market to determine the fair value of the bonds. An increase in interest rates relative to the stated rate makes the bonds less attractive to potential buyers; hence, the price of the bonds will decrease. Alternatively, a decrease in interest rates relative to the stated rate makes the bonds more attractive to potential buyers; hence, the price of the bonds will increase. Since you could sell the bonds for more if they are attractive to potential buyers, you would prefer that interest rates decrease.

CHARACTERISTICS OF END-OF-CHAPTER ASSIGNMENTS

Item	Difficulty	Description
Brief exercises:		
BE11–1	E	Real data: Inferring debt transactions
BE11–2	E	Real data: Bond issuance
BE11–3	M	Real data: Operating and capital leases
Exercises:		
E11–1	M	Disclosing debt and debt covenants
E11–2	M	Annual or semiannual interest payments?
E11–3	E	The relationship among the stated rate, effective rate, and issuance price of a liability
E11–4	M	Computing the proceeds from various notes
E11–5	M	Notes issued at a discount and the movement of interest expense
E11–6	M	Accounting for notes payable with various stated interest rates
E11–7	M	Determining the effective interest rate
E11–8	M	Financing asset purchases with notes payable
E11–9	M	Inferring an effective interest rate from the financial statements
E11–10	M	Computing bond issuance proceeds and the movement of balance sheet value and interest expense over the bond's life
E11–11	M	Accounting for bonds issued at face value
E11–12	M	Accounting for bonds issued at a discount
E11–13	M	Accounting for bonds issued at a premium
E11–14	H	Changing market interest rates and economic gains and losses
E11–15	E	Redeeming bonds not originally issued at par
E11–16	E	Updating amortization and retiring a bond issuance
E11–17	H	Analyzing bond disclosures
E11–18	H	Analyzing bond disclosures
E11–19	M	Accounting for leases
E11–20	H	Accounting for leases and the financial statements
E11–21	H	Financing asset purchases
E11–22	H	Inferring the effective rate of interest
E11–23	M	Appendix 11A: The decision to purchase a bond

Item	Difficulty	Description
Problems:		
P11–1	M	Computing the face value of a note payable
P11–2	M	Accounting for bonds with an effective rate greater than the stated rate
P11–3	M	The balance sheet value of debt and the long-term debt/equity ratio
P11–4	M	Accounting for notes issued at a discount and at face value
P11–5	M	The effects of various notes payable on the financial statements
P11–6	M	The difference between cash interest payments and interest expense
P11–7	M	The effective interest method, interest expense, and present value
P11–8	M	The effective interest method and the straight-line method: effects on the financial statements
P11–9	M	Why the effective interest method is preferred to the straight-line method
P11–10	E	Redemption and updating amortization
P11–11	M	Call provisions and bond market prices
P11–12	H	Tax deductible bond interest and the present value of cash outflows
P11–13	H	Accounting for a capital lease
P11–14	M	Some economic effects of lease accounting
P11–15	M	Financing asset purchases with notes and inferring the effective rate of interest
P11–18	M	Appendix 11A: Determinants of bond market prices
Issues for discussion:		
ID11–1	E	Repurchasing outstanding debt
ID11–2	M	Bonds with a stated interest rate of zero
ID11–3	H	Buy or lease: financial statement effects
ID11–4	E	Financing acquisition with debt
ID11–5	E	Holding debt in times of recession
ID11–6	M	Adjusted ratios for lease accounting
ID11–7	E	Bond prices and economic news
ID11–8	M	Market value of debt and managing risk
ID11–9	H	The annual report of NIKE

CHAPTER 12   Stockholders' Equity

SYNOPSIS

In this chapter, the author discusses the theoretical issues and accounting treatment for both contributed capital and earned capital. Equity is compared and contrasted with debt, and the economic incentives for raising capital through debt versus equity are discussed. The primary contributed capital topics discussed are (1) issuing stock; (2) the rationale for a company repurchasing its own common stock; (3) the cost method of accounting for treasury stock; and (4) stock options. The primary earned capital topics discussed are (1) dividend strategies, (2) accounting for dividends, and (3) stock splits.

The ethics vignette considers whether boards of directors acted ethically when they intentionally handed out hefty stock-option awards just before a proposed FASB rule was expected to take effect. The proposed rule would have required significant reductions in reported net income for stock options.

The Internet research exercise examines the main transactions between Kellogg Company and its shareholders over a three-year period.

The following key points are emphasized in Chapter 12:

1.   The three forms of financing and their relative importance to major U.S. corporations.

2.   Distinctions between debt and equity.

3.   Economic consequences associated with the methods used to account for stockholders' equity.

4.   Rights associated with preferred and common stock and the methods used to account for stock issuances.

5.   Distinctions among the market value, book value, and par (stated) value of a share of common stock.

6.   Treasury stock.

7.   Cash dividends and dividend strategies followed by corporations.

8.   Stock dividends and stock splits.

TEXT/LECTURE OUTLINE

Stockholders' equity.

I.   Nature of stockholders' equity.

    A.   Stockholders have a residual interest in the company. Stockholders' equity consists primarily of:

        1.   Contributed capital—contributions from the company's owners.

        2.   Earned capital—measure of the net assets the company generated through its operations not yet disbursed to the owners as dividends.

    B.   The most common forms of business entities are sole proprietorships, partnerships, and corporations. The primary differences among these three business forms are:

        1.   Liability of the owners.

        2.   Income taxes.

        3.   Returns to owners.

II.   Debt versus equity.

    A.   Characteristics of debt.

        1.   Formal legal contract.

        2.   Fixed maturity date (as specified in the contract).

        3.   Fixed periodic interest payments (as specified in the contract).

        4.   Security (i.e., collateral) in case of default (as specified in the contract).

        5.   Debtholders have no direct voice in management, but they can influence management through debt covenants.

        6.   Interest is an expense.

    B.   Characteristics of equity.

        1.   No formal, legal contract.

        2.   No fixed maturity date.

        3.   Dividend payments are at the discretion of the company's board of directors.

      4.   Residual asset interest.

      5.   Stockholders have a voice in management through their right to vote for the board of directors.

      6.   Dividends are not an expense.

  C. Economic consequences of issuing debt versus issuing equity.

      1.   Dilution of ownership rights.

      2.   Effect on credit ratings.

      3.   Effect on debt covenants.

      4.   Effect on taxes.

III.   Contributed capital.

  A. Authorized, issued, and outstanding shares.

      1.   Authorized shares represent the number of shares of stock that the company is legally entitled to issue as stated in the corporate charter.

      2.   Issued shares represent the total number of shares that have been distributed by the company and not retired. Issued shares equals the shares outstanding plus shares held in treasury.

      3.   Outstanding shares represent the shares currently held by stockholders.

  B. Market value, book value, par value, and stated value.

      1.   Market value is the value at which the stock is currently trading on the open market.

      2.   Book value represents stockholders' equity per share of common stock outstanding. Book value is computed as: (Stockholders' equity - Preferred capital) ÷ Number of common shares outstanding.

      3.   Market-to-book ratio.

         a)   The market-to-book ratio is computed by dividing the market value of a company's common stock by its book value.

         b)   Ratios equal to 1 indicate that a company's net book value (as measured by the balance sheet) is perceived by the market to be a fair reflection of the company's true value. Ratios larger than 1 indicate that the balance sheet is perceived to be conservative.

4.   Par (or stated) value.

    a)   Par value is a legal concept and was created to protect creditors. It no longer has significant economic or legal meaning.

    b)   Owners' contributions in excess of par value are allocated to additional paid-in capital.

C.   Types of ownership interests.

   1.   Preferred stock.

      a)   Preferred stock is usually issued with a par value. Dividends on preferred stock are either stated as a dollar amount or as a percentage of par value.

      b)   Preferred stockholders are entitled to certain preferences (such as on dividends and assets) over common stockholders. In exchange for these preferences, preferred stockholders usually sacrifice certain rights, such as the right to vote for board members.

      c)   Characteristics of preferred stock.

         (1)   Cumulative versus noncumulative.

         (2)   Participating versus nonparticipating.

   2.   Common stock.

      a)   Fundamental rights of common stockholders.

         (1)   Right to receive dividends declared by the board of directors.

         (2)   Right to share proportionately in residual corporate assets in the event of liquidation.

         (3)   Right to exert control over management.

      b)   Common stock is the riskiest ownership interest.

D.   Issuing stock.

   1.   No-par value stock.

   2.   Par value stock.

E.   Repurchasing stock—treasury stock.

   1.   Treasury stock is not considered an asset.

2. Reasons companies repurchase common stock.

   a) To provide a sufficient number of shares to support employee compensation plans.

   b) To concentrate ownership of outstanding shares to make it more difficult for a takeover.

   c) To increase the market price of a company's outstanding stock.

   d) To increase the company's earnings per share.

   e) To retire preferred or common stock. Once common stock has been retired, the shares are considered authorized but not issued.

3. Accounting for treasury stock.

   a) Cost method.

      (1) The cost method is the more common method used to account for treasury stock. Under GAAP, using the cost method is appropriate if the company intends to eventually reissue the shares.

      (2) The treasury stock account has a debit balance and is disclosed in the stockholders' equity section after retained earnings.

      (3) When purchasing treasury stock, Treasury Stock is debited and Cash is credited for the cost of the shares.

      (4) Reissuing treasury stock for more than acquisition cost.

         (a) Treasury Stock is credited for the cost of the shares reissued.

         (b) The excess received over the acquisition cost is credited to Additional Paid-in-Capital, Treasury Stock.

      (5) Reissuing treasury stock for less than acquisition cost.

         (a) Treasury Stock is credited for the cost of the shares reissued.

         (b) The excess of acquisition cost over proceeds is debited to Additional Paid-in-Capital, Treasury Stock. If its account balance is insufficient to absorb the entire excess, the residual excess is debited to Retained Earnings.

   b) Par value method.

F.   Stock options.

    1.   Stock options give the right to purchase equity securities at a fixed price over a specified time period. Stock options are widely used as a form of executive compensation.

    2.   No compensation expense is recorded when granted (except when options are granted at prices below the current market price). An issuance of common stock is recorded when options are exercised.

    3.   Disclosure is required of the amount of compensation expense that would have been recorded if the value of the options granted during the year was recognized.

IV.   Retained earnings.

A.   Dividends.

    1.   Dividend strategies.

    2.   Important dates.

        a)   Date of declaration—the date that the board of directors declares a dividend and the company incurs a liability for the dividend.

        b)   Date of record—the legal owner of the stock on this date is the person or entity entitled to the dividend.

        c)   Date of payment—the date that the company pays the dividend.

    3.   The dividend account is a temporary account that is closed directly into retained earnings during the closing process.

    4.   Cash dividends.

    5.   Stock dividends and stock splits.

        a)   Stock splits.

            (1)   A company issues additional shares of common stock to its stockholders and splits the outstanding shares into smaller units.

            (2)   Stock splits cause the number of shares classified as outstanding to change and the par value per share and market value per share to change. These changes are documented in a memorandum entry. However, the total value of the shares outstanding should, theoretically, remain the same.

b) Stock dividends.

    (1) A company issues additional shares of common stock to its stockholders as a dividend. No assets are distributed to the stockholders.

    (2) After the stock dividend, each stockholder retains the same percentage of ownership interest in the corporation.

    (3) Ordinary stock dividends.

        (a) A stock dividend should be accounted for as an ordinary stock dividend if the number of additional shares to be issued is less than 25 percent of the shares outstanding prior to the stock dividend.

        (b) An amount equal to the fair market value of the common stock issued is allocated from retained earnings to the common stock and additional paid-in-capital accounts.

    (4) Stocks splits in the form of a stock dividend.

        (a) A stock dividend should be accounted for as an ordinary stock dividend if the number of additional shares to be issued is greater than 25 percent of the shares outstanding prior to the stock dividend.

        (b) An amount equal to the par value of the stock is allocated from retained earnings to the common stock account.

c) Reasons companies declare stock dividends and stock splits.

    (1) To reduce the market price per share.

    (2) Publicity gesture.

    (3) To capitalize a portion of retained earnings.

B. Appropriations of retained earnings.

    1. A book entry partitioning retained earnings into restricted and unrestricted retained earnings.

    2. Appropriated retained earnings arise from either the board of directors' discretion or the terms of debt covenants.

C.   Negative retained earnings.

    1.   The retained earnings account is negative if a company's accumulated net losses plus dividends from previous years exceeds the accumulation of its past profits.

    2.   Negative retained earnings (deficits) generally indicate serious problems because they indicate losses. In today's changing environment there are notable exceptions of start-up, high-tech, and Internet companies with accumulated deficits, yet the companies enjoy favorable stock prices, reflecting the market's confidence in their future prospects.

D.   Retained earnings and prior period adjustments.

    1.   Few items are booked directly to retained earnings. These include net income (loss), dividends, appropriations, and certain treasury stock transactions.

    2.   Additionally, correction in the current period of a prior period's accounting error is made by adjusting the misstated asset and/or liability, with a corresponding and offsetting adjustment to retained earnings. The entry to retained earnings is called a prior period adjustment.

V.   Cumulative translation adjustment.

A.   U.S. companies having subsidiaries that operate in other countries and financial statements that are expressed in foreign currencies must translate those statements into U.S. dollars when preparing consolidated financial statements.

B.   Gain or loss due to the translation is referred to as a translation adjustment. These adjustments are disclosed and accumulate in the stockholders' equity section of the balance sheet.

C.   A recent FASB pronouncement requires the current adjustment to be included in the display of comprehensive income, and the accumulated amount to be reflected in accumulated other comprehensive income in the stockholders' equity section.

VI.   Statement of stockholders' equity.

VII.   International perspective.

VIII.   Ethics in the real world.

IX.   Internet research exercise.

LECTURE TIPS

1. A conceptual understanding of why companies would repurchase their own stock and why treasury stock reduces stockholders' equity (as opposed to being an asset) needs to be developed. End-of-chapter issues for discussion 12–3, 12-4, and 12–5 are helpful in developing this understanding. Accounting for treasury stock can be demonstrated with examples such as provided by end-of-chapter exercises 12–4 through 12–8 and problems 12–2 and 12–12.

2. Students usually need extra help in understanding why a company would declare either a stock split or a stock dividend (and the economic difference between the two) as a basis for understanding how to account for each. It should be stressed that the differences in accounting for stock dividends and stock splits arise from the legal differences between the two. End-of-chapter exercises 12–14 and 12–15, problem 12–7, and issues for discussion 12–1 are useful for this demonstration.

OUTSIDE ASSIGNMENT OPPORTUNITIES

Group study of stockholders' equity both across time and within and across industries (continuing assignment for Chapters 6–14)

1. Using the most recent annual report of a major public company in one of the four general industry groupings, identify or compute the items listed below for the two most recent years. Compare the items across time. Relate your findings to the economic characteristics and current conditions in the industry and the company's strategy for competing. Prepare a written summary of your findings. Report findings in a class discussion in which comparisons will be made both across time, and within and across industries.

    Total liabilities as a percentage of total assets
    Contributed capital as a percentage of total assets
    Retained earnings as a percentage of total assets
    Treasury stock as a percentage of contributed capital
    Book value per share of common stock
    Market-to-book ratio
    Nature, classification, and amount of any hybrid securities
        (e.g., redeemable preferred stock)
    Type(s) and amount of dividends: cash dividends, stock dividends
        or splits

Article search: treasury stock transactions

2. Search the financial press (*The Wall Street Journal, Barrons, Fortune, Forbes,* etc.) for an article reporting on recent notable treasury stock activity by a particular company or a particular group of companies. Summarize the nature and amount of the activity, reasons why the shares were repurchased, and any observed consequences of the buybacks.

Article search: application of accounting standards for stock options

3. Search the financial press (*The Wall Street Journal, Barrons, Fortune, Forbes,* etc.) for an article reporting on how companies have responded to the accounting standard issued by the FASB in 1995 for executive stock options. Especially note if any companies have changed the nature of, or extent to which, they continue to use stock options as a form of compensation.

ANSWERS TO END-OF-CHAPTER QUESTIONS

1. Managers may wish to structure financing arrangements as equity rather than as debt to (1) avoid violating existing debt agreements; (2) maintain financial flexibility; and (3) maximize incentive compensation. Existing debt agreements may specify a maximum debt/equity ratio. Issuing additional debt moves the company closer to the restriction, thereby increasing the probability that the company will violate the restriction. Alternatively, issuing equity would reduce the company's debt/equity ratio. If a company has a high level of existing debt, it becomes more difficult, if not impossible, for the company to issue additional debt; the company is simply too risky. The company's only alternative for raising additional capital is by issuing equity. Consequently, structuring financing arrangements as equity provides a company with increased financing flexibility. If management is compensated based on the level of net income, management would prefer to increase net income, holding everything else constant. By issuing debt, the company incurs interest, which reduces net income and decreases management's compensation. On the other hand, if the company issues equity, periodic disbursements to the owners are considered dividends, which do not affect net income.

    A hybrid security is a security that possesses characteristics of both debt and equity. The primary problem that hybrid securities pose to accountants is classifying the security as debt or equity.

2. The primary reason that companies rely more heavily on debt than on contributed capital or earned capital as a source of capital, is that interest on debt is tax deductible. Since the interest is tax deductible, the effective cost of debt is actually less than the interest incurred on the debt. Alternatively, dividends disbursed to the equity owners are not tax deductible. The effective cost of debt is often more attractive than the cost of equity.

    Issuing additional equity shares can also dilute the interests of existing stockholders. This dilution can cause the per share price of the company's stock to decrease, thereby decreasing an existing stockholder's wealth. Companies usually do not want to take actions that adversely affect existing stockholders. Issuing additional equity shares also provides raiders an opportunity to acquire a company's stock, thereby increasing the probability that the raider will be able to take over the company and vote out the existing board of directors and management.

3. Debt covenants exist to protect creditors' financial interests. Creditors want to be assured that the company will have sufficient cash available to meet its interest and principal payments. If the company uses its cash to pay dividends to equity owners or to repurchase its common stock, the company may not have sufficient cash available to make its interest and principal payments. Therefore, creditors would like to restrict the company's ability to pay dividends and to repurchase its common stock. The creditors could achieve this goal by requiring the company to (1) appropriate a portion of retained earnings or (2) simply add a clause to the debt agreement that expressly forbids paying dividends or repurchasing common stock. By restricting dividend payments and stock repurchases, creditors protect their financial interests.

4. Managers must make several trade-offs when deciding whether to acquire capital via debt or equity. First, managers must consider the effect of the financing arrangement on existing debt agreements. If the company has existing debt agreements that specify a maximum debt/equity ratio, issuing additional debt increases the probability that the company will violate the restriction; structuring the financing as equity decreases the probability that the company will violate the restriction.

    Second, managers should consider the effect of the financing arrangement on the company's ability to obtain future financing. If a company has a high level of existing debt, it becomes more difficult, if not impossible, for the company to issue additional debt. So, the company can only raise additional capital through equity issues. Alternatively, raising capital by issuing equity does not seriously decrease the company's financial flexibility.

    Third, managers might consider the effect of the financing arrangement on any existing incentive compensation contracts. If the manager is compensated based on net income, managers would prefer to increase net income, holding everything else constant. If the company issues debt, the associated interest decreases net income, thereby decreasing managers' compensation. On the other hand, if the company issues equity, disbursements to the owners are considered dividends, which do not affect net income.

    Fourth, managers might consider the effect of the financing arrangement on the probability of a hostile takeover. By issuing equity, raiders can acquire an ownership interest in the company; if the raider can acquire a sufficient number of ownership shares, the raider can control the company. Issuing debt does not directly affect the probability of a hostile takeover. However, reporting large amounts of debt can make a company unattractive to corporate raiders because the company would have to be able to generate a sufficient amount of cash to service its existing debt, as well as the new debt that would result from the takeover.

    Finally, managers should consider the effect of the financing arrangement on the probability of the firm going bankrupt. Debt usually requires periodic interest payments and principal payments. If the company is unable to meet interest or principal payments, the company could be forced into bankruptcy. Further, these cash requirements imply that the company will not have this cash available for operating activities. On the other hand, equity financing does not require periodic cash payments to the owners. Dividend payments are at the discretion of the board of directors. Consequently, issuing equity does not increase the probability of bankruptcy.

5. A takeover is when an investor or a group of investors replaces the existing board of directors. Replacing the board requires a majority of the outstanding common shares. Consequently, raiders must either acquire a majority of the outstanding shares or convince existing stockholders to vote with them. Raiders acquire their shares by purchasing the shares through the stock market. Raiders can either purchase their shares from new stock issues or from existing shareholders. If raiders acquire their shares through the former method, the ownership interests of the existing shareholders have been diluted. Dilution means that due to a new stock issue, the existing shareholders own a smaller percentage of the company after the new issue than before the new issue. A takeover also often results in senior management being replaced; consequently, senior managers view takeovers negatively. One way management can prevent raiders from purchasing shares from existing stockholders is to repurchase outstanding shares themselves. Repurchasing outstanding shares concentrates ownership of the company. There are fewer shares now outstanding and the shares outstanding are held by stockholders who do not want to sell their interests in the company. Consequently, the probability that raiders will be able to acquire a sufficient number of shares to oust the current board decreases.

6. Preferred stock and common stock both represent ownership claims in a company. However, the rights and preferences of these two types of stock are different. Preferred stock usually has preferences on dividends and on assets. In other words, preferred stockholders receive dividends prior to the common stockholders and, in the case of liquidation, preferred stockholders are entitled to receive distributions of assets before common stockholders. In some cases, preferred stock may be cumulative and/or participating. Common stockholders are usually considered to be the "true" owners of the company in that they have the right to exert control over corporate management and the right to share in corporate income and losses. Preferred stockholders usually do not enjoy these rights.

   The general claims on the assets of the company are listed in the order of seniority. The claims that will be repaid first in the event of liquidation are listed before the claims that will be paid later. Therefore, liabilities are the first claims to be listed on the balance sheet. Since preferred stockholders have a preference on assets over common stockholders, preferred stock is listed before common stock on the balance sheet. Further, preferred stock often possesses many characteristics of both debt and equity, so it is listed on the balance sheet at the beginning of equity, immediately following debt. In some cases, the characteristics of preferred stock may be so similar to the characteristics of debt that the preferred stock may actually be considered debt.

7. Authorized shares represent the maximum number of shares that a company is entitled to issue. If a company receives authorization for new shares, it indicates that the

company is now entitled to issue additional shares. A company would usually obtain authorization to issue new shares with this intention. If the company does issue additional shares and the existing shareholders do not acquire the additional shares, the existing shareholders' ownership in the company would be diluted.

Issued shares represent the number of shares previously distributed by the corporation that have not been retired; outstanding shares represent the number of shares currently held by stockholders. Shares held in treasury are considered to be issued because these shares had been previously distributed to stockholders. However, shares held in treasury are not currently held by stockholders, so these shares are not considered to be outstanding. The number of issued shares can, therefore, exceed the number of outstanding shares due to treasury stock.

8. Dividends in arrears represent the amount of "missed" dividends on cumulative preferred stock. Preferred stockholders possess preferences on dividends; consequently, preferred stockholders receive their dividends before common stockholders receive their dividends. If the preferred stock is cumulative and the board of directors failed to declare a dividend in a period, the preferred stockholders are entitled to receive the "missed" dividend once the board of directors declares a dividend. Dividends in arrears are not considered liabilities. Liabilities are defined as the probable future sacrifice of assets to settle existing obligations. Since dividends are at the discretion of the board of directors, dividends are not considered to be probable events. It is possible that a company will never declare another dividend.

9. A common stockholder has the right to vote for members of the board of directors. The board, in turn, selects the company's senior managers. Consequently, a common stockholder controls management through the board of directors.

The board of directors serves several roles. The board is responsible for setting general company policy and guiding the direction of the company. In this role, the board is responsible for establishing the company's dividend policy. The board is also responsible for hiring, firing, evaluating, and compensating senior managers. For some companies, the board also establishes an audit committee.

10. Book value of common stock equals total common stockholders' equity divided by the number of common shares outstanding. Total common stockholders' equity is based on conventional accounting practice. Common stockholders' equity, therefore, represents the owners' residual interests in the original cost of net assets. Further, common stockholders' equity does not include certain items of value to the company (such as customer or employee loyalty) because such items are too subjective for financial reporting. Alternatively, a stock's market value reflects the market value of a company's net assets as well as other nonquantifiable net assets. Therefore, a stock's market value will usually exceed its book value due to limitations in conventional accounting practices in calculating book value.

The market-to-book ratio is found by dividing the market value of a company's common stock by its book value. It provides a measure that indicates the extent to which the market believes that the balance sheet reflects the company's true value. Ratios equal to 1 indicate that a company's net book value (as measured by the balance sheet) is perceived by the market to be a fair reflection of the company's true value. Ratios greater than 1, as is more common, indicate that the balance sheet is a conservative measure of the company's true value.

11. Treasury stock is previously issued and outstanding stock (usually common stock) that is reacquired by a company. Treasury stock carries none of the rights of ownership and reduces stockholders' equity. Further, treasury stock is not considered to be outstanding. Since earnings per share is calculated as net income divided by total number of shares outstanding, acquiring treasury stock will increase a company's earnings per share.

Companies reacquire their own common stock for several reasons. The first reason is to provide an adequate number of shares to support incentive stock option plans and employee stock plans. A second reason is to discourage hostile takeovers. By concentrating ownership of its outstanding shares, a company makes it more difficult for raiders to acquire a sufficient number of shares to take over the company. A third reason is to increase the company's earnings per share and/or the market price of the outstanding stock. A final reason is to reduce the scale of operations. Reducing the scale of operations is normally accomplished by retiring the common stock once it has been reacquired.

12. Stock options give the holder the right to buy equity securities at a fixed price over a specified period of time. Companies use stock options to compensate executives because it requires no cash payment, and it motivates executives to act in a manner that maximizes the company's share price. Stock price increases create gains for the executive. Executives desire stock options because there is no risk of loss if the stock declines, but the upside potential can be great.

The company records no compensation expense when the options are granted; an issuance of common stock is recorded when the options are exercised. Many believe that the income statement should be charged for the value of the options when granted, because options have value and companies are giving up something by promising to issue shares at prices that in the future may be below market value. The FASB's 1994 proposal that companies be required to recognize compensation expense was met with much opposition. Opponents argued that capital formation would become more difficult, and that valuation of options is extremely subjective. The FASB compromised by requiring only footnote disclosure of these compensation costs.

13. Companies can follow a multitude of dividend strategies. At the most basic level, the decision is whether or not to pay any dividend. A company can reinvest its profits in the company or it can declare a dividend. If a company declares a dividend, the company must decide how large of a dividend and what type of dividend to declare. Some companies follow a strategy of declaring dividends as a constant percentage of net income, some companies base their decision on the cash needs of the company, and other companies declare a constant amount as a dividend. A company's board of directors must also choose among cash, property, and stock dividends. Companies must also consider whether to increase dividends. If the company is doing well, the company may want to signal its prosperity to the financial community by declaring a larger dividend.

An investment in stock can provide a return to the investor in two different ways. The first way is through a dividend. The second way is through stock appreciation. Companies, particularly young, high-growth companies, do not declare dividends; rather, these companies "plow" their earnings back into the company. As the prospects for the company improves, the price of their stock increases, often dramatically. Once most companies have passed the high-growth phase, they begin paying dividends. Consequently, an investor should be more than willing to invest in a company that does not pay a dividend if the expected stock appreciation or the expected future dividends offset the current dividends foregone.

14. A company has two options in transferring additional shares of stock to existing stockholders without receiving compensation in exchange. The company can issue a stock dividend or declare a stock split. In a stock dividend, the company capitalizes a portion of retained earnings as contributed capital. An ordinary stock dividend is defined as a stock dividend in which the shares to be distributed are less than 25 percent of the shares outstanding prior to the distribution. Since stock dividends do not transfer anything of value to the stockholders, it is unclear why companies declare ordinary stock dividends; the most likely reason is that the company can claim that they declared a dividend. An ordinary stock dividend is simply a publicity gesture. The amount of retained earnings that is capitalized in an ordinary stock dividend equals the market value of the shares distributed. A stock split in the form of a dividend is defined as a stock dividend in which the shares to be distributed are greater than 25 percent of the shares outstanding prior to the distribution. The amount of retained earnings that is capitalized in a stock split in the form of a dividend equals the par value of the shares distributed.

In a stock split, the company makes no formal journal entry. The company simply makes a memorandum entry and adjusts the par value per share and the number of shares outstanding accordingly. The primary reason for declaring a stock split or for declaring a stock dividend is to adjust the company's stock price. If the price of the stock is too high, the cost of investing in the company's stock is prohibitive. By holding the total value of the firm constant and increasing the number of the shares outstanding, the value per share decreases. Consequently, the market value per share drops, thereby lowering the cost of investing in the company. In practice, many companies do not follow the recommended accounting procedures because considerable doubt exists as to the economic exchange between the company and its stockholders with stock splits and stock splits in the form of dividends.

15. In most states, companies are restricted as to the amount of dividends they can declare. Companies are usually not allowed to declare dividends that exceed the balance in retained earnings. By appropriating retained earnings, the company decreases the amount that can potentially be declared as dividends. Appropriating retained earnings is simply a book entry that partitions retained earnings into restricted and unrestricted retained earnings. The only account affected is Retained Earnings; the entry to appropriate retained earnings is:

Retained Earnings (-SE)   XX
    Appropriated Retained Earnings (+SE)   XX
    Appropriated retained earnings.

By appropriating a portion of retained earnings, a company provides information to financial statement users about the company's dividend policy, at least in the short run.

Companies appropriate retained earnings for different reasons. One common reason for appropriating retained earnings is as part of the requirements of a debt covenant. Debt covenants exist to protect the creditors' financial interests. Creditors want to be assured that the company will have sufficient cash available to meet its interest and principal payments. If the company uses its cash to pay dividends, the company may not have sufficient cash available to make these payments. Creditors would, therefore, like to restrict the company's ability to pay dividends. Creditors could achieve this goal by requiring that the company appropriate a portion of retained earnings. A second reason a company might appropriate a portion of its retained earnings is to provide funds for a particular purpose such as plant expansion. The company may set aside cash that it otherwise would have used to pay dividends to finance such expansions.

16. The retained earnings account becomes negative if a company's accumulated net losses plus dividends from previous years exceeds the accumulation of its past profits. Negative retained earnings (deficits) is often a bad sign, but not always necessarily so. Today there are many start-up, high-tech, and Internet companies with accumulated deficits, yet the companies enjoy favorable stock prices, reflecting the market's confidence in their future prospects.

17. U.S. companies having subsidiaries that operate in other countries and financial statements that are expressed in foreign currencies must translate those statements into U.S. dollars when preparing consolidated financial statements. Gain or loss due to the translation is referred to as a translation adjustment. These adjustments are disclosed and accumulate in the stockholders' equity section of the balance sheet. The cumulative amount is called the accumulated translation adjustment. It can be positive or negative, depending on changes in the value of foreign currencies relative to the U.S. dollar. As evidenced by recent activity in the marketplace, these changes can be quite large and go in either direction.

A recent FASB pronouncement requires the current adjustment to be included in the display of comprehensive income, and in the accumulated amount reflected in Accumulated Other Comprehensive Income in the stockholders' equity section.

CHARACTERISTICS OF END-OF-CHAPTER ASSIGNMENTS

Item	Difficulty	Description
Brief exercises:		
BE12–1	E	Real data: Inferring stockholders' equity transactions
BE12–2	E	Stock splits and market values
BE12–3	E	Treasury stock purchases

Item	Difficulty	Description

Exercises:

E12–1	E	Debt, contributed and earned capital, and the classification of preferred stock
E12–2	E	The effects of transactions on stockholders' equity
E12–3	E	Authorizing and issuing preferred and common stock
E12–4	M	The effects of treasury stock purchases on important financial ratios
E12–5	M	Reissuing treasury stock
E12–6	E	Reissuing treasury stock
E12–7	E	Treasury stock exceeds contributed capital
E12–8	M	Book value per share, stock issuances, and treasury stock purchases
E12–9	M	Inferring equity transactions from the statement of stockholders' equity
E12–10	H	Inferring equity transactions from the statement of stockholders' equity
E12–11	H	Inferring equity transactions from the statement of stockholders' equity
E12–12	E	Issuing cash dividends on outstanding common stock
E12–13	E	Cumulative preferred stock and dividends in arrears
E12–14	H	Stock dividends and stock splits
E12–15	E	Why do companies declare stock dividends?
E12–16	E	Appropriating retained earnings

Problems:

P12–1	E	Hybrid securities and debt covenants
P12–2	E	The effects of treasury stock transactions on important financial ratios
P12–3	E	The significance of par value
P12–4	E	Cash and stock dividends
P12–5	M	Dividend payments and preferred stock
P12–6	M	The maximum dividend
P12–7	M	Stock splits and stock dividends
P12–8	M	Miscellaneous stockholders' equity transactions
P12–9	M	Inferring transactions from the balance sheet
P12–10	M	Inferring stockholders' equity transactions from information on the balance sheet
P12–11	H	Stockholders' equity over a four-year period
P12–12	H	Blocking takeovers and treasury stock purchases
P12–13	M	Bankruptcy and protecting the interests of the creditors

Issues for discussion:

ID12–1	H	Do stock dividends represent economic exchanges between a corporation and its shareholders?
ID12–2	E	Dividend strategy
ID12–3	M	Economic consequences of treasury stock purchases and cash dividends
ID12–4	M	Treasury stock purchases
ID12–5	M	Treasury stock
ID12–6	E	Contracts based on net worth

Item	Difficulty	Description
ID12–7	M	Accounting for stock options
ID12–8	M	Exchanging equity for debt
ID12–9	M	Off-balance-sheet financing and preferred stock
ID12–10	E	Corporate dividend policies
ID12–11	E	Stock split and stock prices
ID12–12	E	International accounting standards
ID12–13	E	International financing
ID12–14	M	The annual report of NIKE

CHAPTER 13   The Complete Income Statement

SYNOPSIS

In this chapter, the author provides an in-depth discussion of (1) the different types of business transactions and (2) the income statement. The discussion of transactions focuses on financing, investing, and operating transactions, and how these transactions flow through to the balance sheet and income statement.

The general income statement topics discussed are (1) the economic consequences associated with income measurement and disclosure; (2) the different ways to measure income, including comprehensive income, and how these address the objectives of financial reporting; and (3) the disclosure rules that should be followed when preparing an income statement. The specific issues discussed are operating revenues and expenses; nonoperating revenues and expenses; intraperiod tax allocations; disposal of a business segment; extraordinary items; cumulative effect of a change in accounting principles; and earnings-per-share disclosures.

The ethics vignette considers whether it is ethical for management to consider the impact of the choice between debt and equity financing on its own compensation, where compensation is a function of net earnings after interest expense.

The Internet research exercise examines the income statement of Eastman Kodak Company to evaluate its earnings performance.

The following key points are emphasized in Chapter 13:

1. Economic consequences associated with reporting net income.

2. A framework for financing, investing, and operating transactions.

3. Categories that constitute a complete income statement and how they provide measures of income that address the objectives of financial reporting.

4. Intraperiod tax allocation.

5. Earnings per share disclosure on the income statement.

TEXT/LECTURE OUTLINE

The complete income statement.

I.   Income statement.

    A.   Purpose—to measure the income generated during the accounting period.

    B.   Economic consequences of income measurement and disclosure.

        1.   Income serves as a measure of the company's performance during the accounting period.

        2.   Effect of income on stock and bond prices.

        3.   Role of income in debt covenants.

        4.   Role of income in management incentive compensation.

    C.   Different measures of income for different objectives.

        1.   The objectives of financial reporting are to provide information that is:

            a)   Useful for investment and credit decisions.

            b)   Helpful in assessing future cash flows.

            c)   Reflective of changes in a company's resources.

        2.   No single measure of income can achieve these broad objectives. Elements of financial statements that are key to understanding the different measures are found in the definitions of ten key concepts: assets, liabilities, equity, investments by owners, distributions to owners, comprehensive income, revenues, expenses, gains, and losses.

        3.   Comprehensive income represents a broad definition of income—any change in the company's equity due to nonowner transactions.

            a)   This concept of income includes items not included in the computation of net income, such as foreign currency translation adjustments and unrealized gains and losses on available-for-sale securities (Chapter 8).

            b)   The FASB now requires that comprehensive income and its components be reported and displayed with the same prominence as the other financial statements.

        4.   The definitions distinguish revenues and expenses from gains and losses. The nature of individual transactions must be considered to determine if and how they should be reflected in income.

D. Financing, investing, and operating transactions.

1. Financing and investing transactions principally affect balance sheet accounts. Financing and investing transactions are those transactions associated with the following:

a) Exchanges with stockholders.

b) Exchanges of liabilities and stockholders' equity.

c) Issues and payments of debt.

d) Purchases, sales, and exchanges of assets.

e) Revenues and expenses.

2. Operating transactions are associated with acquiring/selling inventory and/or services. These transactions affect balance sheet accounts (i.e., operating assets and liabilities) and eventually income statement accounts. The five categories of operating transactions are discussed below.

E. Components of the income statement.

1. Operating revenues and expenses.

a) Asset and liability inflows and outflows associated with the acquisition and sale of goods and services.

b) To be considered operating activities, the activities must be both usual (the economic event is part of the company's normal operations; it is associated with the company's central, ongoing activities) and frequent (the economic event is expected to recur in the foreseeable future).

2. Other revenues and expenses.

a) Asset and liability inflows and outflows that are incidental to the company's operating activities.

b) To be classified as other revenue or expenses (i.e., incidental activities), the activities must be either unusual or infrequent, but not both. Both the company and its environment must be considered in deciding whether an item is unusual or infrequent.

3. Gains (losses) from disposing of a business segment.

a) A business segment is defined as a separate line of business, product line, or class of service that represents an operation that is independent of the company's other operations.

        b)   Components of gains (losses) from disposing of a segment.

           (1)   Income (loss) from operating the business segment.

           (2)   Gain (loss) on the disposal of the segment's net assets.

        c)   Gains or losses from the disposal of a business segment are reported net of any tax effect.

    4.   Extraordinary items.

        a)   Extraordinary items are material gains or losses that are both unusual and infrequent. Consequently, such events are not classified as operating activities or incidental activities.

        b)   Both the company and its environment must be considered in deciding whether an item is both unusual and infrequent.

        c)   Extraordinary items are reported net of any tax effect.

    5.   Cumulative effect of changes in accounting principles.

        a)   Reasons for changing an accounting principle.

        b)   The cumulative effect of the change is reported net of any tax effect.

        c)   Voluntary versus mandatory changes.

  F.   Intraperiod tax allocation.

  G.   Earnings-per-share (EPS) disclosures.

    1.   GAAP provides for EPS disclosures for income from continuing operations (after taxes); disposals of business segments; extraordinary items; and the cumulative effect of changes in accounting principles.

    2.   Both "basic" and "diluted" EPS are presented. Diluted EPS gives effect to dilution that may result from additional shares that may be issued for such things as stock options.

II.   International perspective.

III.   Ethics in the real world.

IV.   Internet research exercise.

LECTURE TIPS

1. Students often have trouble applying intraperiod tax allocation, especially with knowing which items should be disclosed net of taxes and the direction of the tax effect (particularly with losses). Care should be taken in explaining why intraperiod tax allocation is used and which items are disclosed net of taxes. End-of-chapter exercises 13–11 and 13–12 and problems 13–6 and 13–8 are helpful in demonstrating the essentials of intraperiod tax allocation.

2. The distinction should be stressed between operating revenues and expenses, nonoperating revenues and expenses, income from continuing operations, disposal of a business segment, extraordinary items, and the cumulative effect of a change in accounting principle, because of the different relevancy of these income statement components for assessing earning power. These differences are associated with earnings persistence. Deciding whether an item is extraordinary requires a great deal of judgment and is difficult even for seasoned professional accountants. Examples illustrating the difficulty of making this decision should be provided.

   End-of-chapter exercises 13–6, 13–8, 13–9, 13–13, and 13–15; problems 13–2, 13–4, 13–5, 13–7, and 13–9; and all the issues for discussion cases are especially useful.

OUTSIDE ASSIGNMENT OPPORTUNITIES

Group study of income statement components both across time and within and across industries (continuing assignment for Chapters 6–14)

1. Using the most recent annual report of a major public company in one of the four general industry groupings, identify or compute the items listed below for the two most recent years. Compare the items across time. Relate your findings to the economic characteristics and current conditions in the industry and the company's strategy for competing. Prepare a written summary of your findings. Report findings in a class discussion session in which comparisons will be made both across time and within and across industries.

   Common-size income statement (see Chapter 3)
   Significant accounting policies affecting recognition of revenue and expenses
   Description and nature of special items: nonoperating revenues and expenses,
       discontinued operations, extraordinary items, and the cumulative effect of
       a change in accounting principles
   Presentation of comprehensive income
   Earnings per share disclosures

Analyzing the quality of earnings

2. Obtain the most recent annual report for a company with several nonrecurring items (such as AT&T Corp. for 1998).   Obtain and read the Comiskey-Mulford-Choi article on analyzing the persistence of earnings referenced below.[1] Use the method discussed in the article to evaluate the company's earnings for the given three years in the annual report in terms of persistence and cash flow. Summarize your conclusions in writing, supported with computations.

ANSWERS TO END-OF-CHAPTER QUESTIONS

1. The term comprehensive income represents a very broad definition of income—any change in a company's equity due to nonowner transactions. There are different ways to measure income, and different measures of income address different objectives of financial reporting.   The notion of comprehensive income reflects changes in a company's resources, which is one of the objectives; it also gives information that can help the user assess future cash flows, another important objective. However, not all changes reflected in this broad measure of income are expected to reflect future cash flows.   For instance, gains and losses that are infrequent and/or tangential to the company's core activities would not be expected to reflect future cash flows, but they would be part of a company's comprehensive income.   Similarly, revaluations of investments in securities and from foreign currency translations would be a component of comprehensive income, but not necessarily representative of future cash flows.

2. Financing and investing transactions involve inflows and outflows of assets, liabilities, and stockholders' equity due to investing and financing activities, such as exchanges with stockholders; issues and payments of debt; and purchases, sales and exchanges of assets.   An operating transaction, alternatively, involves operating activities. These transactions involve inflows and outflows of assets and liabilities associated with the acquisition and sale of goods and services.

3. Usual refers to the normal operations of a company, that is, those activities that are part of the company's central, ongoing operations. Frequent refers to how often an item or event occurs. Specifically, frequent refers to whether an event is expected to recur in the foreseeable future.

    The items or events that are considered to be usual, unusual, frequent, and infrequent vary across companies. However, most companies would classify the following items or events similarly.

---

[1] Eugene E. Comiskey, Charles W. Mulford, and Hyun-Dol Choi, "Analyzing the Persistence of Earnings: A Lender's Guide," *Commercial Lending Review,* Winter 1994/1995, pp. 4–23.

a. A usual and frequent event would be the sale of merchandise inventory for cash.

b. A usual and infrequent event would be the recording of receivables or inventory.

c. An unusual and frequent event would be interest and dividend revenue.

d. An unusual and infrequent event would be a loss due to flood damage in a location where floods are rare.

Usual and frequent items are considered to be part of a company's central, ongoing operations and are, therefore, disclosed on the income statement as part of operations. Usual and infrequent items and unusual and frequent items are both normally considered to be part of a company's continuing operations (but not part of the company's central, ongoing operations) and are, therefore, usually disclosed on the income statement as other revenues and expenses. Unusual and infrequent items are not considered to be part of either the company's central, ongoing operations or part of the company's continuing operations. Consequently, these items are disclosed on the income statement as extraordinary items.

4. A business segment is a separate line of business, product line, or class of customer that represents an operation that is independent from a company's other operations. When a company discontinues a business segment, the company must disclose two items on the income statement associated with the discontinued segment. The first item is the income or loss generated by operating the discontinued segment from the last balance sheet date. The second item is the gain or loss from disposing of the segment's net assets. Both items are disclosed net of the associated tax effect.

5. An extraordinary item is a material event that is considered to be both unusual and infrequent in nature. Determining whether an event is extraordinary requires considerable judgment and depends upon a company's particular environment. What is considered to be unusual for one company may be considered usual for another company. Alternatively, what is considered to be infrequent for one company may be considered frequent for another company. For example, damage from a minor earthquake would probably be considered to be frequent for a company based in San Francisco, but it would probably be considered to be infrequent for a company based in Wisconsin.

6. The principle of consistency states that companies should apply the same accounting principles and methods from one accounting period to the next. Consequently, changing an accounting principle or method is inconsistent with this principle. But, if a company can convince its auditors that the new accounting method is more appropriate than the old accounting method because of a change in the company's environment, the company can change accounting methods. As long as the company's new accounting methods are still in conformance with generally accepted accounting principles, the company does not face a problem.

7. A voluntary accounting change is one that a company voluntarily chooses. A mandatory accounting change is one required by a new FASB standard. Recent changes mandated by FASB standards include accounting for post-retirement health care and insurance costs, income taxes, and pensions. The disclosure requirements and methods of accounting for mandatory changes are generally the same as those required for voluntary changes. However, users should be aware that management's incentives drive voluntary changes, but not those of a mandatory nature. Consequently, voluntary changes should be interpreted much more cautiously because they may be the result of strategies designed to manage the reported numbers.

8. Changes in accounting principles and methods are disclosed in at least three places in a financial report. First, they may be found in the footnotes to the financial statements, and second, as the last item on the face of the income statement before net income, a cumulative effect of a change in accounting principle. They may also be found in the auditor's report. If a company changes an accounting method, the auditor must report that the financial statements were not prepared on a basis consistent with the prior accounting period.

9. Intraperiod tax allocation refers to allocating income taxes among the components of the income statement. The taxes associated with a particular component should be disclosed as part of that component, thereby making it easier to assess a company's long-run earnings potential. Therefore, the taxes associated with continuing operations are disclosed at the end of the continuing operations section. Extraordinary items, disposals of business segments, and cumulative effects of changes in accounting principles are all disclosed on the income statement net of the associated tax effect. On the statement of stockholders' equity, prior period adjustments are disclosed net of the associated tax effect.

10. Earnings-per-share disclosures report selected income statement information on a per-ownership-unit basis, and the disclosures are reported on the face of the income statement, following the formal statement. Since earnings per share provides information on the company's performance per each ownership share, earnings per share provides a convenient device to compare the performances of different companies. Companies are required under generally accepted accounting principles to disclosure earnings-per-share information about (1) income from continuing operations (after tax); (2) disposals of business segments; (3) extraordinary items; and (4) changes in accounting principles.

    Diluted earnings per share adjusts earnings-per-share information for items that could potentially dilute the existing stockholders' ownership rights. For example, assume that a company has issued bonds that the bondholders can convert into common stock. The existing stockholders would own a smaller percentage of the company (i.e., their ownership rights would be diluted) if the bondholders converted their bonds into common stock. Presenting fully diluted earnings per share essentially provides information to stockholders about the "worst case" scenario.

11. Earnings persistence refers to whether a particular earnings dollar amount can be expected to continue (i.e., persist) in the future. Earnings persistence is important because earnings that are expected to continue in the future are sources of future cash flows. The income statement classifications, particularly under the multi-step approach, are important for being able to assess earnings persistence. Items such as disposals of

business segments, extraordinary items, and cumulative effects of changes in accounting principles are "one-time shots." That is, these items do not have earnings persistence, which is one reason why they are disclosed separately from income from continuing operations (i.e., those earnings expected to persist in the future). With the multi-step format, income from continuing operations is further classified as income from operations and as other revenues and expenses. Because income from operations is associated with the company's central, ongoing operations, it will have higher earnings persistence than other revenues and expenses.

12. The major components of the statement of retained earnings are (1) beginning retained earnings, (2) prior period adjustments, (3) adjustments to retained earnings for treasury stock transactions, (4) net income, (5) declared dividends, (6) appropriations of retained earnings, and (7) ending retained earnings. Many companies report these items in a statement of stockholders' equity. This statement explains changes in all the stockholders' equity accounts, not just in retained earnings.

13. International operations pose risks due to currency fluctuations. In addition, the governments in many countries are not very stable, which increases the risk that the governments will change, thereby resulting in changes in the operating conditions for companies with operations in those countries. In the extreme, a new government may decide to nationalize all businesses. Certain countries also experience high inflation. International operations often result in companies reporting special gains and losses on their income statements. It is important that financial statement users analyze such gains and losses carefully so that they understand the ramifications of the underlying events that gave rise to the gains or losses.

CHARACTERISTICS OF END-OF-CHAPTER ASSIGNMENTS

Item	Difficulty	Description
Brief exercises:		
BE13–1	E	Real data: Nonrecurring items
BE13–2	E	Real data: Effects on the basic accounting equation
BE13–3	E	Real data: Following an FASB requirement
Exercises:		
E13–1	E	Which statement is affected?
E13–2	E	Classifying transactions
E13–3	M	Debt covenants expressed in terms of income
E13–4	M	Comprehensive income
E13–5	M	Disposal of a business segment
E13–6	M	Management choices and earnings persistence
E13–7	M	Management choices and earnings persistence
E13–8	M	Accounting for unusual losses
E13–9	M	Economic consequences of an extraordinary item

Item	**Difficulty**	**Description**
E13–10	M	Earnings-per-share disclosure
E13–11	M	Intraperiod tax allocation and the financial statements
E13–12	M	Intraperiod tax allocation
E13–13	H	Covenant restrictions and income reporting
E13–14	H	Stock market reactions to income reporting

Problems:

P13–1	E	Classifying transactions
P13–2	M	Bonus contracts based on income can affect management's business decisions
P13–3	M	Financing, investing, and operating transactions
P13–4	E	Preparing an income statement
P13–5	E	Disclosing extraordinary items
P13–6	M	Intraperiod tax allocation, income tax expense, and income tax liability
P13–7	H	Income effect due to a change in depreciation methods
P13–8	M	Disclosing net of tax, and the earnings-per-share calculation
P13–9	H	Preparing an income statement
P13–10	M	Comprehensive problem

Issues for discussion:

ID13–1	E	Public earnings announcements
ID13–2	E	Changing accounting principles/methods
ID13–3	E	Extraordinary losses
ID13–4	M	Disclosing nonoperating items on the income statement
ID13–5	M	Profits and stock prices
ID13–6	M	Litigation, reported income, and stock prices
ID13–7	E	Management's discretionary reporting and investing decisions
ID13–8	E	Foreign currency fluctuations
ID13–9	M	Analyzing special income statement items
ID13–10	H	Writing off acquisition costs
ID13–11	M	The annual report of NIKE

CHAPTER 14   The Statement of Cash Flows

SYNOPSIS

In this chapter, the author provides a comprehensive discussion of the statement of cash flows. The author discusses (1) the rationale for the statement; (2) using the statement of cash flows to evaluate companies; (3) how the statement complements the income statement and balance sheet; (4) the incentives management has to manipulate cash flows; and (5) the mechanics of preparing the statement of cash flows. Preparing the statement of cash flows focuses on inferring the cash inflows and outflows of transactions from two balance sheets and an income statement.

The ethics vignette considers a company in weak financial condition that manages the timing of its cash receipts and payments to manipulate its reported cash flows (especially from operations) in an effort to delay signaling that weakness to the public.

The Internet research exercise examines the cash flow statements of selected publicly held companies to evaluate the quality of their earnings.

The following key points are emphasized in Chapter 14:

1. The structure and format of the statement of cash flows.

2. Cash flows from operating, investing, and financing activities.

3. How the statement of cash flows complements the other financial statements and how it can be used by those interested in the financial condition of a company.

4. The important investing and financing transactions that do not appear on the statement of cash flows and how they are reported.

5. Economic consequences associated with the statement of cash flows.

6. Preparing a statement of cash flows from the information contained in two balance sheets, an income statement, and a statement of retained earnings.

TEXT/LECTURE OUTLINE

The statement of cash flows.

I.   Purpose.

   A. To explain the change in the cash balance during the accounting period. For purposes of the statement of cash flows, cash can be defined as the following:

      1. Cash only—coin, currency, money orders, certified checks, cashiers' checks, personal checks, bank drafts, and so forth.

      2. Cash plus cash equivalents—usually defined as investments, such as commercial paper, that have maturities of less than three months.

   B. To provide information about the cash flows during the period associated with operating activities, investing activities, and financing activities.

II. Overview of the statement of cash flows.

   A. The change in cash can be explained by summarizing the cash flows from operating and capital transactions.

      1. Operating transactions are associated with acquiring and selling inventories and services. That is, those activities that are part of the company's ongoing central activities. In general, items included on the income statement are considered to be operating activities.

      2. Capital transactions.

         a) Investing activities—associated with purchasing and selling nonoperating (i.e., noncurrent) assets. Investing activities include purchasing or selling long-lived assets, long-term investments, and intangible assets.

         b) Financing activities—associated with cash flows from nonoperating debt and stockholders' equity. Financing activities include issuing long-term debt or equity shares, retiring long-term debt, repurchasing equity shares, and paying cash dividends.

   B. Methods to use in preparing the statement of cash flows.

      1. Direct method.

         a) Cash inflows and outflows from operating activities can be traced directly to the cash account in the general ledger. The actual cash inflow and outflow associated with each income statement item is disclosed on the face of the statement of cash flows.

      b)   Accrual income statement amounts are reported in the body of the statement of cash flows at their cash amounts. That is, the actual cash inflows and cash outflows from individual operating activities are reported on the face of the statement of cash flows.

      c)   A schedule that reconciles net income to net cash flow from operating activities must accompany the statement of cash flows.

  2.   Indirect method.

      a)   Cash flows from operating activities are computed indirectly by adjusting net income.

      b)   Net income is adjusted from an accrual amount to net cash flow from operating activities on the face of the statement of cash flows. Accrual net income is adjusted for noncash charges to noncurrent accounts and changes in current accounts other than cash.

  3.   The choice of methods only affects the way that net cash flow from operating activities is disclosed.

      a)   The dollar amount reported for net cash flow from operating activities is identical under the direct and indirect methods.

      b)   The presentation of the investing activities and financing activities is identical under the direct and indirect methods.

III.   Relation of statement of cash flows to other financial statements.

  A.   Income statement—the operating section of the statement of cash flows and the income statement both provide a measure of the company's operating performance. The income statement measures operating performance on an accrual basis, whereas the operating activities section of the statement of cash flows measures operating performance on a cash basis.

  B.   Balance sheet—the statement of cash flows and the balance sheet both provide information about a company's operating, investing, and financing activities. The information reported in the balance sheet is based on accrual accounting, whereas the information reported in the operating, investing, and financing sections of the statement of cash flows is based on cash inflows and outflows.

IV.   Using the statement of cash flows.

  A.   Assessing a company's ability to generate cash.

    1.   The strength of a company's operating activities.

    2.   Financial flexibility—a company's capacity to borrow, issue equity, and sell nonoperating assets.

B. Assessing a company's effectiveness at managing its cash.

1. Maintaining solvency.

2. Making idle cash productive.

V. Economic consequences of the statement of cash flows.

A. Importance of cash flow information in assessing potential investments.

B. Incentives to window dress the statement of cash flows.

C. Ease of manipulating cash flows.

D. Reasons not to manipulate cash flows.

VI. Operating, investing, or financing activities not involving cash flows.

A. Because the statement of cash flows reports only on cash inflows and outflows, significant operating, investing, or financing activities that do not involve cash flows are not reported in the body of the statement of cash flows.

B. Significant noncash investing and financing activities should be described clearly in the footnotes to the financial statements or in a supplemental schedule to the statement of cash flows.

C. Significant noncash operating activities can be determined by analyzing the adjustments reconciling net income and net cash flow from operating activities.

VII. Deriving cash flows from accrual financial statements.

A. Identify related balance sheet accounts.

B. Adjust accrual numbers for changes in related balance sheet accounts.

C. Prepare the three sections of the statement of cash flows: operating, investing, and financing.

VIII. International perspective.

IX. Ethics in the real world.

X. Internet research exercise.

LECTURE TIPS

1. Students have the greatest difficulty converting from accrual dollar amounts to cash flows, particularly in deciding (1) which balance sheet accounts are related to specific income

statement accounts and (2) how the accounts interrelate. End-of-chapter exercises 14–5, 14–11 through 14–14, and problems 14–8 through 14–11 are useful to demonstrate the process. Exercises 14–15 through 14–20 further emphasize determination of cash flow from operations under both the direct and indirect methods.

2. Some students have trouble classifying transactions as operating, investing, or financing activities. Care should be taken in explaining the distinctions between the different types of transactions and several examples should be provided. End-of-chapter exercises 14–1 and 14–2 and problems 14–1 through 14–4 provide useful practice on the subject.

OUTSIDE ASSIGNMENT OPPORTUNITIES

Group study of statements of cash flows both across time and within and across industries (continuing assignment for Chapters 6–14)

1. Using the most recent annual report of a major public company in one of the four general industry groupings, identify or compute the items listed below for the two most recent years. Compare the items across time. Relate your findings to the economic characteristics and current conditions in the industry and the company's strategy for competing. Prepare a written summary of your findings. Report findings in a class discussion session in which comparisons will be made both across time and within and across industries.

> Net income
> Cash flow from operating activities
> Cash flow from investing activities
> Cash flow from financing activities
> Net change in cash
> Method (direct or indirect)
> Nature of significant noncash transactions

Financial statement analysis using cash flow ratios (repeat of suggestion in Chapter 3)

2. Obtain and read the Giacomino-Mielke article on cash flow ratios referenced below.[1] Compute the nine ratios presented therein for NIKE on a comparative basis for two years using its financial statements in Appendix A and evaluate the results.

Comparative study of cash flow statements: a foreign company compared to a U.S. company

2. Obtain a recent annual report for a publicly held foreign company. Compare the form, content, and terminology used in its cash flow statement to that of a U.S. public company (preferably one in the same industry). Report your findings in writing and/or in a brief presentation to the class.

---

[1] Don E. Giacomino and David E. Mielke, "Cash Flows: Another Approach to Ratio Analysis," *Journal of Accountancy,* March 1993, pp. 55–58.

ANSWERS TO END-OF-CHAPTER QUESTIONS

1. For purposes of the statement of cash flows, cash is either defined as cash or cash plus cash equivalents. Cash consists of coin, currency, demand deposits, and certain negotiable instruments. Cash equivalents are investments that are effectively cash and consist of those investments (such as commercial paper) that have a maturity of less than three months. Since cash equivalents are essentially cash, including cash equivalents in the definition of cash for purposes of preparing the statement of cash flows may be more informative than simply using cash.

2. Cash flows provided (used) by operating activities refers to the cash generated by, or the cash used for, all those activities associated with acquiring and selling the company's inventories and services. Alternatively, net income refers to the flow of net assets into or out of the company associated with acquiring and selling the company's inventories and services. The difference between cash flows from operating activities and net income is, therefore, due to the respective focuses on cash and net assets of these two performance measures. Because cash is only one of numerous assets, net income provides a broader measure of operating performance.

3. The statement of cash flows consists of three sections—cash flows from (1) operating activities, (2) investing activities, and (3) financing activities. Cash flows from selling inventory or services are classified as operating activities; cash flows from selling investments and equipment are classified as investing activities and cash flows from borrowing or issuing equity are classified as financing activities.

   Operating, investing, and financing activities each involve a different aspect of a company. Operating activities are associated with acquiring and selling the company's goods and services; investing activities are associated with building the company's productive capacity; and financing activities are associated with financing the company's productive capacity. Because each activity is associated with a different aspect of the company, the net cash flows from each activity are reported separately.

4. The statement of cash flows and the balance sheet both provide information on the company's operating, investing, and financing activities. The income statement also provides information on the company's operating activities. While all three financial statements provide information on the company's activities, and are, hence, complementary to one another, the information provided by each statement is different. The statement of cash flows provides detailed information about cash flows from the three types of activities. Alternatively, the income statement provides information about net assets flows from operating activities (i.e., accrual-basis income), while the balance sheet provides accrual information about operating, investing, and financing activities. Hence, the statement of cash flows provides information about cash flows that is not readily available from the other financial statements.

5. The statement of cash flows provides information about a company's ability to generate cash and its effectiveness at managing its cash by (1) explaining the change in the company's cash balance; (2) summarizing the cash effects of operating transactions; and (3) summarizing the cash effects of capital transactions.

6. Cash flows are useful in assessing a company's investment potential and solvency. A company's perceived investment potential and solvency are a function of cash flows from the different types of activities: operating, investing, and financing. The importance of cash flows in assessing a company's investment potential and solvency provides incentives for managers to window dress the statement of cash flows.

    Managers can window dress the statement of cash flows by altering the timing of cash payments and receipts. For example, a manager can delay paying suppliers for inventory purchased on account or delay paying employees for back wages, thereby reporting higher cash flows from operating activities. A manager can also time when the company sells assets, acquires assets, issues debt or equity, pays dividends, and retires debt to improve cash flows from investing and financing activities.

    Managers can, however, only delay paying short-term payables and dividends for so long; they must also eventually acquire additional assets, dispose of old assets, issue debt, and retire debt. Thus, managers cannot window dress the statement of cash flows indefinitely. By requiring companies to report the statement of cash flows for at least the previous three years, the FASB has reduced the incentives for managers to window dress the statement of cash flows. This has allowed financial statement users to examine the trend in cash flows from operating, investing, and financing activities.

7. Managers can manipulate the information reported in the statement of cash flows by altering cash inflows and outflows associated with operating, investing, and financing activities. However, manipulating the cash inflows and outflows reported on the statement of cash flows may not be in the managers' best interests for at least four reasons. First, altering the timing of cash inflows and outflows may represent poor business judgment. For example, a manager could boost cash flows by selling some equipment, but if the equipment is used in production or is currently undervalued, selling the equipment may not be wise. Second, altering the timing of cash inflows and outflows may adversely affect the company's future cash position by limiting its financial flexibility and base of productive assets. Third, altering the timing of cash inflows and outflows may reduce the credibility of the company's financial reports, thereby making it more difficult for the company to attract capital. Finally, if a manager fraudulently alters cash inflows and outflows, the manager would be legally liable to financial statement users for any losses.

8. The statement of cash flows reports only those transactions that involve cash inflows or outflows; consequently, any operating, investing, or financing activity that does not involve cash is omitted from the statement. The following transactions are all examples of transactions that would not be disclosed on the face of the statement of cash flows.

    a. Acquiring a building in exchange for a long-term note payable.

    b. Retiring bonds payable by issuing common stock.

    c. Swapping land with another company.

    The FASB realized that investing and financing activities not involving cash are of interest to financial statement users. Consequently, the FASB required that these activities either be disclosed in the footnotes to the financial statements or in a supplemental schedule to the statement of cash flows.

9. The direct method reports, on the face of the statement of cash flows, the actual cash collections and cash payments for each operating activity. These amounts can be traced directly to the company's cash account in the general ledger. The FASB also requires that, as part of the direct method, net income be reconciled to net cash flow from operating activities. With the indirect method, this reconciliation is disclosed on the face of the statement of cash flows. The reconciliation of net income and net cash flow from operating activities is useful because it highlights the differences between net income (which is measured on the accrual basis) and net cash flow from operating activities (which is based on cash flows), and it also explains why these differences exist. Since the direct method directly reports the actual cash inflows and cash outflows for each operating activity, it is probably more straightforward than the indirect method. Further, since the direct method also provides the same reconciliation as presented under the indirect method, the direct method also provides more disclosure.

10. The adjustments to net income to arrive at net cash flow from operating activities can be classified as (1) noncash changes to noncurrent accounts and (2) changes in current accounts. Examples of the first classification are depreciation expense; gains (losses) on sales of nonoperating assets; and gains (losses) on early extinguishment of nonoperating liabilities. Examples of the second classification are increases or decreases in accounts receivable, inventory, prepaid expenses, and accounts payable.

11. These items are all used to calculate net income, which is based on accrual accounting. However, none them directly involve cash inflows or outflows from operating activities. Depreciation and amortization involve the allocation of an asset's cost; they do not involve cash inflows or outflows. Book gains and losses represent the difference between the carrying value of an asset and the disposal price of the asset or between the carrying value of a liability and the retirement price of the liability. Although these underlying transactions involve cash flows, the cash flows arise because an asset was disposed of or because a liability was retired prior to its maturity, not because of the book gain or loss. Since these items are used to calculate net income but do not affect cash flows, net income must be adjusted for these items. Book losses, depreciation, and amortization are deducted from revenues in calculating net income, so these items must be added back to net income to determine cash flows. Book gains are added to revenues in calculating net income so they must be deducted from net income to determine cash flows.

12. It is very unlikely that a financial statement user would find a statement of cash flows in the financial statements provided by companies in foreign countries. Certain countries, such as Britain and France, require a financial statement that is similar to the statement of cash flows but not identical. Probably the most important reason for why companies in foreign countries have not been required to provide a statement of cash flows is that creditors in those countries have more contact with the borrowers, which lessens the need for formal financial statements. However, as the global economy expands—and hence, creditors become more geographically disbursed—more countries will probably require a financial statement similar to the statement of cash flows.

13. Foreign currency exchange gains and losses are used to calculate net income. However, such gains and losses do not involve any cash inflows or outflows. In order to adjust net income to net cash flow from operating activities, it is therefore necessary to adjust net income for foreign currency exchange gains and losses. Since such losses are originally

subtracted in calculating net income, they must be added back to net income to arrive at net cash flow from operating activities. Similarly, since foreign currency exchange gains are originally added in calculating net income, they must be subtracted from net income to arrive at net cash flow from operating activities.

CHARACTERISTICS OF END-OF-CHAPTER ASSIGNMENTS

Item	Difficulty	Description
Brief exercises:		
BE14–1	E	Real data: The indirect presentation
BE14–2	M	Real data: Cash vs. accruals
BE14–3	M	Real data: Inferring inventory transactions
BE14–4	E	Real data: Interpreting the statement of cash flows
Exercises:		
E14–1	E	Classifying transactions
E14–2	E	Operating, investing, or financing activity?
E14–3	E	Cash management policies across companies
E14–4	E	Journalizing and classifying transactions
E14–5	M	Converting accrual to cash numbers
E14–6	M	Depreciation: A source of cash?
E14–7	M	Preparing a statement of cash flows from original transactions
E14–8	M	Preparing a statement of cash flows from the cash account in the ledger
E14–9	M	Computing cash outflows from accrual information
E14–10	H	Reconstructing a transaction and its cash effect
E14–11	M	Computing cash provided by operations from accrual information
E14–12	M	Preparing a statement of cash flows from information contained in two balance sheets, an income statement, and a statement of retained earnings
E14–13	M	Preparing a statement of cash flows from information contained in two balance sheets, an income statement, and a statement of retained earnings
E14–14	H	Computing net income from cash provided by operating activities
E14–15	E	Preparing the operating section of the statement of cash flows: direct and indirect methods
E14–16	E	Preparing the operating section of the statement of cash flows: direct and indirect methods
E14–17	M	Preparing the operating section of the statement of cash flows: direct and indirect methods
E14–18	M	Preparing the operating section of the statement of cash flows: direct and indirect methods
E14–19	H	Preparing the operating section of the statement of cash flows: direct and indirect methods
E14–20	H	Preparing the operating section of the statement of cash flows: direct and indirect methods

Item	**Difficulty**	**Description**

Problems:

P14–1	E	Placing transactions on the statement of cash flows
P14–2	E	Placing transactions on the statement of cash flows
P14–3	E	Classifying transactions and their cash effects
P14–4	E	Classifying transactions and their cash effects
P14–5	E	A company's cash management policy across time
P14–6	M	Deriving the cash effects of investing transactions
P14–7	H	Deriving the cash generated from a common stock issuance
P14–8	H	Converting cash flow numbers to accrual numbers and vice versa
P14–9	H	Reconciling the income statement, the direct method, and the indirect method
P14–10	M	Manipulating dollar amounts on the statement of cash flows
P14–11	M	Preparing the statement of cash flows from two balance sheets and an income statement
P14–12	M	Paying short-term debts: effects on working capital, the current ratio, and the statement of cash flows
P14–13	H	Preparing the statement of cash flows and reconciling the operating section with the income statement
P14–14	H	Preparing the statement of cash flows from two balance sheets and an income statement; book losses and amortized discounts
P14–15	H	Preparing the statement of cash flows from two balance sheets and an income statement; book gains and amortized premiums
P14–16	H	Preparing the statement of cash flows and using it to set dividend policy
P14–17	H	Preparing a complete set of financial statements from a set of original transactions

Issues for discussion:

ID14–1	E	Using the cash flow statement to spot earnings quality problems
ID14–2	E	Equity in unconsolidated affiliates
ID14–3	M	Accrual and cash flow accounting
ID14–4	E	Analyzing the operating section of the statement of cash flows
ID14–5	E	Misunderstandings in the financial press
ID14–6	H	Analyzing the statement of cash flows
ID14–7	M	Mergers and the statement of cash flows
ID14–8	M	Cash management profiles across companies
ID14–9	M	Cash management profiles across time—a mature firm
ID14–10	M	Cash management profile—a young firm
ID14–11	M	The annual report of NIKE

APPENDIX B   The Time Value of Money

In Appendix B, the author discusses time value of money techniques. This discussion encompasses both future values and present values of (1) lump sums, (2) ordinary annuities, and (3) annuities due.

LECTURE OUTLINE

The time value of money.

I. The changing value of money over time.

    A. Factors affecting the time value of money.

        1. Interest—the explicit cost of money. That is, interest is the "rental" fee to use someone else's money.

            a) Simple interest—computed on the principal only. Simple interest equals Principal x Interest rate x Time.

            b) Compound interest—computed on the principal plus any interest earned to date that has not yet been paid or withdrawn. That is, with compound interest, you earn interest on your initial principal plus interest on any interest earned to date.

        2. Inflation.

    B. Fundamental variables affecting the magnitude of the time value of money.

        1. Interest rate.

        2. Number of periods.

        3. Inflation rate.

II.   Types of cash flows.

    A.   Lump sum—a one-time cash inflow or outflow.

    B.   Annuity.

        1.   A flow of cash payments (called rents) of equal nominal amounts paid at periodic intervals.

        2.   Ordinary annuity—the cash flows occur at the end of each period.

        3.   Annuity due—the cash flows occur at the beginning of each period.

III.   Determining the time value of money.

    A.   Future value—the value of cash flows at some future point of time.

    B.   Present value—the value of cash flows at the current point in time.

    C.   Formulas for calculating future and present values.

    D.   Compound interest tables for calculating future and present values.

IV.   Using present values for financial statement purposes.

    A.   Present value is the economic form for valuation.

    B.   A critical problem with using present values for financial statement purposes is that predicting future cash flows is extremely subjective.

    C.   If future cash flows can be objectively determined, such as in a contractual agreement, then using present value for financial statement purposes is acceptable.

LECTURE TIPS

1.   Some students grasp the concept of time value of money immediately, while other students struggle. Some students have prior experience from math or finance courses and have used financial calculators or computer programs to solve time value problems. Consequently, lectures on this topic have to acknowledge this wide range of understanding. Use of the tables during lecture puts all students on a common plane. Engaging and relevant examples can make the topic more interesting to all students.

2. The use of time diagrams is especially helpful in complex problems to help identify known quantities; the type of problem (e.g., future vs. present value); the number of periods; and the interest rate involved.

CHARACTERISTICS OF END-OF-CHAPTER ASSIGNMENTS

Item	Difficulty	Description
Exercises:		
EB–1	E	Future value/single sum
EB–2	E	Present value/single sum
EB–3	E	Future value/ordinary annuity
EB–4	E	Future value/annuity due
EB–5	E	Present value/ordinary annuity
EB–6	E	Present value/annuity due
EB–7	M	Present value of different payment patterns
EB–8	M	Present value of different payment patterns
EB–9	M	Future and present values
EB–10	H	Present value of future bond payments—ordinary annuity and annuity due
EB–11	M	The highest present value
EB–12	H	Comparing ordinary annuities and annuities due
EB–13	M	Different terms of financing
EB–14	M	Saving for a college education—future value
EB–15	M	Saving for a college education—future value
Problems:		
PB–1	M	The value of common stock
PB–2	M	Computing future value, present value, and equivalent value
PB–3	M	Computing present value and equivalent value of contract cash flows
PB–4	M	The highest present value?
PB–5	H	Computing equivalent values
PB–6	H	Present and future values
PB–7	M	Present value of a note receivable and inferring the effective interest rate

CHECKLIST OF KEY FIGURES
FOR SELECTED END-OF-CHAPTER MATERIALS

Chapter 2

E2-4   1997 Dividends, $12
         1999 Beginning Retained Earnings, $110
         1998 Expenses, $500

E2-5   1997 Expenses, $650
         1998 Dividends, $144
         1999 Revenue, $1,300
         Profits as a Percentage of Sales
           1997: 27.8%
           1998: 30%
           1999: 30.8%
         Dividends as a Percentage of Net Income
           1997: 40%
           1998: 40%
           1999: 40%

E2-7   Method 1 New Working Capital, $9,500
         Method 2 New Working Capital, $9,500
         Method 3 New Working Capital, $14,500

E2-8   1999 Net Cash Flow from Financing Activities, $3,000
         1998 Net Cash Flow from Operating Activ., $(4,000)
         1997 Net Cash Flow from Investing Activities, $(8,000)

E2-9   1999 Net Cash Flow from Investing Activ., $(30,000)
         1998 Net Cash Flow from Financing Activ., $(11,000)
         1997 Beginning Cash Balance, $15,000

E2-10 Increase in Cash Balance, $3,500

E2-11 Increase in Cash Balance, $0

E2-12 Net Income, $500
         Ending Retained Earnings, $(300)
         Total Assets, $10,700
         Increase in Cash Balance, $2,700

E2-13 Net Income, $(2,000)
         Ending Retained Earnings, $(3,000)
         Total Assets, $42,000
         Increase in Cash Balance, $2,000

P2-3   Total Assets, $358,600

P2-4   1996 Contributed Capital, $700
         1996 Net Income, $600
         1996 Dividends, $200
         1997 Inventory, $700
         1997 Expenses, $700
         1997 Dividends, $0
         1998 Accounts Receivable, $500
         1998 Expenses, $800
         1998 Dividends, $400
         1999 Accounts Payable, $900
         1999 Net Income, $500
         1999 Sales, $1,100
         Current Ratio
           1996: 5
           1997: 4.33
           1998: 2.20
           1999: 1.78
         Working Capital
           1996: $800
           1997: $1,000
           1998: $600
           1999: $700

Debt/Equity Ratio
         1996: .64
         1997: .75
         1998: 1.44
         1999: 1.33
Return on Equity
         1996: .55
         1997: .33
         1999: .42

P2-5   2000 Total Assets, $15,000
         1999 Total Assets, $13,900
         1998 Total Assets, $13,700
         2000 Net Income, $2,000
         1999 Net Income, $3,000
         1998 Net Income, $2,000
         2000 Ending Retained Earnings, $1,500
         1999 Ending Retained Earnings, $2,500
         1998 Ending Retained Earnings, $1,500
         Current Ratio
           2000: .81
           1999: .54
           1998: .50
         Working Capital
           2000: $(500)
           1999: $(1,200)
           1998: $(1,700)
         Debt/Equity Ratio
           2000: .81
           1999: .49
           1998: .65
         Return on Equity
           2000: .24
           1999: .32
           1998: .24

P2-6   Current Ratio
         2000: 2.00
         1999: 2.00
         Working Capital
         2000: $7,000
         1999, $6,000
         Debt/Equity Ratio
         2000: 1.06
         1999: 0.96
         Operating Cash Flow to Total Debt
         2000: 0.45
         1999: 0.33
         Net Profit Margin
         2000: 0.34
         1999: 0.19
         Total Asset Turnover
         2000: 0.55
         1999: 0.58
         Return on Assets
         2000: 0.19
         1999: 0.11
         Return on Equity
         2000: 0.39
         1999: 0.21

P2-7   Current Ratio
      2000: 1.29
      1999: 2.00
   Working Capital
      2000: $2,000
      1999, $4,000
   Debt/Equity Ratio
      2000: 1.45
      1999: 0.92
   Operating Cash Flow to Total Debt
      2000: 0.75
      1999: 1.36
   Net Profit Margin
      2000: 0.15
      1999: 0.19
   Total Asset Turnover
      2000: 3.41
      1999: 3.87
   Return on Assets
      2000: 0.52
      1999: 0.74
   Return on Equity
      2000: 1.27
      1999: 1.42

P2-8   b. Value of Eat and Run, $6,000

P2-9   a. Additional Investment in Land, $34,000
   b. Total Assets, $107,000
      Current Ratio, 2
      Total Liabilities/Total Assets, .74
   c. Total Assets, $125,000
      Maximum Dividend, $22,000
      Total Liabilities/Total Assets, .75

ID2-3 a. Net Income %
      1996: 8.5%
      1997: 8.7%
      1998: 4.2%
   e. Dividends as a Percentage of Net Income
      1996: 14.3%
      1997: 12.7%
      1998: 31.9%

ID2-7 Cash from Operating Activities
      1995: 526
      1996: 459
   Cash from Investing Activities
      1995: (396)
      1996: (325)
   Cash from Financing Activities
      1995: (216)
      1996: (140)

Chapter 3

E3-1   Return on Equity
      1999: .390
      2000: .324
   Return on Sales
      1998: .313
      1999: .201
      2000: .200
   Current Ratio
      1998: 1.29

      1999: 1.08
      2000: 1.00
   Debt/Equity Ratio
      1998: .56
      1999: .74
      2000: .65

E3-2   Return on Equity
      1999: .344
      2000: .327
   Return on Sales
      1998: .324
      1999: .303
      2000: .272
   Current Ratio
      1998: 1.880
      1999: 1.467
      2000: 1.333
   Debt/Equity Ratio
      1998: .632
      1999: 1.094
      2000: 1.740

E3-3   Return on Equity
      1999: .548
      2000: .507
   Return on Sales
      1998: .263
      2000: .262
   Current Ratio
      1999: 2.00
      2000: 2.33
   Debt/Equity Ratio
      1999: 1.065
      2000: .825

E3-4   a. Return on Equity, .504
      Return on Assets, .22
      Earnings per Share, $8.25
      Return on Sales, .275
      Interest Coverage, 6.0
      Current Ratio, 2.36
      Quick Ratio, 1.27
      Receivables Turnover, 6.86
      Inventory Turnover, 1.82
      Financial Leverage, .284
      Debt/Equity Ratio, 1.71
      Price/Earnings Ratio, 4.36
      Dividend Yield, .125
      Return on Investment, .35

E3-5   a. Current Ratio
      1997: 2.40
      1998: 2.50
      1999: 2.92
      2000: 3.00
   b. Gross Profit
      1997: .43
      1998: .45
      1999: .44
      2000: .44
   c. Inventory Turnover
      1997: 1.67
      1998: 1.83

1999: 1.92
2000: 1.93
Average Days Supply of Inventory
1997: 218.56
1998: 199.45
1999: 190.10
2000: 189.12
d. Receivables Turnover
1997: 5.00
1998: 5.33
1999: 4.09
2000: 2.94
Average Number of Days Outstanding
1997: 73.00
1998: 68.48
1999: 89.24
2000: 124.15
E3-6 a. Cash from Operating Activities, $(322)
Cash from Investing activities, $(150)
Cash from Operating Activities, $130
E3-7 a. Current Ratio
1999: 2.26
2000: 0.87
Quick Ratio
1999: 0.794
2000: 0.717
b. Receivables Turnover
1999: 8.00
2000: 8.65
Number of Days Outstanding
1999: 45.625
2000: 42.197
E3-8 a. Return on Equity
1997: 5.10
1998: 2.51
1999: 1.70
2000: 1.22
b. Inventory Turnover
1997: 12.00
1998: 5.93
1999: 4.85
2000: 4.09
Days' Supply
1997: 30.42
1998: 61.55
1999: 75.26
2000: 89.24
E3-9 a. Current Ratio
1997: 2.500
1998: 1.846
1999: 1.240
2000: 1.167
Debt/Equity Ratio
1997: 0.767
1998: 1.200
1999: 1.250
2000: 1.207
Return on Assets
1997: 0.272

1998: 0.238
1999: 0.239
2000: 0.224
E3-11 a. Debt/Equity Ratio, 1.40
b. Additional Debt, $20,000
c. Maximum Dividend, $13,333
d. Maximum Dividend, $20,000
E3-12 a. 1996: 60.00%
1997: 41.67%
1998: 40.00%
1999: 30.00%
2000: 40.00%
b. Price/Earnings Ratio
1997: 14.58
1998: 15.00
1999: 14.80
2000: 12.60
Dividend Yield
1997: .029
1998: .027
1999: .020
2000: .032
Return on Investment
1997: .200
1998: -.120
1999: .258
2000: .171
c. Overall Return from Beginning of 1994
to the End of 1997 is 52.93%
E3-13 a. Earnings per Share, $12.68
Price/Earnings Ratio, 2.76
Dividend Yield, .286
Return on Investment, .50
P3-1 Current Ratio, 1.872
Quick Ratio, 1.359
Earnings per Share, $25
Interest Coverage, 8.576
Return on Assets, .584
Inventory Turnover, 9.00
Return on Equity, .952
P3-2 a. Return on Equity
1999: .389
2000: .562
Return on Assets
1999: .288
2000: .357
Common Equity Leverage
1999: .952
2000: .883
Capital Structure Leverage
1999: 1.444
2000: 1.888
Profit Margin
1999: .327
2000: .404
Asset Turnover
1999: .865
2000: .833

b. Return on Equity, .335
   Return on Assets, .349
   Common Equity Leverage, .978
   Capital Structure Leverage, 1.849
   Profit Margin, .424
   Asset Turnover, .814

P3-3   a. Total Assets Dollar Change, $(5,000)

P3-4   (1) Return on Equity
          1999: .855
          2000: .658
       (2) Return on Assets
          1999: .421
          2000: .409
       Financial Leverage
          1999: .434
          2000: .249
       (3) Current Ratio
          1999: 3.673
          2000: 3.379
       Quick Ratio
          1999: 2.673
          2000: 2.190
       (4) Earnings per Share
          1999: $30.29
          2000: $26.15
       Price/Earnings Ratio
          1999: 2.278
          2000: 2.065
       (5) Accounts Receivable Turnover
          1999: 7.525
          2000: 6.533
       Number of Days Outstanding for Receivables
          1999: 48.505 days
          2000: 55.870 days

P3-5   Return on Equity
          1999: 1.294
          2000: 1.391
       Return on Sales
          1998: -.058
          1999: .312
          2000: .272
       Current Ratio
          1998: 7.0
          1999: 2.0
          2000: 1.286
       Debt/Equity Ratio
          1998: .556
          1999: .917
          2000: 1.455

P3-6   a. Return on Equity
          Hathaway, .433
          Yakima, 1.687
       b. Return on Assets
          Hathaway, .387
          Yakima, .409
       c. Earnings per Share
          Hathaway, $10.94
          Yakima, $21.57

P3-7   a. Return on Equity
          Robotronics, .607

          Technology, 1.163
       b. Return on Assets
          Robotronics, .211
          Technology, .989
          Financial Leverage
          Robotronics, .396
          Technology, .174

P3-8   Net Sales, $312,500
       Cost of Goods Sold, $187,500
       Expenses, $100,000
       Ending Inventory, $75,000
       Ending Accounts Receivable, $78,125
       Cash, $21,875
       Net Income, $25,000
       Total Current Assets, $175,000
       Total Current Liabilities, $200,000

P3-9   a. Total Current Assets % of Total Assets
          1999: 56.59
          2000: 60.00
       Total Current Liabilities % of Total Liabilities and
       Stockholders' Equity
          1999: 17.43
          2000: 19.66
       Gross Profit
          1999: 38.71
          2000: 34.23
       Net Income
          1999: 7.02
          2000: 7.94

P3-10 a. Return on Equity
          1999: .361
          2000: .588
       Current Ratio
          1999: 3.247
          2000: 3.052
       Quick Ratio
          1999: 2.180
          2000: 2.190
       Return on Assets
          1999: .220
          2000: .345
       Receivables Turnover
          1999: 9.400
          2000: 12.769
       Earnings per Share
          1999: $26.73
          2000: $31.29
       Price/Earnings Ratio
          1999: 1.684
          2000: 2.237
       Debt/Equity Ratio
          1999: .880
          2000: .766
       Return on Sales
          1999: .081
          2000: .085
       Financial Leverage
          1999: .141
          2000: .243

Dividend Yield
  1999: .020
  2000: .548
Return on Investment
  1999: -.082
  2000: 1.409
Interest Coverage
  1999: 7.846
  2000: 19.200
Inventory Turnover
  1999: 12.214
  2000: 19.585

P3-11 Current Ratio
  Selig Equipment, 1.74
  Mountain Bike, 1.86
Quick Ratio
  Selig Equipment, .561
  Mountain Bike, 1.400
Receivables Turnover
  Selig Equipment, 4.67
  Mountain Bike, 3.46
Average Number of Days Outstanding
  Selig Equipment, 78.16
  Mountain Bike, 105.49
Inventory Turnover
  Selig Equipment, 2.48
  Mountain Bike, 4.92
Average Days Supply of Inventory
  Selig Equipment, 147.18
  Mountain Bike, 74.19

P3-12 a. Alternative 1
      Earnings per Share, $3.41
      Return on Equity, .1304
      Return on Assets, .1070
      Financial Leverage, .0234
      Debt/Equity Ratio, .609
    Alternative 2
      Earnings per Share, $3.53
      Return on Equity, .1354
      Return on Assets, .1076
      Financial Leverage, .0278
      Debt/Equity Ratio, .768
    Alternative 3
      Earnings per Share, $3.46
      Return on Equity, .1328
      Return on Assets, .1073
      Financial Leverage, .0255
      Debt/Equity Ratio, .685
    c. Alternative 1
      Net Income, $660,000
    Alternative 2
      Net Income, $0
    Alternative 3
      Net Income, $330,000

P3-13 a. Total Stockholders' Equity, $600,000
      b. Total Liabilities, $240,000
      c. Total Assets, $840,000
      d. Interest Expense, $96,000
      e. Net Income Before Taxes, $681,818

f. Net Sales, $2,250,000
g. Credit Sales, $1,800,000
h. Accounts Receivable, $72,000
i. Cost of Goods Sold, $1,237,500
j. Inventory Turnover, 30
k. Inventory, $41,250
l. Current Liabilities, $84,000
m. Current Assets, $252,000
n. Marketable Securities, $28,000
o. Noncurrent Assets, $588,000
p. Common Shares Outstanding, 28,125 shares

ID3-1
  1. Kelly Services
  2. Microsoft
  3. Toys R Us
  4. J. P. Morgan

ID3-2
  1. Hershey Foods
  2. Lands End
  3. Disney
  4. Ford

ID3-12
  Return on Equity, .125
  Return on Assets, .081
  Financial Leverage, .044
  Earnings per Share
    1996: 1.93
    1997: 2.76
    1998: 1.38
  Return on Sales
    1996: .089
    1997: .090
    1998: .046
  Times Interest Earned
    1996: 22.8
    1997: 24.8
    1998: 10.9
  Current Ratio
    1997: 2.05
    1998: 2.07
  Quick Ratio
    1997: 1.178
    1998: 1.046
  Debt/Equity
    1997: .699
    1998: .655

ID3-13
  Return on Equity, .130
  Return on Assets, .058
  Financial Leverage, .072
  Earnings per Share
    1995: 2.63
    1996: 2.69
    1997: 3.12
  Return on Sales
    1995: .039
    1996: .035
    1997: .036

Times Interest Earned
   1996: 5.648
   1997: 6.931
Current Ratio
   1996: 1.068
   1997: 1.087
Quick Ratio
   1996: .843
   1997: .833
Debt Equity
   1996: 1.60
   1997: 1.574

ID3-14
   #1 Wal-Mart
   #2 Sun Microsystems
   #3 Merck

Chapter 4

E4-1 Cost of Basket of Goods at End of Period, $53,000
     Change in Cost of Basket of Goods for Period, $3,000

E4-2 a. $15,000 Cost per Parcel of Land
     b. Economic Loss of $9,000
     c. Total Land in 1981 Dollars, $24,375
       Total Land in 1996 Dollars, $39,000

E4-5 a. Revenue Recognized at the End of the Project
       Period 1, $0
       Period 2, $200,000
      Revenue Recognized During Production
       Period 1, $150,000
       Period 2, $50,000
      Revenue Recognized When Payments Are Received
       Period 1, $100,000
       Period 2, $100,000
     b. Total Income Under All Alternatives, $200,000

E4-6 Net Book Value
     1999, $20,000
     2000, $15,000
     2001, $10,000
     2002, $5,000
     2003, $0

E4-8 b. Adjusted Net Income
     1997, $21,000
     1998, $19,000
     1999, $18,000
     2000, $15,000

P4-1 a. Gain, $10,000

P4-2 a. Interest Revenue, $240

P4-3 a. Asset A Total Cash Flows
       Option 1, $1,500
       Option 2, $5,500
       Option 3, $2,500
      Asset B Total Cash Flows
       Option 1, $500
       Option 2, $2,000
       Option 3, $2,500
      Asset C Total Cash Flows
       Option 1, $3,000
       Option 2, $4,500
       Option 3, $2,500

P4-4 a. 81.8% Increase in Sales from 1998 to 2000

     b. 2000 Sales in 1998 Dollars, $139,130
       Real Change in Sales, $59,130
       Real Percentage Change in Sales, 74%

P4-5 a. Purchase Price, $33,901

P4-6 a. Total Present Value, $138,313
     b. Net Income, $15,000
       Total Assets, $105,000
     c. Present Value, $132,144.40
       Economic Income, $13,831.40

P4-7 a. Book Value, $96,000
     b. Total Present Value, $153,734.60
     c. Liquidation Value, $96,000

P4-8 a. Net Income, $24,000
     b. Net Income, $26,000
     c. Economic Income, $15,373.80

P4-9 a. Revenue
       Assumption 1, Year 4, $200,000
       Assumption 2, Year 4, $200,000
       Assumption 3, Year 4, $600,000
     b. Costs
       Assumption 1, Year 4, $95,000
       Assumption 2, Year 4, $95,000
       Assumption 3, Year 4, $285,000
      Net Income
       Assumption 1, Year 4, $105,000
       Assumption 2, Year 4, $105,000
       Assumption 3, Year 4, $315,000
     c. Total Net Income
       Assumption 1, $1,260,000
       Assumption 2, $1,260,000
       Assumption 3, $1,260,000

P4-10 a. Revenue
       Year 1, $20,000
       Year 2, $20,000
       Year 3, $10,000
     b. Revenue
       Year 1, $15,000
       Year 2, $20,000
       Year 3, $15,000
     c. Assumption 1 Net Income
       Year 1, $12,000
       Year 2, $12,000
       Year 3, $6,000
      Assumption 2 Net Income
       Year 1, $9,000
       Year 2, $12,000
       Year 3, $9,000

P4-12 b. Expected Cost of a Type 1 Error, $8,000
      Expected Cost of a Type 2 Error, $10,000

ID4-4 a. Net Income
       1992, $1,872
       1993, $269
       1994, $2,211

Chapter 5

E5-1 Assets, $41,000
     Liabilities, $9,000
     Stockholders' Equity, $32,000

E5-2 Cash, $13,000
     Accounts Receivable, $8,000

Land, $20,000
Notes Payable, $9,000
Contributed Capital, $30,000
Retained Earnings, $2,000

E5-3   Net Income, $2,500
Ending Retained Earnings, $2,000
Total Assets, $41,000
Increase in Cash Balance, $13,000

E5-4   Assets, $25,600
Liabilities, $13,000
Stockholders' Equity, $12,600
Net Income, $3,000
Ending Retained Earnings, $2,600
Total Assets, $25,600
Increase in Cash, $17,600

E5-6   Net Income, $17,000
Ending Retained Earnings, $23,000
Total Assets, $86,000

E5-7   a. Ending Cash, $43,000
b. Increase in Cash Balance, $34,000

E5-8   b. Ending Cash Balance, $11,600
c. Increase in Cash Balance, $6,600

E5-9   a. Cash, $8,600
Accounts Receivable, $4,000
Land, $7,000
Notes Payable, $5,000
Contributed Capital, $12,000
Retained Earnings, $2,600
Net Income, $4,800
Ending Retained Earnings, $2,600
Total Assets, $19,600
Increase in Cash Balance, $8,600

E5-10 a. Ending Cash Balance, $27,500
b. Increase in Cash Balance, $19,500

E5-13 c. Total Wage Expense, $70,000
Total Cash Outflow Associated with Wages, $70,000

E5-14 a. Book Value on 12/31/00, $16,000
Book Value on 12/31/01, $8,000
Book Value on 12/31/02, $0
b. Total Depreciation Expense, $24,000
Total Cash Flow Associated with Purchase of Press, $24,000

E5-15 b. Prepaid Insurance Ending Balance, $9,000
Supplies Inventory Ending Balance, $16,000
Rent Payable Ending Balance, $6,000

E5-16 a. Net Income, $1,800
Net Cash Incr. Due to Oper. Activ., $4,200

E5-17 b. Cash Ending Balance, $12,370
c. Increase in Cash Balance, $8,370

E5-18 a. Year 1 Net Income, $3,000
Year 2 Net Income, $7,000
Year 1 Increase in Cash Balance, $26,000
Year 2 Decrease in Cash Balance, $(26,000)
b. Total Net Income, $10,000
Total Net Cash from Oper. Activ., $10,000

E5-19 c. Long-term Investment, $400

E5-20 a. Final Trial Balance, $81,900
b. Net Income, $10,200
Ending Retained Earnings, $10,200

Total Assets, $79,900
Increase in Cash Balance, $4,200

E5-21 a. $13,000
b. $24,000
c. $21,000

P5-3   c. Net Income, $38,800
Ending Retained Earnings, $12,800
Total Assets, $182,800
Increase in Cash Balance, $81,800

P5-4   c. Net Income, $3,000
Ending Retained Earnings, $10,200
Total Assets, $29,200
Increase in Cash Balance, $2,200

P5-9   Case 1, $200
Case 2, $(3,300)
Case 3, $900
Case 4, $0
Case 5, $(2,600)
Case 6, $(300)

P5-10 a. Total Insurance Revenue, $240,000
Total Cash Receipts, $240,000
b. Total Insurance Expense, $240,000
Total Cash Payment, $240,000

P5-12 a. Current Ratio, 2.50
Debt/Equity Ratio, .50
Book Value, 6.67
b. Stock Issuance
Current Ratio, 2.50
Debt/Equity Ratio, .36
Book Value, 7.33
Long-term Note
Current Ratio, 2.50
Debt/Equity Ratio, .88
Book Value, 6.67
Open Account
Current Ratio, 1.00
Debt/Equity Ratio, .88
Book Value, 6.67

P5-16 c. Net Loss, $(209,500)
Total Assets, $768,000

P5-17 c. Final Trial Balance, $2,785,720
f. Net Income $243,859
Ending Retained Earnings, $609,859
Total Assets, $2,362,220
Decrease in Cash Balance, $(161,000)

P5-18 Cash Payments Due to Operating Activities, $8,400

P5-19 Total Revenue Generated from Adver. Display Sales
1999, $38,700
2000, $40,800
Total Revenue Generated from Consulting Services
1999, $37,300
2000, $48,700

P5-20 Gain on Sale of Equipment, $5,600

ID5-8 a. Cash Received for Sale of Goods, $9,618.60
b. Inventory Purchases, $6,123.50
c. Land Purchases, $2.20

Chapter 6

E6-5   Ending Balance, $26,000

E6-6   a. Beginning Allowance Balance, $187,500
       b. Ending Accounts Receivable, $8,600,000
E6-7   b. Ending Allowance Balance, $54,200
E6-8   a. Write-offs, $1,261
E6-9   Total Uncollectible Amount, $22,740
P6-2   b. Annual Interest Rate of Forfeiting a Cash Disc., 73%
P6-3   b. December 31, 2000 Allowance Balance, $550
P6-4   b. Ending Allowance Balance, $44,500
       d. Ending Allowance Balance, $0
P6-5   a. Net Loss, $(17,000)
          Total Assets, $80,000
P6-6   a. Fees Earned, $230,000
          Accounts Receivable, $58,000
          Allowance for Doubtful Accounts, $5,800
          Current Ratio, 1.42
          Working Capital, $27,600
          Net Income, $2,600
P6-7   a. Current Method
             2000 Bad Debt Charge, $90,000
             2000 Accounts Receivable, $1,095,000
          Allowance Method
             2000 Bad Debt Charge, $79,200
             2000 Accounts Receivable, $943,240
       b. Current Method
             Total Bad Debt Charge, $250,000
          Allowance Method
             Total Bad Debt Charge, $401,760
P6-8   b. Ending Allowance Balance, $69,800
       c. Beginning Accounts Receivable Balance, $3,675,000
       d. Total Uncollectible Amount, $335,000
P6-9   c. Bad Debt Charge as a % of Accounts Receivable
             1998: 9.09%
             1999: 12.50%
             2000: 6.20%
P6-10 a. Value of Transaction in U.S. Dollars
             (1) $640,000.00
             (2) $2,333.33
             (3) $33,333.33
             (4) $133,333
       c. Exchange Gain (Loss)
             (1) $(106,666.67)
             (2) $166.67
             (3) $(2,083.33)
             (4) $33,333.33
P6-11 a. Carrying Value of Receivable, $68,000
       b. Exchange Rate, 1.575
       c. Exchange Rate, 1.574
ID6-3 a. Working Capital
             1992: $168.70
             1993: $(37.50)
             1994: $(5.50)
ID6-4 a. Bad Debt Expense
             1997: 878
             1996: 887
             1995: 453
       b. Write-Offs, %
          Domestic Consumer Loans: $1,085, 1.5%
          Domestic Commercial Loans: $154, .2%
          Foreign Loans: $66, .2%

Chapter 7
E7-4   a. 12/31/97
             Purchase Discounts, $5,000
             Ending Inventory, $125,000
             Cost of Goods Available for Sale, $180,000
          12/31/99
             Beginning Inventory, $130,000
             Purchase Discounts, $15,000
             Ending Inventory, $110,000
          12/31/00
             Purchases, $55,000
             Cost of Goods Sold, $80,000
E7-5   a. Cost of Goods Sold, $71,300
       b. Cost of Goods Sold, $69,300
E7-6   a. Error in Cost of Goods Sold, $9,000 Over.
       b. Error in Cost of Goods Sold, $18,000 Under.
       c. Total Error in Cost of Goods Sold by 2000:
             $9,000 Understatement
E7-7   a. Gross Profit, $5,200
          Ending Inventory, $23,100
       b. Gross Profit, $3,600
          Ending Inventory, $21,500
E7-8   a. FIFO Cost Flow Assumption
          Cost of Goods Sold, $61,750
          Gross Profit, $68,250
          Ending Inventory, $36,000
          Averaging Cost Flow Assumption
          Cost of Goods sold, $66,881.10
          Gross Profit, $63,118.90
          Ending Inventory, $30,868.20
          LIFO Cost Flow Assumption
          Cost of Goods Sold, $70,750
          Gross Profit, $59,250
          Ending Inventory, $27,000
E7-10 a. LIFO, $658,000
          FIFO, $658,000
          Average Cost, $657,900
E7-11 b. Accumulated Tax Savings, $1,120
       c. 2000 Net Income Under FIFO, $41,400
E7-12 b. Item #1 Total Profit, $10
          Item #2 Total Profit, $10
P7-3   1998 Correct Cost of Goods Sold, $45,000
          1999 Correct Cost of Goods Sold, $35,500
          2000 Correct Cost of Goods Sold, $54,700
          2000 Correct Net Income, $8,300
          1999 Correct Net Income, $22,500
          1998 Correct Net Income, $20,000
P7-4   a. Cost of Goods Available for Sale, $47,500
          Number of Units Available for Sale, 37,000
          FIFO Cost Flow Assumption
          Ending Inventory, $17,200
          Cost of Goods Sold, $30,300
          LIFO Cost Flow Assumption
          Ending Inventory, $11,000
          Cost of Goods Sold, $36,500
          Averaging Cost Flow Assumption
          Ending Inventory, $14,124
          Cost of Goods Sold, $33,376
          FIFO Net Income, $6,790

Averaging Net Income, $4,637
LIFO Net Income, $2,450

b. Tax Savings, $1,860
c. Ending Inventory at Market Value, $14,850
d. Cost of Goods Available for Sale, $52,500
Number of Units Available for Sale, 37,000
FIFO Cost Flow Assumption
Ending Inventory, $13,600
Cost of Goods Sold, $38,900
LIFO Cost Flow Assumption
Ending Inventory, $17,600
Cost of Goods Sold, $34,900
Averaging Cost Flow Assumption
Ending Inventory, $15,609
Cost of Goods Sold, $36,891
FIFO Net Income, $770
Averaging Net Income, $2,176
LIFO Net Income, $3,570

P7-5 a. Adjusting Entry for Ending Inventory
using LIFO, $393,250
b. Adjusting Entry for Ending Inventory
using FIFO, $491,735

P7-6 a. FIFO Current Ratio, 2.22
LIFO Current Ratio, 1.56
b. FIFO Net Income, $17,500
LIFO Net Income, $9,100
c. Tax Dollars Saved, $3,600

P7-7 a. Total LIFO Layers, $112,500
b. Net Income, $843,500
c. Net Income, $210,000

P7-8 a. FIFO Net Income, $37,500

P7-9 a. Net Income, $20,860
b. Net Income, $14,350

Chapter 8

E8-2 a. Change in the Wealth Level
Wearever Fabrics, $12,000
Frames Corp., $2,000
Pacific Transport, $(24,000)
Video Magic, $13,000
b. Holding Gains and Losses
Wearever Fabrics, $20,000
Frames Corp., $(10,000)
Pacific Transport, $(20,000)
Video Magic, $10,000

E8-3 b. Total Cost, $460
Total Market Value, $385

E8-4 a. Total Income, Trading, $70
Total Income, Available-for-Sale, $70
b. 12/31/01 Balance Sheet Value, $120

E8-5 a. Tom Miller Total Assets, $8,220
Larry Rogers Total Assets, $8,220
b. Tom Miller
Net Income, $0.00
Working Capital, $6,720.00
Current Ratio, 5.48
Larry Rogers
Net Income, $720.00
Working Capital, $6,720.00

Current Ratio, 5.48

E8-9 b. Book Value of Invest. on 12/31/00, $177,250

E8-10 a. Tumbleweed's Total Net Income 1999, $40,000
b. Total Div. Decl. by Tumbleweed, $26,667

E8-11 b. Goodwill Amortized in Year 1, $8,250

E8-12 (1) Purchase Price, $9,000
(2) Net Market Value in Excess of Book Value, $0
(3) Net Book Value, $5,000
(4) Goodwill, $2,000
(5) Purchase Price, $6,000
(6) Goodwill, $0

E8-13 a. Number of Common Shares Outstanding, 3,000
b. Market Value per Share, $17

E8-14 Goodwill, $16,000
Minority Interest, $32,000

E8-15 Consolidated Balance Sheet, $1,298,000

P8-1 Total Effect on 1999 Income, $2,785

P8-2 b. Marketable Securities, $41,000

P8-6 a. Trading Securities
Total Real. Gain of $100 on Income Stmt.
Total Unreal. Gain of $1,440 on Income Stmt.
b. Available-for-Sale Securities
Total Real. Gain of $100 on Income Stmt.
Total Unreal. Gain of $1,440 on Bal. Sheet

P8-7 a. Total Assets on January 1, 1999, $160,000
1999 Net Income, $37,000
Total Assets on December 31, 1999, $193,000
2000 Net Income, $8,000
Total Assets on December 31, 2000, $207,000
b. Total Assets on January 1, 1999, $160,000
1999 Net Income, $38,000
Total Assets on December 31, 1999, $198,000
2000 Net Income, $9,000
Total Assets on December 31, 2000, $207,000

P8-8 a. Total Assets on December 31, 1999, Consolidated
Balance Sheet, $244,000
b. 1999 Goodwill Amortization, $1,000
c. Total Assets on December 31, 1999, Consolidated
Balance Sheet, $180,000
d. Debt/Equity Ratio
Purchase Method: 1.71
Equity Method: 1.00

P8-9 a. Total Short-term Investments as of 12/31/00, $290
$280 is in Trading Securities and $10 is in
Available-for-Sale Securities
b. Balance Sheet Carrying Value of Trading Securities
Sold During 2000, $130
c. Total Income of the Affiliate, $100
Total Number of Shares Outstanding, 125,000
Earnings per Share of the Affiliate, $.80
d. Per Share Dividend Declared by the Affiliate, $.20

P8-10 b. Consolidated Balance Sheet, $1,116,000

P8-11 b. Consolidated Balance Sheet, $1,150,000

P8-12 b. Consolidated Balance Sheet, $1,150,000

P8-13 Consolidated Balance Sheet, $1,266,000

P8-15 Company X, Minority Interest, $21,200
Company Y, Minority Interest, $13,600
Company Z, Minority Interest, $4,750

P8-16 a. Debt/Equity Ratio, Post Acquisition: 1.185

ID8-2 d. Cost of Securities Sold
           1997: $23,398
           1996: $154,036
           1995: $293,038

Chapter 9
E9-2   Lot 1 Net Income, $32,000
       Lot 2 Net Income, $24,000
       Lot 3 Net Income, $12,000
       Lot 4 Net Income, $12,000
E9-3   a. Land, $97,000
          Land Improvements, $32,000
          Building, $140,000
E9-5   a. Expensed Immediately
             2002 Net Income, $45,000
             2001 Net Income, $45,000
             2000 Net Income, $5,000
             2002 Total Assets, $185,000
             2001 Total Assets, $140,000
             2000 Total Assets, $95,000
          Amortized Over Two Years
             2002 Net Income, $45,000
             2001 Net Income, $25,000
             2000 Net Income, $25,000
             2002 Total Assets, $185,000
             2001 Total Assets, $140,000
             2000 Total Assets, $115,000
          Amortized Over Three Years
             2002 Net Income, $31,666
             2001 Net Income, $31,667
             2000 Net Income, $31,667
             2002 Total Assets, $185,000
             2001 Total Assets, $153,334
             2000 Total Assets, $121,666
       b. Method 1 Total Net Income, $95,000
          Method 2 Total Net Income, $95,000
          Method 3 Total Net Income, $95,000
E9-6   a. 12-Year Useful Life Net Income, $23,750,000
       b. 6-Year Useful Life Net Income, $22,500,000
       c. 12-Year Useful Life Dividends, $7,125,000
          6-Year Useful Life Dividends, $6,750,000
E9-7   a. Depreciation Expense per Year, $9,600
          Book Value After Three Years, $31,200
       b. Depreciation Expense, $3,840
E9-9   a. (1) Straight-Line Depr., $60,000 per Year 1999-2002
          (2) Double-Declining-Balance Depreciation
             1999: $150,000
             2000: $75,000
             2001: $15,000
             2002: $0
E9-10 b. (1) Straight-Line Depr., $53,000/Year for 1999-2003
          (2) Double-Declining-Balance Depreciation
             1999: $134,000
             2000: $80,400
             2001: $48,240
             2002: $2,360
             2003: $0
E9-11 (1) Depreciation Expense per Mile, $0.4/mile
       (2) Depreciation Expense per Year, $16,000/year
E9-12 c. $800,000

E9-13 a. Cumulative Difference
             1999: $95,000
             2000: $70,000
             2001: $45,000
             2002: $20,000
E9-14 a. Accumulated Depreciation-Office Equip., $300,000
E9-15 Book Value
             1997: $15,000
             1998: $9,000
             1999: $5,400
             2000: $5,000
             2001: $5,000
E9-16 a. Orig. Cost of Equip. Sold in 2000, $7,200
       b. Relat. Acc. Depr. on Equip. Sold in '00, $3,900
E9-17 a. Relat. Acc. Depr. on Equip. Sold in '00, $3,100
       b. Equipment Purchased During 2000, $11,800
E9-18 b. Amortization Expense, $1,125
E9-19 a. (3) Amortization Expense, $50,000
       b. (3) Loss on Patent, $50,000
P9-2   a. Cost Allocation
             Building, $250,000
             Office Equipment, $125,000
             Cranes, $125,000
             Land, $500,000
       b. Depreciation Expense—Building, $8,750
          Depreciation Expense—Office Equipment, $30,000
          Depreciation Expense—Cranes, $19,000
       c. Total Property, Plant, and Equipment, $799,000
P9-3   a. Cost, $1,180,000
       b. Depreciation Expense
             Double-declining-balance, $590,000
             Straight-line, $282,500
       c. Loss on Sale of Equipment
             Double-Declining-Balance, $340,000
             Straight-Line, $647,500
P9-4   b. 1997 Net Income Understated by $48,000
          1998 Net Income Overstated by $12,000
       c. 1997 Net Income Understated by $48,000
          1998 Net Income Overstated by $32,000
P9-5   c. 1996 through 1999 Deprec. Expense, $18,000
          2001 through 2003 Deprec. Expense, $44,500
P9-6   c. Depreciation Expense, $50,500
P9-7   a. Depreciation Expense per Year, $15,000
          1/1/99 Accumulated Depreciation, $75,000
          1/1/99 Book Value, $105,000
P9-8   a. Straight-Line Depreciation Expense Total, $60,000
          Double-Declining-Balance Depr. Exp. Total,$60,000
       b. Straight-Line Depr., Years 1 through 4, $16,250
          Double-Declining-Balance Depreciation
             Year 1 Net Income, $0
             Year 2 Net Income, $13,000
             Year 3 Net Income, $26,000
             Year 4 Net Income, $26,000
       d. Straight-Line Depr. Present Value, $27,736.36
          Dble-Decl.-Bal. Depr. Present Value, $25,865.63
P9-9   a. S-L Depreciation (10-year life)
          Net Income, $47,600
          Bonus Amount, $3,808
          Dividend Amount, $35,700
          DDB Depreciation

Net Income, $20,400
Bonus Amount, $1,632
Dividend Amount, $15,300
S-L Depreciation (5-year life)
Net Income, $20,400
Bonus Amount, $1,632
Dividend Amount, $15,300

P9-10 b. 1999 Depletion, $240,000
2000 Depletion, $300,000
2001 Depletion, $260,000
c. Depletion Expense, 1999-2001, $7,000
d. 1999 Depletion, $240,000
2000 Depletion, $300,000

P9-11 a. Gain on Sale of Machinery, $65,000
b. Depreciation Expense, $40,000
c. Land, $210,000 (FMV of Asset Received)
Land, $250,000 (FMV of Asset Given Up)

ID9-1 d. Cost of Hotel, $67,000,000
Depreciation per Year, $2,680,000

Chapter 10

E10-1 a. Present Value, $39,868.80
E10-2 a. Current Ratio 2.25
b. Current Ratio 1.875
c. Current Ratio 1.625
E10-3 Adjusted Current Assets, $25,100
Adjusted Current Liabilities $20,050
Adjusted Net Income, $3,550
E10-4 b. Interest Expense, $250
E10-6 c. 2000 Ending Balance, $16,000
E10-8 a. Bonus Expense, $10,000
E10-9 b. Net Income (Loss)
Contingency Basis
1999: $46,000
2000: $0
Cash Basis
1999: $48,600
2000: $(2,600)
E10-10 b. Pension Liability, $10,000
E10-11 a. Income Tax Liability, $22,750
b. Income Tax Liability, $19,500
E10-12 a. Conservatism Ratio 1.36
E10-13 a. Conservatism Ratio .898
P10-1 Total Current Liabilities, $343,000
P10-2 Total Assets $2,120,000
P10-3 b. Current Assets, $139,000
Current Liabilities, $65,000
c. Current Assets, $139,000
Current Liabilities, $75,000
P10-4 c. Contingent Loss on Lawsuit, $742.00
P10-5 d. Year-End Warranty Liability, $16,100
P10-6 a. Promotion Expense
1999: $400
2000: $560
b. Ending Balance
1999: $100
2000: $260
P10-7 b. Total Amount Funded through 1999, $176,000

P10-8 a. Income Tax Liability
1995: $26,250.00
1996: $30,625.00
1997: $32,812.50
1998: $32,812.50
b. Income Tax Liability
1995: $26,250.00
1996: $30,625.00
1997: $18,750.00
1998: $18,750.00
c. Income Tax Liability
1995: $26,250.00
1996: $21,875.00
1997: $28,437.50
1998: $30,625.00

P10-9 Owen-Foley Taxable Income, $139,444
Amerton Taxable Income, $151,389

Chapter 11

E11-2 c. (1) Total Present Value, $300,000
(2) Total Present Value, $300,000
E11-4 Present Value of
Note(1) $735.00
(2) $3,525.00
(3) $5,368.45
(4) $3,000.00
(5) $12,945.00
E11-5 a. Present Value Factor 0.5674
E11-6 b. Discount on Notes Payable, $1,141.60
c. Discount on Notes Payable, $285.62
E11-7 a. Present Value of Periodic Interest Payments
(1) $356.65
(2) $347.11
(3) $338.01
E11-8 b. Present Value
(1) $581,856.66
(2) $550,124.19
(3) $520,657.83
E11-9 b. Credit to Discount on Notes Payable, $2,400
E11-10 Discount/Premium
a.   Bond A, $0
Bond B, $59,512
Bond C, $48,668
E11-11 d. Present Value of Interest Payments, $17,535
e. Present Value of Interest Payments, $16,257
E11-12 a. Discount, $40,536
b. Interest Expense, $18,378.56
E11-13 a. Premium, $14,878
b. Interest Expense, $3,446.34
c. Balance Sheet Values as of 12/31/00, $114,324.34
E11-14 a. Total Present Value, $21,403.76
b. Total Present Value, $18,706.56
E11-15 a. Cash paid to redeem bonds, $505,000
b. Gain on Redemption, $2,000
E11-16 a. Interest Expense, $4,822.70
b. Discount on Bonds Payable, $2,723.30
E11-17 a. Annual Effective Interest Rate, 8%
b. Annual Effective Interest Rate, 6%
c. Unrealized Holding Loss, $3,517

E11-18   a. Annual Effective Interest Rate, 6.92%
         b. Annual Effective Interest Rate, 8.83%
         c. Unrealized Holding Gain, $6,580
E11-19   b. 1999 Lease Liability, $39,927
            1999 Depreciation Expenses, $7,985.40
            1999 Interest Expense, $3,194.16
E11-20   b. Present Value of Lease Payments, $3,790,800
         c. Interest Expense, $379,080
E11-21   a. Lease Payment, $26,439.32 (rounded)
         d. Bal. Sheet Value after 2nd Pay., $131,340.95
E11-22   Effective Interest Rate
         Note 1   8%
         Note 2   14%
         Note 3   9%
         Bond 1   4%
         Bond 2   8%
E11-23   a. Present Value of Interest Receipts, $404.24
         b. Present Value of Interest Receipts, $433.51
P11-1   b. Face Value, 24,201
P11-2   c. Interest Expense, $218.85
P11-3   a. L-T Debt/Equity Ratio, .40
         c. Proceeds, $47,918
P11-4   a. Discount
            Note A, $7,582
            Note B, $3,734
            Note C, $0
         d. Note B, Interest Expense, $3,126.60
P11-5   b. Total Interest Expense, Years 1-3
            Note A, $12,434
            Note B, $15,000
            Note C, $13,973
         c. Total Return, Years 1-3
            Note A, $15,211.52
            Note B, $20,246.40
            Note C, $18,232.69
P11-6   c. Interest Rate 13% (rounded)
P11-7   a. PV of Cash Interest Payments, $5,631.06
         b. PV of Cash Interest Payments, $5,256.30
         d. Interest Expense, $724.92
P11-8   b. Interest Expense, $420.97
         c. Interest Expense, $412.64
P11-9   a. Total Present Value, 12/31/00
            Note A, $1,073.34
            Note B, $1,000.00
            Note C, $930.58
         b. Book Value, 12/31/01
            Note A, $1,037.73
            Note B, $1,000.00
            Note C, $963.63
         c. Book Value, 12/31/01
            Note A, $1,035.63
            Note B, $1,000.00
            Note C, $966.84
P11-10   a. Loss $7,400
         b. Loss $27,400
         c. Loss $42,022
P11-11   a. Discount on Bonds Payable, $351.42
         e. Credit Discount on Bonds Payable, $205.35
P11-12   a. Balance Sheet Value 12/31/02, $94,554.05
         b. Total Cash Outflow, $124,000

         c. Total Cash Outflow, $115,840
         d. Total Cash Outflow, $80,481
P11-13   a. Leasehold Obligation 12/31/01, $53,497.94
P11-14   Present Value of Lease Payments, $18,023.90
P11-15   b. Effective Interest Rate is 8%
         a. 12/31/00 Net Book Value, $18,012
P11-16   b. Present Value of Interest Payments, $331.20
         c. Present Value of Interest Payments, $364.99
ID11-2   d. 5% Stated Rate; Issue Price $110,253,200
            18% Stated Rate; Issue Price $226,923,520
ID11-3   a. Effective Interest Rate is 10%
ID11-6   a. Liabilities/Total Assets Ratio
            Albertson's   .53
            Safeway   .88
         b. Adjusted Liabilities/Total Assets Ratio
            Albertson's   .53
            Safeway   .88

Chapter 12
E12-1   b. (1) Debt/Equity .278
            (2) Debt/Equity .878
E12-4   b. Debt/Equity Before 1.05
            Debt/Equity After 1.08
E12-5   b. Total stockholders' equity, $1,038,000
E12-6   a. Total stockholders' equity, $153,000
         b. Additional Paid-In Capital Attributable to
            Treasury Stock, $3,000
E12-7   b. Total stockholders' equity, $4,450,000
E12-8   a. Book Value per Share, $26.00
         c. Book Value per Share, $24.00
E12-9   c. Debit Cash for $30.00
E12-10   a. Number of Shares Issued, 2,000
         b. Purchase Price of Treasury Stock, $20/Sh.
         e. Per Share Dividend Rate, $1.354
E12-11   a. Issue Price per Share, $5.00
         b. Purchase Price of Treasury Stock, $12/Sh.
         d. Per Share Cash Dividend Rate, $.519
E12-12   a. 325,000 Shares Eligible for Dividend
E12-13   b. Dividends in Arrears
            December 31, 1996: $25,000
            December 31, 1997: $20,000
            December 31, 1998: $0
            December 31, 1999: $10,000
            December 31, 2000: $0
E12-14   e. Ratio Prior to Entries, 2.27
            After (a), 3.02
            After (b), 2.27
            After (c), .00
            After (d), 2.27
E12-15   a. Additional Paid-In Capital, Common Stock
            Option 1: $37,500
            Option 2: $75,000
P12-1   a. Debt/Equity, .58
         b. Debit/Equity, 1.06
P12-2   a. Par Value per Share, $6.00
         b. Book Value, $10.89
         c. Average Price, $8.00
P12-4   a. 47,000 Shares Eligible to Receive a Dividend
         c. Debit to Stock Dividend, $235,000

P12-5   a. Dividend Per Share   Preferred   Common
        1994: $4.33 $0.00
        1998: $5.00 $1.00
        2000: $5.00 $0.48
        b. Dividend Per Share   Preferred   Common
        1994: $4.33 $0.00
        1998: $7.00 $0.40
        2000: $5.00 $0.48

P12-6   a. Maximum Cash Dividend, $25,000
        b. 7,200 Shares
        d. Cash Dividend, $150,000

P12-7   a. Addtnl. Paid-In Capital on Bal. Sheet, $639,000
        b. Addtnl. Paid-In Capital on Bal. Sheet, $525,000
        c. Addtnl. Paid-In Capital on Bal. Sheet, $639,000
        d. Addtnl. Paid-In Capital on Bal. Sheet, $639,000

P12-8   b. Retained Earnings, $4,405
           Total Stockholders' Equity, $12,785

P12-9   a. Number of Shares Issued, 900 Shares
           Average Issue Price, $227.78/Share
        b. Number of Shares Issued, 15,000 Shares
           Average Issue Price, $21.13/Share
        c. Average Repurchase Price, $22.00/Share

P12-10 a. Number of Shares Issued, 4,000 Shares
        b. Average Issue Price, $41.25/Share
        c. Dividends Declared, $1,275,000
        g. Reissue Price per Share, $300

P12-11 b. Total Stockholders' Equity, $2,510,000

P12-12 c. Total Assets, $13,569,950
        d. Debt/Equity Ratio
           Before: .087
           After: .631

P12-13 b. Debit to Liabilities
           Alternative: (1) $400,000
                        (2) $250,000
                        (3) $400,000
           Debit to Treasury Stock
           Alternative: (4) $650,000

ID12-1 c. Total Value of Quantum, $540 Million
           Post-Dividend Value/Share, $19.61
        d. After Stock Dividend, 918,000 shares

Chapter 13

E13-3   a. (1) $36,560
           (2) $26,160
           (3) $21,760
           (4) $30,000

E13-4   a. Net Income, $26,000

E13-5   b. Discontinued Operations, $123,500

E13-6   a. Net Income, $650,000
        b. Net Income, $625,300

E13-7   a. Net Income, $1,355,900
        b. Net Income, $1,270,750

E13-8   b. Debit to Income Tax Liability, $813,750

E13-9   Bonus
        a. $24,960
        b. $62,400
        c. Gain Not Extraordinary, $99,840
           Gain Extraordinary, $62,400

E13-10 Net Earnings Per Share
        a. $1.00
        b. $0.60
        c. $0.50

E13-11 a. Net Income, $31,980
        b. Ending Retained Earnings, $85,980

E13-12 a. Net Income, $275,600
        b. Ending Retained Earnings, $662,600

E13-13 a. Maximum Dividends, $29,205
        b. Maximum Dividends, $37,687.50

E13-14 a. Income Tax Expense, $326,200
           Net Income, $546,650

P13-2   a. Bonus, $280,000
        b. Bonus, $300,000

P13-3   b. Net Income, $265,000
        c. Net Income, $265,000

P13-4   b. Net Income, $164,450

P13-6   a. Net Income, $464,750
        b. Income Tax Expense, $250,250
        c. Ending Retained Earnings, $1,548,750
        d. Tax Liability Balance 12/31/00, $120,250

P13-7   a. Total Depreciation, 1995-1998
           Straight-Line, $1,000,000
           Double-Declining, $1,771,200
        b. Debit to Cum. Loss from Acct Change, $771,200
           Debit to Income Tax Liability, $269,920

P13-8   c. Net Earnings Per Share, $2.79

P13-9   Disposal of Business Segment, $260,000
        Net Income, $3,887,000

P13-10 b. Net Loss, $22,750
           Net Earnings (Loss) per Share, $(0.11)
        c. Ending Retained Earnings, $515,250

ID13-2 a. Gain of $122.13 million

ID13-3 c. Debit to Income Tax Liability, $33,231,000

Chapter 14

E14-7   b. Net Income, $22,000
           Ending Retained Earnings, $20,000
           Total Assets, $125,000
        c. Ending Cash Balance, $25,000

E14-8   b. Ending Cash Balance, $67,000

E14-9   Insurance Purchases, $5,800
        Wages Paid, $2,500

E14-10 b. Gain on Sale of Machinery, $2,000

E14-11 b. Net Cash Increase Due to Oper. Activ., $11,100

E14-12 Net (Decrease) in Cash, $(2,000)

E14-13 Net Increase in Cash, $7,000

E14-14 Accrual-Basis Sales, $56,000
        Accrual-Basis COGS, $36,000

E14-15 Net Cash Increase Due to Operating Activ., $7,700

E14-16 Net Cash Increase Due to Oper. Activ., $10,800

E14-17 Net Cash Increase Due to Oper. Activ., $20,500

E14-18 Net Cash Increase Due to Oper. Activ., $2,300

E14-19 Net Cash Increase Due to Oper. Activ., $10,900

E14-20 Net Cash Increase Due to Oper. Activ., $30,300

P14-6   a. Case 1, Cost of Building Sold, $130,000
           Case 2, Accum. Depr. on Equip. Sold, $25,000
           Case 4, Cost of Building Sold, $670,000

P14-7   Cash Received, $33,000
P14-8   b. Net Purchases, $355,000
P14-9   Accrual COGS, $11,000
P14-10   Cash Payments, 1998
              a. $4,000
              b. $4,000
              c. $1,000
          Cash Collections, 1999
              a. $13,000
              b. $9,000
              c. $13,000
P14-11   Cash Collections from Customers, $34,500
P14-12   b. Net Income, $7,400
              Ending Retained Earnings, $4,400
              Total Assets, $88,400
              Ending Cash Balance, $25,000
P14-13   a. Cash Collections, $955,000
          b. Net Cash Increase Due to Oper. Activ., $332,000
P14-14   Proceeds from Sale of Fixed Assets, $125,000
P14-15   Direct Method:
              Cash Paid to Suppliers for Inventory, $199,000
              Proceeds from Sale of Plant Equipment, $90,000
              Purchase of Plant Equipment, $25,000
              Proceeds from common stock issue, $65,000
              Payment of Dividends, $30,000
P14-16   Total Cash Collections from Customers
              1999: $8,570,000
              2000: $4,295,250
P14-17   a. Ending Cash Balance, $1,524,600
              Ending Retained Earnings Balance, $628,140
          c. Net Income, $728,140
              Total Assets, $3,399,200

Appendix B
EB-1   5 Periods
              5%, $191.44
              10%, $241.58
              15%, $301.70
        10 Periods
              5%, $244.33
              10%, $389.06
              15%. $606.83
        15 Periods
              5%, $311.84
              10%, $626.59
              15%, $1,220.56
EB-2   5 Periods
              5%, $7,835.26
              10%, $6,209.21
              15%, $4,971.76
        10 Periods
              5%, $6,139.15
              10%, $3,855.44
              15%, $2,471.85
        15 Periods
              5%, $4,810.17
              10%, $2,393.92
              15%, $1,228.94

EB-3   5 Periods
              5%, $828.84
              10%, $915.77
              15%, $1,011.36
        10 Periods
              5%, $1,886.68
              10%, $2,390.61
              15%, $3,045.56
        15 Periods
              5%, $3,236.78
              10%, $4,765.87
              15%, $7,137.06
EB-4   5 Periods
              5%, $870.29
              10%, $1,007.34
              15%, $1,163.06
        10 Periods
              5%, $1,981.02
              10%, $2,629.68
              15%, $3,502.39
        15 Periods
              5%, $3,398.62
              10%, $5,242.46
              15%, $8,207.62
EB-5   5 Periods
              5%, $43,294.80
              10%, $37,907.90
              15%, $33,521.60
        10 Periods
              5%, $77,217.30
              10%, $61,445.70
              15%, $50,187.70
        15 Periods
              5%, $103,796.60
              10%, $76,060.80
              15%, $58,473.70
EB-6   5 Periods
              5%, $45,459.50
              10%, $41,698.70
              15%, $38,549.80
        10 Periods
              5%, $81,078.20
              10%, $67,590.20
              15%, $57,715.80
        15 Periods
              5%, $108,986.40
              10%, $83,666.90
              15%, $67,244.80
EB-7   a. $154.15
        b. $385.24
        c. $192.39
        d. $146.15
EB-8   a. $157.61
        b. $416.06
        c. $207.78
        d. $157.85
EB-9   a. 10%, 4 periods, $36,603
           12%, 3 periods, $51,425
           15%, 5 periods, $103,434

EB-10 a. $438,552.80
b. $463,130.80
EB-11 Option 1, $4,256,780
Option 2, $4,500,000
Option 3, $4,566,941
EB-12 a. Ordinary Annuity, $1,740.80
Annuity Due, $1,914.88
b. Ordinary Annuity, $1,914.88
Annuity Due, $2,106.36
c. Ordinary Annuity, $2,106.36
Annuity Due, $2,317.00
d. Ordinary Annuity, $2,317.00
Annuity Due, $2,548.70
EB-13 a. Option 1, $240,000
Option 2, $201,940
Option 3, $193,182
Option 4, $230,239
c. Option 1, $240,000
Option 2, $270,135
Option 3, $277,914
Option 4, $249,636
EB-14 a. Present Value of College Expenses in 15 Years,
$139,474; Present Value of College Expenses
Today, $33,389
b. Annuity Payment, $4,532.43
c. Present Value of College Expenses in 15 Years,
$143,084; Present Value of College Expenses
Today, $45,106
Annuity Payment, $5,471.21
EB-15 a. $49,706.40
b. $7,956.98
c. $61,529.70
PB-1 Present Value, $82.85
PB-2 a. Investment 1 Future Value, $10,759.26
Investment 2 Future Value, $33,200.40
b. Current Investment, $14,153.69
PB-3 a. Contract 1 Present Value, 62,413.52
Contract 2 Present Value, $14,439.40
Contract 3 Present Value, $14,947.16
b. Contract 1 Fut. Value After 5 Per., $83,523.44
Contract 2 Fut. Value After 5 Per., $25,447.32
Contract 3 Fut. Value After 5 Per., $24,072.72
Contract 1 Fut. Value After 10 Per., $111,773.12
Contract 2 Fut. Value After 10 Per., $44,846.80
Contract 3 Fut. Value After 10 Per., $38,769.37
PB-4 Option 1 Present Value, $25,000
Option 2 Present Value, $30,112.20
Option 3 Present Value, $29,417.46
PB-5 a. $52,222
b. $63,189
c. $76,458
d. $84,104
PB-6 Present Values
a. $10,000
b. $11,493.28
c. $13,916.30
d. $11,978.13
e. $14,587.25

f. $5,349.78
g. $11,133.04
Future Values
a. $13,604.90
b. $21,273.26
c. $17,530.55
d. $25,859.91
e. $25,000.00
f. $6,240.00
g. $14,024.44
PB-7 a. Present Value of Annual Receipts, $13,518.04
Present Value of Lump-sum Receipt, $115,662.00
Total Present Value, $129,180.04

Appendix C
Case 3

		Technic	Sonar-Sun
1998	Current Ratio	2.50	1.16
1999	Current Ratio	2.14	1.04
1998	Quick Ratio	1.64	.36
1999	Quick Ratio	1.92	.39
1998	Liabilities/Equity	1.26	1.59
1999	Liabilities/Equity	2.19	1.82
1999	Receivables Turnover	2.44	9.39
	ROA	.09	.13
	ROE	.25	.36
	Return on Sales	.17	.12
	Times Interest Earned	2.53	5.64
	Inventory Turnover	3.37	1.75

Case 4 (Avery Corporation)
Return on Equity
1998   .078
1999   .063
Return on Assets
1998   .040
1999   .037
EPS
1998   3.75
1999   1.90
Return on Sales
1998   .046
1999   .056
Times Interest Earned
1998   1.95
1999   2.76
Current Ratio
1997   4.23
1998   6.22
1999   3.79
Quick Ratio
1997   2.04
1998   4.19
1999   1.95
Receivables Turnover (days)
1998   89
1999   110

Receivables Turnover (times)
1998   4.12
1999   3.32
Inventory Turnover (days)
1998   228
1999   302
Inventory Turnover (times)
1998   1.60
1999   1.21
Debt/Equity
1997   1.58
1998   .73
1999   .66
Financial Leverage
1998   .038
1999   .026
Questions
1. Number of Outstanding Shares
    12/31/99 3,850,000
5. Cash Collected from Customers, $105,050
    Cash Paid to Suppliers, $67,700,000

8. Value of Buckeye's PPE acquired $50,000,000
9. Book Value of Equipment, $14,000,000
10. Cash Contribution, $8,000,000

Case 6

		Wellington	Wagner
1997	Current Ratio	1.09	3.43
1998	Current Ratio	.47	1.97
1997	Quick Ratio	.58	1.80
1998	Quick Ratio	.39	.82
1997	Debt/Equity	.62	1.51
1998	Debt/Equity	.85	1.81
1998	Rec. Turnover	9.85	8.65
Inventory Turnover		9.00	1.93
ROA		-.08	.09
ROE		-.15	.30
Return on Sales		-.13	.13
Times Interest Earned		-2.31	9.02